Archetypal Processes in Psychotherapy

Edited by Nathan Schwartz-Salant and Murray Stein

Chiron Publications ● Wilmette, Illinois

The Chiron Clinical Series
ISBN 0-933029-12-8

General Editors: Nathan Schwartz-Salant, Murray Stein
Managing Editor: Harriet Hudnut Halliday
Book Review Editor: Peter Mudd

Chiron Publications gratefully acknowledges the help of the Chicago Society of Jungian Analysts, the Inter-Regional Society of Jungian Analysts, and the International Association for Analytical Psychology in making this series possible.

Printed in the United States of America

Book design by Elaine M. Hill

Library of Congress Cataloging-in-Publication Data

Archetypal processes in analysis.

    (Chiron clinical series)
    Includes bibliographies.
    1. Jung, C. G. (Carl Gustav), 1875–1961. 2. Psychoanalysis. I. Schwartz-Salant, Nathan, 1938–   . II. Stein, Murray, 1943–
BF173.J85A83   1987   150.19'54   87-17895
ISBN 0-933029-12-8

Contents

The Chiron Clinical Series
Policy on capitalizing the term "Self"

Jung's understanding of the Self is significantly different from how
this term is often used in other contemporary psychoanalytic literature. The
difference hinges primarily on the understanding of archetypes: The
Jungian conceptualization of the Self sees it as rooted in the transpersonal
dimension. Hence the frequent capitalization of this term. Since the
clinical concern with the Self often relates more narrowly to the sphere of
ego-consciousness, however, it can be more mystifying than edifying
always to allude to the archetypal level in the literature. Consequently the
editors of *Chiron* have chosen to allow authors to exercise an option on
the question of capitalization. They may choose to capitalize Self and
thereby to emphasize its transpersonal, archetypal base; or, they may
choose to employ the lower case, signifying by this that they are discussing
issues that have to do principally with ego-identity and the personal
relation to this central factor of psychic life, which may be less precisely
articulated by reference to the archetypal substratum.

Archetypal and Personal Interaction in the Clinical Process

Edward Whitmont

Were not the eye to sun akin,
The light we never could behold.
Filled not a God's strength us within
How would the divine hold us enthralled?
                                             J. W. von Goethe

The organism confronts light with a new formation, the eye, and the psyche meets the process of nature with a symbolical image, which apprehends the nature process just as the eye catches the light. And in the same way as the eye bears witness to the peculiar and independent activity of living matter, the primordial image expresses the unique and unconditioned creative power of the spirit.

                                             C. G. Jung

This paper seeks to explore the interface between the classical archetypal or symbolic mode and the biographical or personalistic ap-

Edward Whitmont, M.D., is Chairman of the Board of the C. G. Jung Training Center of New York and maintains a private practice of analytical psychology in New York City and Irvington, New York. A graduate of the University of Vienna, he is a founding member and member of the teaching staff of the C. G. Jung Training Center of New York, as well as a founding member of the International Association for Analytical Psychology. He is the author of *The Symbolic Quest; Psyche and Substance: Essays on Homeopathy in the Light of Jungian Psychology;* and *The Return of the Goddess: Desire, Aggression and the Evolution of Consciousness.*

proach. To call the latter "clinical" in contradistinction to the former would seem to imply, obliquely at least, that the archetypal approach is not clinical. It has even been claimed that so-called archetypal experience is nothing but defense against object loss (Satinover 1985, pp. 65 ff).

There is also the opposite, equally radical, archetypal position that tends to dismiss altogether the value of reductive analysis of damage to children (Hillman 1979). Both of these extreme positions tend to identify with one exclusive aspect of what is in fact an interdependent field of complementary dynamics. The following is an attempt to trace the structural interrelationships within such a postulated unitary field process.

A Clinical Question

Some time ago I began to treat a middle-aged, highly successful business executive who suffered from intermittent spells of depression and feelings of alienation and emptiness, which alternated with almost manic periods of excited fury and destructive hostility. In between, his life was filled by work ambitions, prestige urges, and artistic interest in paintings and music.

During the early phase of his analysis he brought the following dreams, which appeared to him as rather "crazy" dreams. In the first dream it was announced to him that because long ago he had left his wife and children, his business partner would now have to declare bankruptcy. In the second dream the family cat went on a wild rampage, biting and clawing at whatever got in its way. The dreamer felt that this was because he had failed to pay attention to the animal. As he tried to restrain the cat she grew bigger and bigger, attaining the size and shape of a lion. He felt there was a threat to life and limb unless he could propritiate her by returning her rattle to her.

Both dreams show that something is seriously amiss: bankruptcy, a dangerous rampage. The calamity is said to be a consequence of a separation from family in one dream and neglect of the cat anima in the other. In the dreamer's associations, the business partner represented the dreamer's orientation toward power and success, his emotionally closed-off persona-identified ego. From early childhood on the dreamer had had to learn to rely on himself at the price of feelings, and to strive for independence and financial security. Neither he nor his family had ever owned a cat, and it meant nothing to him.

As we worked through the first dream, we elicited memories and affects of his childhood struggles to separate himself from the threat of suffocation by his overly possessive and seductive mother and of his feel-

ing of having been flooded at times by her depression and hysterical violence. Obviously this brought about the state of alienation from emotion
and instinct in respect to which both dreams seem to concur.

Yet what about the second dream? Subsequent to the working
through of the first dream, there appears to be little if any additional information forthcoming or insight gained from the second dream. In fact,
except for the peculiar lysis (returning the rattle), the second dream
would seem merely to restate in more general terms what the first dream
already had alluded to more specifically, separation from family. To be
sure, the violent cat could perhaps be expected to connect him emotionally with the memories of his mother's (and his own) temper; as a matter
of fact, it did not. He merely felt that the cat was a "crazy beast." Beyond
that there was no further response when we discussed the dream. On the
other hand, he was able to identify with the business partner and this released a flood of memories and affects. Cats and lioness may point to instinctual and even archetypal dynamics, but how is this of help at this
point?

Put in more general terms, the question is why our dreams so frequently state essentially identical messages on two different levels, one
personal, allegoric, and symptomatic, the other general, archetypal, and
symbolic. To be sure, we do not dream merely to satisfy the needs of
therapy. But then, we *also* do that; our dreams do respond to the therapy's requirements. Hence it may not be too far off the mark to assume
that there might be a point and purpose to the fact that dreams tend to
render the same or like messages in personal, symptomatically specific
terms *and* in general archetypal, symbolic terms.

Even if we grant that the archetypal mode is significant, there is still
the further question of its practical clinical significance above and beyond working through the disturbed complexes (in terms of here and
now as well as in relation to the childhood originations of need frustration, abandonment, and other traumatisms.) What do we gain by relating
to cat and lioness not simply as embodiments of the patient's or his mother's violence, but also as mythological figures, Sekhmet and Bast? Why is
this violence depicted in animal form, analogous to the theriomorphic
divinity figures rather than as the angry dreamer himself or a personal
mother figure? One might speculate that the anger is too unconscious
and too unassimilated to take human form. Yet my client's anger was
quite close to the surface, for he would flare up at the slightest provoca-
tion. (He was painfully aware of this.) On the other hand, tendencies that
may be quite remote from consciousness—such as shaman and power
magician, to name but two typical ones—may appear in human form in
our dreams.

Lastly, what do we make of the fact that my client's association to the rattle was to a toy of his childhood which, as he remembered, his mother took away from him because the "noise bothered her." On the other hand, he described the rattle of his dream as "something like an upside-down horseshoe with a handle." The allusion to Bast's sistrum is obvious, though totally unknown to the dreamer.

Does the concern with archetypal elements as transpersonal factors sidetrack the dreamer and allow him or her to avoid dealing with affect and interpersonal relationships and therefore make it advisable to disregard them and deal with personal feelings and relationships only? Or are archetypes genuine healing factors, thus perhaps making it unnecessary to concern oneself with personal reduction?

The thesis I propose to explore is that transformation and healing are brought about by being moved and touched by, and by striving to actualize—that is, to personalize—the significance of the transpersonal or archetypal elements that arise from the Guidance Self. Expressed symbolically, healing comes about through meeting or envisioning one's God or daimon. However, for such an encounter to be effective, it must be approached and experienced in personal terms, by means of working through personal symptoms, affects, and relationships as well as by reductive understanding and by reliving the effects of past traumatisms.

As a means of unifying personal and transpersonal, archetypal dimensions I propose an overall view of life in terms of a dramatic story or myth that "stages" psychic evolution in alternating phases of dynamic quantum leaps of creation and breakdown: birth, death, and rebirth. This model both supersedes and includes the traditional mechanistic view of pathology as caused by a trauma that interferes with a postulated "normalcy." As in modern physics, the mechanistic cause-and-effect, entropy pattern is seen as a special but only partially valid and subordinate aspect of the quantum dynamic of constant evolution and involution.

As a first step toward illuminating these interconnections, it will be necessary to clarify our concepts of archetype, symbol, and Self, and also to try to get a better understanding of the healing process.

Archetype, Symbol, Self

What do we really mean when we speak of the archetypal approach to clinical issues? In our clinical usage this has come to mean, by and large, the use of mythological amplification. This equation is too simplistic and misses an essential point. The use of myth and fairytale for illustration, amplification, and interpretation is merely one way of relating to archetypal dynamics. Frequently it is helpful; often it is indifferent or even hindering. The extant corpus of mythology represents a precipitate of the mythmaking function inherent in the unconscious psyche, but its formulations pertain to other individuals and cultures. Being an expression of a collective unconscious, mythologies have some relevance for everybody, at least potentially, but they are also rooted in past stages of culture and psychic evolution. A particular historical myth may offer viable channels of psychic energy to an individual, but this is not universally the case. The extant mythologems offer us no more than a way to see how others have related to archetypal energies. They are not that energy itself nor are they necessarily our way of relating to it. Our own innate dynamic tends to create our own myths that freely use motifs of our own life contexts, along with pieces of this or that past myth and personal or collective memory to weave our own story that connects us with transpersonal dynamics. This fact has been emphasized by Jung and has led to his differentiating between archetypal image and archetype as such, as well as to his definition of symbol and Self.

In his own words:

> The archetypal representations, images and ideas must not be confused with the archetype as such. They are very varied structures which point back to essentially unrepresentable basic forms. . . . The real nature of the archetype is not capable of being made conscious. . . . It is transcendental . . . but has effects which make visualizations of it possible. (Jung 1969, p. 417)

> The archetype can no longer be regarded as psychic, although it manifests itself psychically. Although there is no form of existence that is not mediated to us psychically and only psychically, it would hardly do to say that everything is merely psychic. We must apply this argument logically to the archetype as well. Since their essential being is unconscious to us and still they are experienced as spontaneous agencies, there is probably no alternative but to describe their nature, in accordance with their chief effect, as spirit. (*Ibid.*, p. 420)

Yet, what is "spirit"? Here we are at a loss for a rational definition. At best we can intuit spirit as a principle of nonmaterial and suprapersonal order to which we associate creative intelligence and power. Hence, Jung speaks of it as a "kind of higher consciousness [which] . . . in its inscrutable superior nature can no longer be expressed in the concepts of human reason; our powers of expression have recourse to other means: they create a *symbol*" (*ibid.*, p. 643). Jung went on to speak of a symbol as

> an image that describes in the best possible way the dimly discerned nature of the spirit. A symbol does not define or explain; it points beyond itself to a *meaning* that is darkly divined yet still beyond our grasp, and cannot be expressed in the familiar words of our language. (*Ibid.*, p. 644; italics added)

What emerges here is a notion of transcendental *essence* or quintessential distillate, representable and reachable only symbolically. This transcendental essence effectively expresses itself as a source of awe, through patterns of form, perception, emotion, and behavior.

What we call archetypal refers to fundamental principles, to basic ordering systems of transpersonal, even suprapersonal, creative power; to thematic field configurations asking to be consciously realized and related to in respect to their structural and ordering implications within, as well as between, people and physical objects.

As creative powers they are felt to be numinous and awesome. As creative order they are experienced as sources of meaning or significance. The structuring of form and ordering of relationship in terms of our personal lives are felt to be activities of the central archetype, the archetype of archetypes, as it were, which, when it is perceived transcendentally, has been called god or daimon or angel; when perceived predominantly as immanence, it is called Self.

The notion of such quintessentially active transcendental principles behind perceptible phenomena, akin to Plato's ideas, is now also expressed in the modern physicist's concept of "form behind anything that *has* form," "creations within the wave field . . . imagined or visualised 'as if it were permanent material reality'" (Schroedinger 1966, p. 56), or the concept of reality as *unfolded* or *explicate order,* special forms contained within an emerging from a more general totality of existence, the *enfolded* or *implicate order* (Bohm 1980). More recently, in biology such a priori form potentials have been postulated as morphogenetic fields, unrepresentable potencies that are "responsible for organization and form of material systems" (Sheldrake 1981, p. 130) and that perpetuate the morphogenesis of new systems by *morphic resonance,* "an effect of form upon form across space and time (which) would resemble energetic resonance in its selectivity, but . . . could not be accounted for in terms of any known types of resonance, nor would . . . involve a transmission of energy" (*ibid.*, p. 95).

The reaction of consciousness to the impact of transpersonal power is fear of inundation and extinction. To avoid this, the energy is either partially assimilated by means of symbolic images or neutralized by rationalization and denial. The former response results in the creation of religious and mythological forms and rites; the second hopes to minimize the threat of the numinosum by reducing it to a romanticized aesthetic abstraction or by explaining it away as "nothing but" a defense against the fear of death or object loss. In this case the magic-level dynamics are equated with psychopathology. In either case the power of transpersonal archetypal agencies in shaping our destinies in adult life, childhood and birth events as well as our interpersonal relationship problems, is denied and missed.

Keeping in mind these considerations, we must differentiate Jung's concept of the Self from the way it is conceived by psychoanalysis and personalistic psychological systems. A good deal of confusion, of which Jung himself is not entirely innocent, prevails here in Jungian writing. Unfortunately Jung has not been consistent in the use of Self. When he says, "Natural man is not a 'self' . . . that is why since time immemorial he has needed the transformation mysteries. . . ." (Jung 1968, p. 104), he uses self in the psychoanalytic sense, thus confusing and contradicting his own definition. In terms of his definition as central archetype, no one can ever "be" the Self, for that would mean assimilation of ego to Self or of Self to ego, thus courting inflation and dissolution of ego (*ibid.*, Pt. 2, pp. 45–48).

Jung defines the Self as

> A construct that serves to express an unknowable essence which we cannot grasp as such, since by definition, it transcends our powers of comprehension. It might equally well be called the "god within us." The beginnings of our whole psychic life seem to be inextricably rooted in this point and all our highest and ultimate purposes seem to be striving towards it. (Jung 1960, p. 399)

Here again there is a reference to an undefinable essence, which manifests as thematic form-setter for the empirical person, unrepresentable as such except through symbol

This particular entity of the implicate order has been called Higher Self or Spirit Self in esoteric tradition. I prefer to call it Guidance Self. This Guidance Self is something other than the psychoanalytical self, which refers to the empirical personality and its complexes, to the explicate definable and describable order, and which in esoteric tradition has been called "lower self." I propose to call the empirical personality the "complex self." The Guidance Self is implicate order; it is of the nature of archetype. It includes the notions or symbols of karma or destiny. As archetypal order it can be postulated as dialectically interacting with complex self and ego.

Symbol, Similarity, and Healing

Whenever in order to point toward implicate or quintessential order we use the symbolic mode, we use the principle of similarity or analogy. When, for instance, a person is called wolflike, we do not claim that he *is* a wolf with four legs and a tail, etc., but that something in his being or behavior is like or similar to a wolf. That something may be clearly definable, for example, his hunger or greed, or it may be a more subtle, imponderable something, an undefinable essence that reminds us of a like sense induced by a wolf. Genuine meaningful (*sinnbildliche*) similarity

rests upon the fact that things that appear different in terms of shape, behavior, space, or time may share some essential quality. Thus they are
different manifestations or reflections of the same time/space-indepen-
dent reality.

When the thematic likeness is based on an explicate fact such as concrete hunger or greed, we use allegory. In the symbolic stance we ad-
dress ourselves to the essentially unknown, to the *implicate essence* itself.
This is obvious when the wolf stands for a deity—such as Mars or Apollo
—or functions in the initiatory identification of a man with a wolf. The
animal cult postulates a particular undefinable essence, transpersonal,
godlike, and relatively "pure" in the particular animal, yet presumed to
be only partially alive and diluted by other factors in humans. In the initiatory symbolic evocation through ritual enactment, the godlike wolf
essence—the wolf archetype—is *potentized* (to borrow a term from the
analogous homeopathic technique); its spirit is evoked and assimilated in
its pure form in order to strengthen its corresponding similar quality in
the warrior about to meet the enemy. The potentially faltering wolflike
strength of the warrior is "healed" by encountering its archetypal essence
through the simile of the symbolic image of that animal, which is felt to
embody that essence in its pure unconditioned manifestation.

Likewise, in the ancient incubation mysteries of Aesculapius it was
held that healing was vouchsafed by encountering in a vision or dream a
likeness of the god who was both the giver as well as the healer of illness,
or, in psychological language, that aspect of the Guidance Self that constellates the particular thematic configuration that underlies both illness
and its healing. Numbers 21:6–8 provides an apt example:

> Then the Lord sent fiery serpents among the people and they bit the people,
> so that many people of Israel died. and the people came to Moses and said,
> "We have sinned for we have spoken against the Lord; pray to the Lord that
> he take away the serpents from us." So Moses prayed for the people. And the
> Lord said to Moses, "Make thee a fiery serpent and set it on a pole; and every
> one who is bitten, when he shall see it shall live. So Moses made a bronze
> serpent and it set on a pole; and if the serpent bit any man he would look at
> the bronze serpent and live.

When Job can say: "I have heard of Thee by the hearing of my ear but
now my eyes see Thee . . . ," he is healed by Him who had given him the
illness. And, according to the Kabbalah, when Adam Kadmon beheld his
reflected image in the world, the fall of man, as well as illness and misery,
began. In turn, one may say that when world and man can see themselves
reflected in Adam Kadmon, healing ensues. Healing, in other words, is
postulated to occur by virtue of a rectifying or rebalancing encounter

with that similar or analogous form-pattern that "out there" in the object world embodies the particular archetypal essence, the inner subjective embodiment of which has been unbalanced or disrupted. Can we point to any concrete practical evidence to show that this is more than just mythological fantasy, that we really state an operative dynamic of healing? It is in the practice of homeopathy that we find experimental verification on the biological level of the dynamic we have just described.

Homeopathy and Archetypal Meaning

Homeopathy uses specially prepared potentized—essentially dematerialized—substance derivatives for the treatment of illness. They are prescribed on the basis of the "law of similars." In this system substances are *proven,* that is, tested for their effects on human beings by *provers* of average physical health. The substance to be tested is introduced—introjected, as it were—into the organism in repeated doses until symptoms appear. These symptoms show the ways in which the particular substance affects or causes an imbalance in organismic functioning. Nontoxic or presumably inert substances are proven in potentized, dematerialized form; in this way they also exhibit definite effects.

Those symptoms that are elicited by a majority of provers are considered to express the characteristic pathogenetic effects of that particular substance. When the symptom complex of any spontaneous illness is compared with the induced symptom complexes produced by the provings, there often will be found an extraordinarily close resemblance between disease pictures and proving pictures. And the drug whose symptomatology represents the closest resemblance to the symptom complex of the sick person, the *simulimum,* has been found clinically to be the most successful means to heal this condition when it is administered in potentized form. In contradistinction to the allopathic method, this healing effect is holistic and not limited to one target organ; it affects the whole person constitutionally and psychosomatically, in the sense of reordering and integrating. This healing is often preceded by therapeutic regressions and healing crises. Accordingly, the similarity that leads to the therapeutic choice has to be expressive of the total complex pattern of the personality and illness dynamics, not merely of isolated symptoms. The term "genius" has been used in homeopathic writing to denote the sense of a gestalt core of a substance or remedy, which would be representative of the essence pattern shared by patient and medicine.

Imagine, for example, a condition of dammed-up grief, worry, or anxiety in an over-disciplined and overly responsible and repressed person. A condition may ensue that is characterized by depressive irritability, brooding listlessness, hopelessness, or in more extreme forms, by a tendency to suicide or substance addiction. Organic expressions may range from headaches and hypertensive states to chronic indigestion, biliary disorders, and disturbances of the heart function and circulation (Weiss and English 1949, pp. 339, 347, 430).

Such a state is duplicated, often down to minute details, in a person who proves gold in a suitable assimilable form. Regardless of the external exciting factors, the gold-prover becomes subject to depression and anxiety, to brooding, pessimistic, hopeless, and suicidal moods, and he or she may develop a craving for alcohol or other mind-altering substances. Physically, the gold-proving produces circulatory and cardiac pathology as well as digestive, biliary, and rheumatoid disorders. Most significantly, people of stature, power, responsibility, and discipline are more likely than others to respond symptomatically to gold in the proving experiment and with therapeutic response when ill.

Rounding out our example, we may recall that the symbolic range of the gold archetype as we know it from alchemy includes not only the principles of individuation and indestructible value, but also, on the more secular level, power, wealth, and security. Moreover, it also represents the solar principle and the heart, the "sun" of the organism, from which radiates the circulation.

Since every existing substance is potentially productive of both pathology (in a proving or poisoning) and healing (when used on the basis of symptom similarity), we can see that the whole range of human functional patterns is mirrored in macrocosmic fields of form that are embodied in mineral, plant, and animal substances. Their healing essences can be activated and connected with on the basis of symbolic likeness or similarity. As "wolfness" is assimilated through the enacting of the wolf ceremony or meditation on wolf power, so the solar principle embodied in gold and heart can be assimilated through the potentized, dematerialized preparation of (and probably meditation on) gold. Weakness, fear of death, and the need for bravery, which yet may be lacking, are responses to feeling threatened or unbalanced by wolf-being; they are the wolf pathology, as it were. Cardiac or circulatory disorder, depression, and loss of value ensue as a result of being unbalanced by the gold or solar archetype.

Likewise our chief psychological archetypal thematic fields—father, mother, hero, animus/anima, shadow, adversary, birth, death, etc.—are aspects of macrocosmic dynamics as well as microcosmic incarnation: predispositions, expectations, and response readiness. As with external substances, their incarnation is never perfect. No crystal, for instance, is a perfect embodiment of the archetypal form. Every mother, father, or hero is flawed in comparison to the archetypal, ideal expectation. Yet this flawed embodiment is what is introjected. The introjects of father, mother, etc., are the analogs to the toxic introjection of external substances or their field processes that bring about dis-ease. The introject of the tyrannical or tyrannically perceived personal father unbalances; it flaws the incarnation and functioning of the father archetype. The personal explicate and the archetypal implicate or essential realities are linked by the similarity of their patterns, namely the fact that they share essential or typical structural code elements. Father introject and Father archetype share Father "essence."

This similarity enables the morphic resonance effect, the projection and projective induction, whether this occurs through image or symbol or, organically, through potentized substances. Yet the awareness of the pattern in question can be gained only through evaluation and awareness of the symptomatic picture, both in the here and now as well as in its genetic development, psychologically and organically. Biologically this occurs by virtue of gathering and evaluating the symptom totality until a meaningful pattern arises that would point to the genius of a remedy substance; psychotherapeutically it occurs by means of working through the totality of presenting and past symptoms, memories, affects, etc., both reductively and in their here and now effects, until a pattern of meaning arises that links up with the healing effect of archetypal essence.

The assimilation of the symbolic image of the archetypal father, Zeus or Jehovah or whichever image may present itself, reconnects with the *similar* unconditioned essence and thus can heal the effects of the introject. Thus, at crucial phases of the process of working through of personal material, archetypal images tend to emerge in dreams or visions. They offer meaning of transpersonal order to complexes encountered, or panoramic overviews of areas covered or still to be encountered, as well as a connection with a transpersonal healing essence. Where there is an image, the situation can be understood—not only by the mind but also by the heart. Thence it can be borne more easily. To conceive of the lioness as Sekhmet's anger in response to the human hubris of disregarding transpersonal psychic autonomy, and to realize that the psyche *is* autonomous and not subject to arbitrary manipulation by the ego—also that play and joy can be divine—has nonrational effects on deep emotional strata. It subtly affects the patient's attitude.

At other times, however, such material may be more significant for the therapist's orientation than the patient's, such as when the patient's capacity for adequately assimilating its meaning may still be limited. Then it is important that the therapist can open his or her mind and heart to the significance of the messages, even though little or no interpretation or amplification may be possible or indicated.

At such times the therapist is made aware not only of the theme played on the patient's life stage, but also of its enactment in transference and countertransference and the role assigned to himself or herself in the play. The therapist's understanding openness must serve now as a channel of force through which a reordering simile for the present subphase can be constellated in the interpersonal situation between her or him and the patient.

A special contingency is the acute flooding that sometimes dominates the scene in acute stress in borderline and psychotic situations. In those instances the transpersonal power breaks forth directly without mediation; or, owing to the lack of personalization, ego boundaries may be threatened. The power is toxic, not healing. Now we have to neutralize and mitigate the potentially destructive effect of the images and their induced affects by companioning the patient and offering whatever interpretation and personalization can be assimilated.

Drama and Death/Rebirth as Healing Agents

The major stumbling block that persistently stood in the way of testing the homeopathic evidence by pre-Einsteinian scientific methods was its unique way of processing the substance material by essentially destroying its materiality. By rhythmed dilation called potentization, it is reduced to levels of dispersion that are way beyond Avogardro's limit of molecular presence. Yet the paradoxical fact is that with increasing dematerialization, their effect becomes not less but more powerful and more specific to person and substance, acting within minutes and even seconds in highly acute conditions. Moreover, substances ordinarily considered medically inert, such as table salt, quartz, or clay, become highly potent medicines when they are destroyed and essence extract is used in accordance with the simile principle.

It is as though by destroying materiality the spirit is distilled out of substance. This is akin to the *solve et coagula* of alchemy, the extraction and precipitation of the lapis. Matter is destroyed and reborn, transformed into "potency of form prior to anything that has form" (Schroedinger, p. 33). This potency is then precipitated onto a new vehicle; in homeopathy sugar globules are the usual substratum. Like the lapis or the wafer of the mass, which also is considered a vehicle for healing the soul and body, this potentized, *pure form* medicine is now an embodiment of an aspect of transcendental essence; the gross material aspect of the carrier (solvent and sugar pill) has become irrelevant relative to its function as a carrier of the spirit.

I believe that precisely this "unacceptable" or unbelievable dynamic points to the very heart of the healing process. Archetypal field configurations give rise to disturbances in the form of acted-out complexes and their distortive features. They restore order and give meaning, hence healing, when assimilated in potentized nonmaterial form, that is, in symbolic perception. The creation of a symbolic image is the analogue to the alchemistic *solve* and the substance *death* of the homeopathic preparation. Images, symbols, and their dramatic representations are derivatives of, and borrowed from, the elements of the object world. Yet, like the homeopathic potencies, they are desubstantialized image likenesses of the objects, but not their materiality. They are not to be confused with the object in its concreteness; they are similes that point to spiritual essence, to order and meaning, to that which is behind visible form. They are windows to and channels of transcendental power. We mortify our urges toward acting out by inhibiting them in order to gain a sense of symbolic significance. The stuff of the symbol is conscious mind and emotion, not physical substance; but the symbol mobilizes unconscious transpersonal power and brings about transformational, and indeed even also physical, effects. When we find images for our complexes, we can live with them and begin to handle them. The processing of the potentized simillimum on the psychological level ranges from symbol creation, which is the *solve,* the desubstantializing extractive death phase, to the *coagula,* the rebirth phase of incarnating the symbolic pattern in ritual, dramatic expression, and symbolic, responsible living.

Drama and death and birth patterns, therefore, are two chief vehicles for connecting ego, complex self, and Guidance Self in the healing process. Together they constitute the basis of the initiation process (which always consists of drama, ritual, and death/rebirth ceremonies) aimed at transubstantiation and transformation. This also means healing. In reference to individuation, illness can be seen as an initiatory steppingstone, a means toward reaching an evolutionary *telos.* Job's illness is shown to exist not because he is at fault, but as an initiatory test in order to reach the vision of God. Jesus' reply to the disciples, when asked whether the man's blindness from birth was because of his or his parents' sin, answers, "Neither has this man sinned nor his parents, but that the works of God should be made manifest in him" (John 9:2, 3). C. Hering, a pioneer homeopath, spoke of disease symptoms as "the cry for simillimum," the spirit essence.

The Life Drama

Dramatization is the organization of events into an action pattern that includes cause-and-effect relationships and is characterized by alternating tension-and-release rhythms that convey meaning and a message and move our affects and feelings. Every myth or story is a drama. The mythopoetic function is a dramatizing function. Even the reductive explaining of childhood events—abandonment, deprivation, oedipal responses—is a dramatic ordering; if it were not, it would be meaningless and would not affect us emotionally.

Drama and theater present ritualized or mythologized symbols of human psychology and event. Ritual and myth are symbolic psychodrama. Drama depicts existential meaning, the "just so" of life. It is tragic or funny, staged, as it were, by the gods, in terms of human affect, behavior, and destiny. Modern drama, a secularization of the ancient sacred drama, is still cathartic. Translated literally, drama means that which is being done, action, represented on the stage of "theatron." That word is derived from *theoein*: to behold or witness with awe and wonder, to behold the spectacle of the gods (*theos*) as the spectacle of life. The unrepresentable is made visible through symbolic human action, through foibles and suffering, death and rebirth, failure and redemption, aggressive assertion and forced or blissful surrender, separation and loving union. All are variants of the one leitmotif: transformation. In beholding drama, therefore, one sees one's suffering as drama and connects with potentized simillima. As in the example of the wolf ritual, a corrective emotional experience is channeled through the symbol.

The effectiveness of a symbol therefore depends on its dramatic relevance. Once this is lost, the symbol is dead. A genuinely moving drama carries symbolic significance; an effective symbol is dramatic.

The chief features of a drama are a) an initial situation in need of change or in the process of being altered by the intrusion of new factors; b) an ensuing development that leads to a crisis; and c) its denouement or solution, which amounts to the birth of a new situation following the death of the old one. Hence drama requires awareness and understanding of personal action and its symptomatology. To act without understanding the action's place and function within the overall intended context, which is both "because of" and "in order to," is devoid of meaning.

Only when seen in relation to the actions of the complex self can the trends and intents of the Guidance Self be comprehended. In order to grasp the *telos* toward which the dramatic development aims, we must understand the meaning of the action as it unfolds as well as the situations out of which it logically arises. In order to understand Hamlet's wavering, we must understand not only what he intends to do—to avenge his father's death—but also how he got into the situation that does not allow him to make up his mind one way or another, having been prompted by an apparition whom he cannot quite trust. We must comprehend the exposition that derives the present from the personal past, the present back-and-forth movement out of which the crisis tends to develop, in order to perceive and be touched by the possible lysis.

As in dreams and in the birth process, an initial impasse, a state of being hemmed in, is necessary to get the action going. If "they lived happily thereafter" were to be the undisturbed beginning of the play, nothing much of interest could happen; no development would be possible. An expositional disturbance, a Luciferian ("light bringer") serpent of paradise, a spoiler and disturber of the peace, is an essential ingredient of life's drama; the devilish antagonist is the initiator and architect of destiny, the assigner of the karmic task.

The nature of this exposition of a basic fault must be established by reductive analysis and therapeutic regression. It is to be made present by working through in the setting of transference and countertransference, which help to establish the similar formal pattern through which the healing essence, the archetypal motif of meaning with its *telos,* can become constellated. Only in this way can we understand the paradox that digging up and reactivating old and forgotten pains and wounds and the experience of a negative, not only a positive, transference can have healing effects.

The child's archetypal predispositions embody themselves through its experience of parental figures and its relationship to them. Since these people are human and all too human, they make for flawed introjects. They inevitably resonate only partially and dampen the child's archetypal patterns. Like the potential toxicity of every external substance in the homeopathic experimental model, the exogenous influence upon ourselves that comes to us from parents and other significant figures is, inevitably, both potentially supportive as well as toxic to varying degrees, even when there is no gross abuse or abandonment. Gross brutality or catastrophic traumatization, of course, impose their destructive disordering effects regardless of individual patterning, albeit in different degrees, depending upon predispositions. At worst, they can produce psychotic flooding. We find the biologic analogue in gross poisonings and epidemics. A sufficiently powerful "daimon" of illness can overrule and impose itself over and above individual predisposition.

Transference and countertransference stage and eventually ritualize the basic themes of the life drama. The play may start out as initial acting out on both sides. One hopes that the therapist catches on sooner or later and becomes aware of the role that his or her own complex patterns, as well as projective identification, have been inducing in her or him. In consciously enacting the assigned roles in ways other than those dictated by the client's projections, he or she not only introduces a corrective emotional experience but also constellates to the patient's complexes the objectified symbolic archetypal simillimum.

The transference drama thereby embodies and mediates archetypal healing power. Here again it is necessary to understand the personal symptomatology and defenses through reductive interpretation, in order to grasp the significance of the dramatic interaction.

The Birth Archetype

Birth and death are the chief dramatic pacesetters of our life dramas. Birth is the first incarnation of our life theme. The birth experience frequently includes and merges with a sense of dying or the threat of death and with "memories" of past lives and deaths. It is not surprising, then, that the particular way in which the birth process is experienced and re-called in the course of therapeutic regression carries a fundamental significance for the way in which life and selfness are experienced and the way complexes are structured. In the reexperiencing of the birth process, the personal biographical material merges with and leads to the symbolic archetypal and transegoic dimension.

We have St. Grof to thank for an extensive mapping of the psychological implications of the birth experience (1975, 1983). My own limited experiences with therapeutic regressions in various states of light trance and guided imagination fully bear out his observations. In the birth experience, personal and transpersonal levels are fused; out of the concrete personal arises symbolic essence. The one implies the other, and interpretation is usually superfluous. While St. Grof originally gathered most of his material through the use of LSD, it can also be reached reductively via therapeutic regression in full consciousness by means of body techniques and guided imagination. In the birth memories we often touch the core material of the complexes, the pacesetters appointed by the Guidance Self as our karma or destiny for the unfolding life span.

Each stage of biological birth appears to have a specific spiritual counterpart. For the undisturbed intrauterine existence it is the experience of cosmic unity. The onset of delivery is paralleled by feelings of universal engulfment. The first clinical stage of delivery, the contractions in a closed uterine system, corresponds with the experience of "no exit" or hell; the propulsion through the birth canal in the second stage of clinical delivery has its spiritual analogue in the death/rebirth struggle, with ecstasies of aggression, surrender, and sexual arousal; and the metaphysical equivalent of the termination of the birth process in the third clinical stage of delivery is the experience of ego death and rebirth.

It is significant that contrary to what we would expect, the first, blissful, pleromatic experience of uterine containment already includes negative aspects of both a personal and a transpersonal nature: good or bad womb, good or bad maternal feelings and environmental factors, positive awareness of inner reality but also visions of wrathful deities as described in the *Tibetan Book of the Dead,* adverse destiny or karma or malefic cosmobiological or astrological influences (St. Grof 1975, p. 153). St. Grof remarks:

> It is not easy to explain why certain kinds of events have such a powerful traumatic effect on the child that they influence his psychodynamic development for many years or decades. Psychoanalists have usually thought in the connection about constitutional or heredity factors of an unknown nature. LSD research seems to indicate that this specific sensitivity can have important determinants in deeper levels of the unconscious, in functional dynamic matrices that are inborn and transpersonal in nature. Some of these factors, when brought to consciousness . . . have the form of ancestral, racial or phylogenetic memories, archetypal structures or even past incarnation experiences. Another important factor might be the dynamic similarity between a particular traumatic incident in childhood and a certain facet of the birth trauma. . . . In this case, the traumatic import of a later situation would actually be due to the reactivation of a certain aspect of the psychobiological memory of the birth. (*Ibid.,* p. 72)

> It is not uncommon for a dynamic constellation to comprise material from several biographical periods, from biological birth, and from certain areas of the transpersonal realm, such as memories of a past incarnation, animal identification and mythological sequences. Here the experiental similarity of these themes from different levels of the psyche is more important than the conventional criteria of the Newtonian Cartesian world view, such as the fact that years or centuries separate the events involved, that an abysmal difference appears to exist between the human and the animal experience or that elements of "objective reality" are combined with archetypal and mythological themes. (*Ibid.,* 1985, p. 97)

Clinical Conclusions and Illustrations

While clinically it is both justified and usually also necessary to treat personal pathology initially *as if* it is caused by biographical traumata of early childhood or later life, we are now discovering that actually these traumata are but stagings of the developing drama. The roots can lie much further back in prebirth and even preconception formal thematic patterns that are activated as somatic and imaginal cores during pregnancy and birth. Subsequently they are projected on and, by psychic induction and morphic resonance, invoked and called forth in the behavior of relevant people to whom one is selectively attracted in accordance with their similarity and their fitting-in with the a priori expectations. This would seemingly apply even to the personal parents who appear to be chosen, as the fact of "astrological inheritance" seems to indicate. Children share major horoscopic features with parents and grand-parents. These constellations correspond to characterological, hence genetic, predispositions. The latter, being established shortly after conception, happen to "time" the actual birth moment so as to correspond with the appropriate celestial position nine months later. Since, thus, it is evident that the moment of birth is not accidental, but rather is "chosen" in accordance with genetic predisposition, it no longer appears far-fetched and incredible to think that the genetic predisposition might be "chosen" to fit in with parental patterning and stellar positions nine months later, all expressing a priori thematic patterning of the life drama to be staged.

During the further life experiences, the complexes thus structured continue to attract similar, corresponding experiences. We have here the snowball or onion skin-like phenomenon of repetition compulsion and self-fulfilling prophecy that endlessly restages and reconfirms the central essential themes. The process of therapy obviously has to progress in the opposite direction if the pathological trend is to be reversed. It is like playing in reverse a musical theme with variations. In such a musical form a theme is stated at the outset and subsequently modulated, varied, shortened, or enlarged to seemingly ever new forms that nevertheless are but derivatives of the original theme. Thus also proceeds the formation of a complex. Therapy has to play it backwards, from the last—often unrecognizable variations, the shells of complexes, back to the first still relatively simple variations, the early traumata, whence a notion of the theme can arise. In the musical form the original theme is stated for all and sundry to hear; in human life it is sounded but in the archetypal realm, inaudible to our conscious hearing. Through mirroring and reductively interpreting the presenting symptoms, working through transference and therapeutic regression, we eventually can constellate a vision of thematic essence, a dramatic theme which, by virtue of similarity, mediates the daimon, god, or archetype that has been giver of pathology and now, through conscious assimilation, may heal. As in the homeopathic model, it is necessary to work through the totality of symptoms; when they can be seen as an organic unit, they point to the "genius" of the problem, the intentions of the Guidance Self.

For illustration I now shall describe two clinical situations. The first is the case of a Catholic priest who felt that he had to come to a decision as to whether to renounce the priesthood in order to marry a former nun with whom he had developed a close, loving relationship, or whether to renounce the longing of his heart and body and remain a priest. For a long time he was unable to make up his mind; he felt genuinely stuck. All along, his lifestyle had been based on compromising and avoidance of hard decisions. In working this through to his childhood we came upon his need to please his mother, who saw in him her redeemer and spiritual fulfillment through his becoming a priest. Always he had to smooth out the atmosphere of conflict between his parents and find compromises. As this was worked through we had insights and understanding of why he could not make up his mind, but he still felt stuck as before. While being careful to show me that he agreed with all and every interpretation, he nevertheless did not move an inch. At the same time I became aware of an increasing sense of frustration and of being stuck with him, myself. I felt annoyed at him for not moving and annoyed at myself for not being able to find a way out of the impasse. Stuckness and impasse seemed to fill the interpersonal space with a sense of paralysis. My annoyance was the induced equivalent of the failure of his assertion. I expressed this to him and he was "dismayed" and "sorry for making me feel this way."

Then in a subsequent session he brought a dream in which I offered him a homeopathic (sic) treatment by making him curl up and lie down between father and mother in a most uncomfortable position, buttocks up. His associations led to the need to compromise between the warring parents and feeling stuck there. Indeed, with respect to getting more out of the dream, we were stuck again. I now asked him actually to assume the uncomfortable position that I had put him in in the dream, in order to dramatize it and thus make it more "like real." He tried, and responded by saying, "I can't, I can't." At the same time I noticed that his breathing became labored, he began to hold in his breath and to clench his fists. I now suggested that he pay attention to and intensify all those responses and keep continuing to say, "I can't, I can't." As he did so his discomfort increased steadily, he became quite spastic, indeed convulsive, rolled onto the floor and in a state of extreme agony went through a reliving of his physical birth he felt himself stuck in the birth canal in a breech position. Then he shifted into identity with his mother who, asked to press in order to promote expulsion, responded with, "I can't, I can't."

Again as himself, he felt stuck, unable to move and afraid he would die or hurt his mother in forcing his way to delivery. With suggestion and encouragement from the therapist, he was eventually able to go through to full delivery and completion of the birth process. This brought about a tremendous sense of relief and a total change of disposition. He subsequently felt able and free to make his own decision, to be his own man, no longer needing to please and remain stuck in "mother" church, nor, for that matter, in continued analysis—all this without any need for interpretation from the therapist.

After first acting out and projectively inducing his pattern and having it mirrored back by the therapist, he had now, at last, "homeopathically" assimilated its "essence" in the "similar" image experience: stuckness in the birth canal, the leitmotif of his life drama. This now enabled him to proceed into the next phase of "delivery." No doubt there will be further stuck episodes in his life; he may need further analytic working through as the dramatic theme keeps repeating itself. But it is to be hoped that each time there will be a somewhat easier delivery.

The second example concerns a woman in her late thirties, of midwestern background, a rather prosaic and rational housewife, very depressed, phobic, and with periodic suicidal moods. During these phases she tended to seclude herself from husband and children, to brood and angrily complain about being invaded and pursued. In between, she tried "dutifully" to "do her best" to be a good wife and mother, yet feared and resented it and wished she could get away from all of it. At the same time she felt guilty about wanting to give up her "obligations." She could remember of her dreams only vague nightmarish images of persecution by sinister black-clad male figures. Her childhood memories led us back to a dreary, dull life in a parochially narrow upbringing; a punishing, sadistic father, strict, stern and despotic; and a remote, sullenly submissive mother who was hospitalized for several years, probably in connection with alcoholism, and then died when the patient was six or seven. She felt that her stepmother and stepsiblings were strangers to her. She felt "ganged up" on and felt the need to protect herself by secreting and hiding herself away. This in turn was considered by the father to be insubordination to himself. The stepmother and stepbrothers felt she was being disloyal to the family, and she was punished, thus confirming and intensifying her persecution phobia. Several times she thought of suicide; instead she tried to run away from home. The last time, at age 16, she got herself a job at a ski resort and when her father threatened to fetch her back, hurriedly got married to her present husband.

The insights gained by working through those painful memories helped her understand her marriage impasse and somewhat lightened her load by helping her comprehend how it repeated the story of her childhood relations and feelings. But it did little to relieve her depression, paranoic fears, and the urge to get away. She considered the idea of divorce, but rejected it as a betrayal of her obligations and also because she did not know what to do with herself. On the other hand, staying felt like doom. Suicide beckoned as the only way out of the impasse. What the therapist picked up was an atmosphere of fear, gloom, darkness, and hopelessness. I began to dread the sessions and wondered what the message of that was. Through all of this she had a peculiar sense that somewhere there was something significant that was missing, some event vaguely felt as if from her early childhood, that somehow was relevant to the present impasse. But try as she might, she could not remember it. Since her infrequent dreams dealt merely with a vague sense of repression and persecution, they were not much help. We decided to try to recapture that vaguely sensed material by means of trance regression and guided imagination. In that state she was invited to go back in time until she came upon that significant point in her past, whatever and wherever it happened to be.

In contradistinction to the conventional active imagination, guided imagination has the advantage of enabling the therapist to refocus the patient whenever there should be a tendency to wander off prematurely or go into grandiose archetypal imagery as a defense against facing a frightening affect. Otherwise the same freedom of image creation obtains as in active imagination. The therapist ought not to go so far as to prescribe images of his or her choice.

Presently the patient described being addressed by a voice and arguing with "her." She was asked to report or describe this argument. The following conversation ensued:

> Voice: Remember! Remember! I told you (or I warned you), don't go down, don't get mixed up with them!
> Patient: But I must.
> Voice: They are awful. Don't go down to them!
> Patient: But I must. I have to fight it out.
> Voice: Then don't do it again. Remember. Remember!
> I asked: Now whose is the voice? To whom are you talking?
> Patient: My sister.
> Now, I never had heard about her having a sister throughout the whole time, so I asked: How old is she?
> Patient: She is dead. She died before I was born.
> Nonplussed, I asked: And how old are you?
> Patient: I have not yet been conceived.

Now, that struck me as rather weird, so I felt I might at least get more details. I asked: What is it then that you are to try not to do? What are you to remember? Go back in the time scale to whatever or wherever that significant event is to be remembered from.

At that the patient became rather anxious and visibly tense. She cowered and pulled herself into a sort of curled up position. I asked, "What is going on? Where are you?" She muttered, "Under the bridge. They are going to catch us." I asked her to describe what was happening, who was catching her, and to describe all details. I have found it to be of great help in grounding and concretizing fantasies of this sort if one asks for details and descriptions of surroundings, clothing, and particularly of footwear whenever possible. What developed was a description of herself as a Jewish refugee, originally from well-to-do circumstances, hiding under a bridge somewhere in Denmark. She was eventually caught and beaten up by black-clad storm troopers or police and shipped to a concentration camp, where she committed suicide and—after death (*sic*)—felt that that was an "inappropriate" cowardly act of deserting one's fellow victims instead of trying to help. The forgotten thing, then, was the resolve not to commit suicide again but to stick it out under adversity, as it were, and to help others in like circumstances. To this end, purportedly, she had to "come down" into these awful circumstances of childhood.

Coming out of the fantasy, the patient was visibly shaken and profoundly impressed but also confused and, in view of her rather nonmetaphysical orientation, quite skeptical. In response to her question regarding what to make of all of that, I replied that I thought she should relate to it in "as if" terms, like a symbolic summing up of the meaning of her life drama, her life myth, no matter what the historical reality might or might not be.

As a result of this experience, she became aware on quite a deep level that staying in a marriage entered into for the purpose of getting away from home and without any basic affinity to her husband felt like a concentration camp, as did her childhood. This evoked the suicide reflex. At first we thought that perhaps that insight might help her to withdraw the concentration camp projection from the marriage, but it was all too apparent that in the choice of her mate she had picked another likeness of her despotic father and thus made sure that the deadly impasse would ever recreate itself. Now she realized that she had to gain a sense of her own separate space if she was not to regress into suicidal despair. She chose the alternative of divorce and entered training for a helping profession.

The main effect of such a "reliving" is its emotional impact. Paradoxically, such birth, pre-conception, or past life fantasies mobilize affect dynamics that are far more intense than those of "bona fide" childhood memories. (In my experience, only group encounters have a similar, comparable degree of intensity.) To the understanding already gained by prior reductive work is added an existential sense of "just so" regarding what perhaps feels like an extended role in a drama that transcends current ego boundaries, hence a sense of being connected to a larger context of being and becoming, of being in touch with essence.

I have described these cases in order to illustrate how the pursuit of the biographical material, followed persistently into past originations, leads to the emergence of "high points" that could be likened to a condensation, of the meaning essence into a motif or motifs or dramatic representation. In the priest's instance it was the motif of "being stuck in the narrow passage" of mother's anxiety, and fear of injuring her, and finding the courage to trust and go with the forward movement. This was dramatized in birth process and the breech position (an actual event that he subsequently was able to confirm from his mother's account).

The second case is clearly one of the archetype of the persecuted victim, the scapegoat who is to bear his or her own cross and help others with theirs: the problem of facing suffering, hardship, and despair, and yet not giving up on life.

In all of this material, the personal experiences as they are gathered together by pursuing the symptomatic material through *reductio ad primam causam* (which, however, turns out to be a potentially rather infinite process rather than one primal causal point) eventually arrange themselves into personal mythologems or dramatic patterns that present verisimilitudes of the disturbed dynamic and hence can convey archetypal primal essence of healing. They are made up of varying proportions of personal biographical, historical, and collective mythological imagery. In subsuming the high points of these images into a dramatic story of exposition, peripeteia, crisis, and lysis, a developmental goal—a *telos*—can be discerned or postulated, toward which psychological development would seem to be striving. Supportive meaning, even guidance, can be experienced in what otherwise might be felt as pointless suffering and misery, through encountering the guiding "genius," often tragic, of one's transpersonal life pattern. One becomes a witness, a participating onlooker of the life drama, the play of one's destiny.

We have wandered far afield from our starting point, the two dreams presented at the beginning of this paper. I believe that the question raised there—why two levels: one personal, the other archetypal—has been answered. Applying these answers to those dreams we can assume that cat and lioness, images of the deities Bast and Sekhmet, set forth the overall life themes, the possible goal and resolution at that moment: the threat of violence and destruction owing to the disregard of transpersonal power and the possibility of its transformation into joy and play. The personal dream of the bankrupt business partner presents us with the personalized "how" and fictional "why"—fictional in the sense that this "why" is the necessary peripeteia and crisis of the dramatic fiction or story, the necessary premise for the action and dynamic progression of the drama. Out of the critical position of bankrupt haggling with power control and defensive shunning of feeling and emotion, the dreamer is to learn to play with and enjoy life in both its beautiful and its terrible aspects, thus rendering the sistrum, the rattle of his squashed childhood play, back to the divinity in acknowledgment of the transpersonal sovereignty of what has been theriomorphically represented by the goddess as cat and lioness.

*   *   *

In the course of diligent working through of personal biographical and complex material, eventually a vision of a gestalt pattern arises that expresses symbolically the essence of the dominant life theme or themes in image, drama, or mythical form. The unrepresentable magic, pre-image level is converted into image. By virtue of encountering this analogue or mirror image, archetypal Self is met and the "similar" objectified pattern rebalances the imbalanced or dis-eased dynamic by subsuming it into transpersonal order. Thus, healing can ensue.

If we can but free ourselves from the bias of Cartesian positivistic tradition, we can see that nothing happens in our personal lives that is not either an unconscious acting out or a conscious enactment (these are our only "free" choices) of the unrepresentable order of archetype, spirit, or destiny, whatever we chose to call them. And no way or access exists to the implicate order of Self and Spirit other than through the conscious living and working through of the explicate given order—our personal lives, complexes, symptoms, relationship problems, and what have you—through perceiving and living life metaphorically and symbolically in terms of "Formation, Transformation, Eternal Spirit's Eternal Recreation" (Goethe 1950, p. 6286–7).

References

Bohm, D. 1980. *Wholeness and the implicate order*. London: Routledge & Kegan Paul.
Goethe, J. W. von. 1950. *Faust*. George M. Priest, trans. New York: Alfred Knopf. *Collected Writings*. Insel verlag Leipzig. Vol. 1. Gedichte, Spruche.
Grof, S. T. 1975. *Realms of the human unconscious*. New York: Viking Press.

———. 1985. *Beyond the Brain.* New York: University of New York Press.

Jung, C. G. 1953. *Two essays on analytical psychology.* In *Collected works,* vol. 7. Princeton: Princeton University Press, 1966.

———. 1959. *Aion: Researches into the phenomenology of the Self.* In *Collected works,* vol. 9:ii. Princeton: Princeton University Press.

———. 1968. *Psychology and alchemy.* In *Collected works,* vol. 12. Princeton: Princeton University Press.

———. 1969. *The structure and dynamics of the psyche.* In *Collected works,* vol. 8. Princeton: Princeton University Press.

Schroedinger et al. 1961. *On modern physics.* New York: Clarkson N. Potter.

Sheldrake, R. 1981. *A new science of life.* Los Angeles: J. P. Tarcher.

Weiss and English. 1949. *Psychosomatic medicine.* Philadelphia.

The Archetypal Foundation of the Therapeutic Process

Barbara Stevens Sullivan

An archetypal perspective on therapeutic work tells us the patient's psyche itself is the primary healer. The psyche rests on the archetypes, "typical basic form[s] of . . . ever-recurring psychic experiences . . . [that] formulate them in . . . appropriate way[s] . . ." (Jung 1921, p. 444). The archetypal layer of the patient's psyche functions as "an inherited organization of psychic energy, an ingrained system, which . . . facilitates [the operation of the energic processes]" (*ibid.*, p. 447). This inherited organization of energy is the collective unconscious, the matrix of the archetypes. When life is not working in one way or another, we try to turn in the direction of the archetypes, knowing that they contain the patterns of human behavior that could get us back on the right track.

Viewing the work of analysis from an archetypal perspective, the analyst tries to understand, first and foremost, where the patient's life force is heading—in what direction are native energies trying to move the patient, in what direction are they trying to move the analytic work? This does not ordinarily imply *talking about* archetypes with the patient. The

Barbara Stevens Sullivan, M.S.W., is a member of the Northern California Society of Jungian Analysts, with a private practice in Berkeley. She is the author of papers that have appeared in the *San Francisco Jung Institute Library Journal* and teaches at the Jung Institute of San Francisco.

fact that mythic motifs or archetypal images are being discussed does not necessarily indicate that the analyst takes an archetypal perspective on the analytic process; it indicates an attempt to attend to the archetypal layer of the patient's psyche. When therapists take an archetypal perspective on the process, they try to see the thrust of the psyche's own healing instincts and to align themselves with that thrust rather than attempting to channel the psyche's growth according to ego-based conceptions about how the psyche does or should grow.

This unfortunately implies that a given Jungian analyst may not, or even cannot, take an archetypal perspective on the work. It is completely possible to block the route that the individual's psyche tries to take through a "Jungian" theory about the direction of the patient's development, even a theory based on some mythological parallel to the individual's situation. Conversely, an increasing number of non-Jungian analysts are investigating the archetypal processes that analysis mobilizes as well as the archetypal layer of the psyche—without, however, using that particular word.

In this paper I will try to elucidate the "typical basic form" of the therapeutic process that "formulates [it] in an appropriate way." We know that within each individual lie the seeds of one's own personal healing, based on the needs generated by particular wounds. Beyond this, a general pattern underlies and guides all successful therapeutic work. Jungians often analyze the individual patient from an archetypal perspective: the patient is caught in the archetype of the *puer*, or the trickster, or the *senex*, for example; and therefore development is needed in this or that direction. In this paper, I am looking not at the *patient* from an archetypal perspective, but at the analytic *process*. Does analysis—all analysis, analysis as a form—follow an archetypal gradient that we could identify and thus more easily align ourselves with?

I will examine this question by surveying a number of analytic writers who have directly or indirectly addressed it. I hope to demonstrate that a variety of Jungian and non-Jungian analysts have all described the same basic pattern structuring the work. The analysts whose work I will try to correlate with each other on this topic are C. G. Jung, Donald Sandner, Sylvia Brinton Perera, Michael Balint, D. W. Winnicott, and Heinz Kohut.

Joseph Campbell: The Monomyth

As a backdrop for my exploration of the work of these clinicians, Campbell's description of the skeletal structure of the universal hero myth is worthy of mention. He suggests that all hero (or heroine) myths follow the same pattern in which the hero, leaving his ordinary world, descends into the underworld where he confronts hostile and helpful forces in a variety of forms. After any number of preparatory adventures, the hero undertakes his ultimate ordeal and gains his reward. Whatever concrete form that reward may take, it symbolizes "an expansion of consciousness and therewith of being" (Campbell 1949, p. 246). The final stage of this universal myth deals with the return of the hero to the ordinary world where the treasures of the underworld rejuvenate life (*ibid.*, pp. 245–46).

It is common to use this mythic pattern as a template for the individuation process. Through the course of one's life, one makes any number of mini-descents to the underworld and several major ones. Any night's descent into sleep/unconsciousness and the retrieval of a dream may be seen as sketching in the bare outline of the monomyth. Life's major crises and initiations also conform to this general pattern. The more deeply they are experienced, the more clearly we can see the congruence between the drama of the myth and that of the individual's life. A depth analysis is a major initiatory experience, and this monomyth is an excellent template for one. I hope to describe in this paper how an analyst-patient dyad will subjectively experience the monomyth's various elements as they unfold in the course of a therapeutic venture.

C. G. Jung: *The Psychology of the Transference*

Jung's monograph on the transference uses a particular set of alchemical engravings and maintains that they describe "the 'classical' form of transference and its phenomenology" (1946, p. 164). The question that Jung is addressing corresponds closely to mine: What is the universal form that guides the development of any particular person's therapeutic experience?

The central image in Jung's work is the *coniunctio*. The woodcuts of the *Rosarium Philosophorum* depict a king and queen meeting, fully dressed in court clothing, standing rather far apart. By the third image in the series, the king and queen, though still separate, face each other naked. As the series proceeds, they lower themselves into a bath where they have sexual intercourse. The result of this union is one person with two heads lying dead in the bath, which now resembles a tomb. Their soul leaves the body and rises heavenward. From heaven, a healing moisture waters the dead body, and the soul returns to reanimate the corpse. The last picture in the series shows the king and queen, now a unified hermaphrodite, risen from the tomb, reborn.

These pictures capture both the relationship between the patient and the therapist and the relationship between the patient and the patient's self. The therapeutic process that occurs within the patient is mirrored in the transference; the unfolding of the transference reflects the patient's inner development. Following Jung, I will translate this picture story into a description of the natural progress of the therapeutic endeavor.

The therapist and patient meet each other with the intention of exploring the patient's suffering, a unique pain contained in the endlessly flowing fountain of humanity's eternal suffering (see fig. 1, The Mercurial Fountain). Knowing very little about each other, they make a commitment to one another (fig. 2, King and Queen) and relax their guards. They come to know each other as undefendedly and authentically as possible (fig. 3, The Naked Truth). They immerse themselves in the patient's suffering (fig. 4, The Bath), gingerly at first, then more and more deeply until the distinction between the two individuals is lost (fig. 5, The Conjunction). This union is possible—or unavoidable—precisely because the patient's suffering reverberates with humanity's and thus with the therapist's as well. "Doctor and patient . . . find themselves in a relationship founded on mutual unconsciousness" (1946, p. 176). An experience of "unconscious identity" (*ibid.*, p. 183) arises between them. Jung says of this stage that the two participants "have gone back to the chaotic beginnings" (*ibid.*, p. 247). A therapeutic regression is in progress.

The result of this union, this loss of interpersonal and intrapsychic boundaries, is a state that is labeled "Death" (fig. 6), a word that captures the adult ego's experience of a deep regression and merger. This picture and the next (fig. 7), in which the soul ascends to heaven, leaving behind the lifeless body, images the depths of disorientation and despair which any successful treatment must navigate. Depression is an inherent part of life. If the patient's presenting complaint involves depression, the work will, of course, be imbued with it. If the patient is not depressed at the start, he or she will become depressed as manic defenses give way, facilitating a confrontation with the pain that existence necessarily involves. A descent to the underworld will be experienced at least partly as a depression.

If the patient can reach the nadir of pain, however, and come to accept it, something new may appear out of the depths. A healing moisture washes away the blackness (fig. 8, Purification). The patient's patience is rewarded with hope (fig. 9, Return of the Soul) and with some measure of resolution (fig. 10, The New Birth). Neither the therapist nor the patient has *done* anything, but something has *happened*. We could think of this as the result of the patient's "working through" his complexes, pro-

vided that we remember that "working through" is a fancy term for
"suffering." When the individual "accept[s] the conflict just as it is, with all
the suffering this inevitably entails" (1946, p. 194), the conflict will resolve itself, and the individual can move on.

In translating these alchemical pictures into a modern, depth psychotherapeutic form, we must remember that in any given case, the order, duration, and intensity of the stages will vary considerably (1946, p.
322). The general sequence in which stages of intense suffering are relieved by hopeful developments in the individual's inner and outer life
(figs. 6–10) repeats itself many times, always in the atmosphere of (fig. 5)
the *coniunctio*. Whether one is in the *nigredo* (the blackness) or the *albedo* (the whitening or purification) is always a question of degree. Eventually the transference more or less wears itself out. This particular descent resolves itself and the analysis as an interpersonal event is over,
although the intrapsychic *opus* continues throughout one's life.

Donald Sandner: Patterns of Symbolic Healing

In looking for the archetypal pattern that underlines psychoanalysis,
we are struck by the fact that analysis, as a new procedure, fosters an
emotional experience that seems unique, as any involved analysand will
attest. Does analytic work nevertheless have roots in human history? Are
we looking at an intensified form of a procedure that has a past?

The most obvious forerunner of analysis would be the symbolic
healing practices of primitive societies—the work of medicine men and
shamans who, like modern psychotherapists, seek to cure the ills of the
soul. Donald Sandner has studied primitive healing practices extensively.
He has outlined a structural pattern that all symbolic healing practices
follow and a set of experiences through which symbolic healers commonly take their patients (Sandner 1979). Like Jung's alchemical imagery,
Sandner's stages parallel Campbell's description of the universal monomyth.

Sandner differentiates symbolic and scientific healing: Scientific
healing (i.e., modern medicine) attempts to achieve a concrete cure,
while a symbolic healing procedure such as analysis "explains, or at least
provides a context for, the sufferings of [the patient]" (Sandner 1979, p.
11). The "cure" that proceeds from this attempt may be much less tangible than the cure mediated by penicillin. Jung does not even strive for
cure, focusing instead on wholeness. The results of a successful analysis
are similar in some ways to those of primitive healing ceremonies: The
patient "feels better"; the process "helps some." There is still pain and

suffering, but they become tolerable, meaningful, and even enriching instead of tormenting and chaotic.

Sandner (1979, pp. 20–22) suggests that symbolic healing practices move through five stages:

1. Purification: of the doctor and the patient and perhaps of the space within which the healing rituals are to be held.

2. Presentation or Evocation: in which the relevant symbolic images are presented in visual or audible forms and are invested with the numinous power that underlies them.

3. Identification: both the doctor and the patient become identified with the powers that have been evoked. "The medicine man symbolically becomes the supernatural power, and at the same time may take into himself the evil or bad part of the patient that is causing the sickness" (*ibid,* p. 21).

4. Transformation: The healer "wins the battle, banishes the disease, expels the evil, counteracts the sorcery, or recovers the soul" (*ibid.,* p. 21).

5. Release: The healer and the healed are ritually returned to their ordinary lives, divested of the numinous symbolic power with which they have been imbued during the ceremony.

In trying to imagine how this pattern might manifest itself in analytic work, we need to ask first what the "relevant symbolic images" might be that are evoked in the second stage and that dominate the remainder of the work. In primitive healing practices these symbols are presented in visual or audible forms, forms that the culture has developed and passed on from one generation to another. As Jung indicates in *The Psychology of the Transference*, underlying depth psychological treatment is the image of the *coniunctio*, symbolizing the individual's union with the deeper self. Psychoanalysis constellates this symbol in emotional forms that are invisible and inaudible. We call these invisible emotional forms "the transference relationship." The analyst and the patient live the symbol out, and the analysis consists in large measure in studying the various transformations of the symbol which their relationship embodies. Alternatively, we could say that analysis consists of a quest for the symbol initially presented in invisible form. Via a long-term experience of incarnating the symbol, its image may become manifest in a dream or vision.

The invisibility of the symbol is a function of the fact that analysis, unlike primitive symbolic healing practices, is a completely individual affair. The analyst is concerned with a particular person's descent and union with himself or herself, with finding the specific images that capture this unique marriage with the self; the medicine man attempts to guide every person's descent into the tribe's collective pattern.

We can now see how Sandner's stages guide modern psychotherapy. Purification involves the establishment of the analytic contract and frame. A container is created, set apart from the ordinary world. The alchemists enjoined the worker to make sure the alchemical *vas* was hermetically sealed lest any part of the wholeness they sought be lost. Between Jung's second and third pictures we see this purification in the shift in the connection between the king and queen: In the second image, when the king and queen first meet, they symbolize their connection by joining their left hands and holding in their right hands each end of a flowering branch over which hovers the Holy Ghost. Jung suggests that the left-handed connection indicates the secretly incestuous nature of their bond. In the third picture, their left-handed connection has changed; and they hold the flowering branch with *both* hands, indicating that their connection in all areas now proceeds through the Holy Ghost. The boundaries of their container have been firmly established. Impure instinctual behavior is banished from the work which now will be exclusively spiritual/symbolic in nature.

At some point after the container has been established, the transference clicks into place; we have moved into the second stage of Presentation or Evocation. On a personal level, the analyst embodies the patient's particular original objects. On an archetypal level, the same instinctual energies that initially bound the infant-patient to his or her parents now bind patient to analyst. As the intensity and power of the bond grows, we move more deeply into stage three, Identification. Willingly or otherwise, the analyst must "take into himself the evil or bad part of the patient that is causing the sickness" and carry these projections through Sandner's stage of Transformation—the stage of "working through." As the patient's inner self realigns itself in a stronger, more harmonious pattern, the final stage of Release or termination is navigated. This stage, in which the power of the transference is reabsorbed by the patient, is often lengthy and difficult, and it is never really complete. Analysts, like parents, cannot become absolute peers; but when enough movement in that direction takes place, the analyst and patient are freed from their interpenetrating connection, allowing the patient to leave and go on with life.

In addition to describing the cross-cultural stages of symbolic healing practices, Sandner describes the four central principles of the Navajo healing ceremonies, principles that he suggests may be basic to healing in other cultures as well. These four elements—principles inherent in Campbell's universal hero myth—are:

1. return to origins
2. confrontation and manipulation of evil
3. death and rebirth
4. restoration of the universe (Sandner 1979, p. 4).

In analysis, the four elements overlap and interpenetrate. The Return to the Origins—the hero's descent—is experienced as a therapeutic regression. On a personal level, the patient feels infantile and dependent on the therapist. A substantial amount of time and energy is ordinarily spent exploring the particular forms the patient's childhood suffering took. On an archetypal level, the patient descends into the unconscious, immersing him or her self in the alchemical bath. Consciously or unconsciously, the descent is experienced as a merger with the analyst comparable to the infant's merger with the mother.

In the primitive healing ceremonies that Sander examines, the different elements of the work are collective rather than individual in nature, so that the patient is returned to *tribal* origins via the culture's particular mythology. Discussing this common healing procedure, Mircea Eliade says, "We get the impression that for archaic societies life cannot be *repaired*, it can only be *re-created* by a return to sources" (quoted in Sandner 1979, p. 111, italics in original). A similar situation exists in analysis. Sandner describes the primitive's experience of this return to the origins of the tribe: "[T]he presentation of the origin myth . . . allow[s] the patient to identify with those symbolic forces which once created the world, and by entering into them to re-create himself in a state of health and wholeness" (*ibid.*, p. 111). In analysis patients return to their individual origins and connect with the archetypal forces within that once—in infancy—created the world. Out of this experience, they can achieve their own re-creation.

Sandner's second element, the confrontation with and manipulation of evil, is pictured in Campbell's monomyth as various encounters between the hero and negative underworld forces. In analysis, the patient confronts and deals with the question of human evil in the regressed state induced by the return to origins. The parents' evil is uncovered, evil which the patient has heretofore arranged to not notice; and the patient's rage emerges. Through the experience of rage and other negative emotions directed at all the people who can be blamed for the pain of existence, the patient begins to face his or her own evil (e.g., rage) and to come to terms with it. Jungians call this working with the Shadow.

The entire analysis is experienced as a Death and Rebirth. The descent into the unconscious and its attendant emotional regression to the individual's origins feels like a death. The Confrontation with Evil occurs in this disoriented, abnormal state. The renewal that eventually emerges is a rebirth that leads to and supports a new ordering of the individual's life, both inside and out, a Restoration of the Universe that leads ultimately to the end of the analysis. The parallels between Sandner's stages and principles, Jung's alchemical images, and Campbell's monomyth are outlined in Table 1.

Sylvia Brinton Perera: *Descent to the Goddess*

Sylvia Brinton Perera's monograph uses the myth of Inanna as a template for feminine development, amplifying the myth with clinical examples. By examining feminine development *in the context of analysis*, she offers us a sense of what an analyst with a patient of either sex might experience as the archetypal pattern underlying human development unfolds in a late twentieth-century consulting room.

Inanna, the Sumerian goddess of heaven and earth, journeys to the underworld, Ereshkigal's realm, and demands admission. She is brought naked into Ereshkigal's inner sanctum. Here her soul is judged, and Ereshkigal kills her. She is hung on a peg where her body turns into rotting meat.

When Inanna fails to return, her aide sets out to organize a rescue. The great father gods refuse to help, but Enki, the god of water and wisdom, is responsive. He creates two mourners from the dirt stuck under his fingernails, and they slip into the underworld unseen by its guardians, carrying with them the food and water of life. Penetrating to Ereshkigal's throne, the mourners find the dark goddess consumed by her own pain. They empathize with her compassionately, and, as their empathy relieves her suffering, she rewards them by returning Inanna's corpse.

The mourners revivify Inanna, and she returns to the upper world charged with the task of finding a substitute to take her place. She comes upon her primary consort, Dumuzi, who sits enjoying himself on his throne, unaware of her absence. Sacrificing the one she has loved best in this world, Inanna fixes on Dumuzi the same eyes of death that Ereshkigal fixed on her and condemns him to take her place in the land of the dead. We have here the tale of a female hero that corresponds in form to Campbell's monomyth.

As a template for the analytic process, the myth presents the movement of the work toward its core as a disrobing: At each of the underworld's seven gates, one article of Inanna's clothing is removed until she enters the central chamber naked. Perera suggests that a similar process occurs in analysis as the adaptive defenses that protect and hide the pa-

<table>
<tr><th>Campbell's Monomyth</th><th colspan="2">Jung's Psychology of the Transference</th><th>Sandner's Stages</th><th colspan="2">Sandner's principles</th></tr>
<tr><td>Preparation for the journey</td><td></td><td>The Mercurial Fountain
King & Queen
The Naked Truth</td><td>Purification</td><td></td><td></td></tr>
<tr><td>Descent of the hero</td><td rowspan="3">T
H
E

C
O
N
J
U
N
C
T
I
O
N</td><td>The Bath</td><td>Presentation
or
Evocation</td><td rowspan="3">D
E
A
T
H

&

R
E
B
I
R
T
H</td><td>Return to origins</td></tr>
<tr><td>Encounters with underworld forces</td><td>Death
Ascent of the Soul</td><td>Identification</td><td>Confrontation and manipulation of evil</td></tr>
<tr><td>A successful ultimate ordeal</td><td>Purification
The Return of the Soul</td><td>Transformation</td><td></td></tr>
<tr><td>Return to the upper world</td><td></td><td>The New Birth</td><td>Release</td><td></td><td>Restoration of the universe</td></tr>
</table>

Table 1

tient's essential nature peel slowly away. The central experience of the work is one of unraveling. Subjectively experienced, a journey to the underworld—to the world beneath our conscious adult world—is a passage to the world on top of which we built our adult selves, that of childhood. The deeper the layers we are compelled to explore, the more infantile the experience becomes. The patient is returning to a preverbal core. It is frightening, for the therapist as well as the patient, to allow this process to unfold. The myth reassures us of the experience's ultimate value. During Inanna's descent, the earth is barren and appears to have died. We must tolerate the patient's loss of competence—especially within the hour, but also occasionally in the context of his or her life—if we are to hold the patient through this regression into rebirth.

Only when the therapist feels secure can the patient allow regression to proceed. As the regression deepens, the analysand suffers "the dismembering dissolution of her own old identity" (Perera 1981, p. 53) in a powerful depression. Rather than seeking a cure for this depression, Ereshkigal "demands death, complete destruction of differentiations and the felt sense of individuality, and total transformation. She demands a terrible empathy, one that surrenders, waits upon and groans with her" (*ibid.*, pp. 26–27). The patient and the therapist are called upon to worship the Black Madonna, the Death Mother, the Old Crone. To the extent that one can revere her, her poisonous side can turn to the service of life.

Similarly, the anlaysand must learn Enki's view of the *prima materia* of the work, the dirt caught under one's fingernails. This worthless initial stuff, out of whith healing ultimately emerges, is the patient's

> unpremeditated, raw, basic reactiveness . . . the small, potent, autonomous flickers of emotion, the gripping, vibrant, and painful concrete details, the compelling fantasies . . . the autonomous psyche as it is revealed in the small personal, here-and-now, affect-laden facts . . . the despised slag of life's processes. (1981, p. 69)

In what is always a difficult and painful development, the patient's attitude toward his or her own infantile aspects must shift from rejection and disgust to acceptance and respect. We see the parallel here with alchemical instructions, which always tell the worker to begin the transformative work with something disgusting like the menstruum of a whore.

In a variation on this theme, Enki's mourners affirm Ereshkigal's suffering rather than trying to smooth over the negative aspects of existence. Like these mourners, the therapist's task is to

> trust the life force even when it sounds its misery. Complaining is one voice of the dark goddess . . . It does not, first and foremost, seek alleviation, but

> simply to state the existence of things as they are felt to be to a sensitive and vulnerable being. (1981, p. 70)

To facilitate the regressive unfolding within which the patient can experience the full range of aliveness—of vibrancy, miserable and ecstatic by turns—both patient and therapist are called upon to take a receptive stance that conflicts with many of our heroic ideals. Inanna undertakes her journey to witness the funeral of Gugulana, the Great Bull of Heaven: the heroic attitude that must die for individuation/analysis to proceed. Inanna, our universal analysand, must submit to a transformative process that works upon her, that she cannot control, that manifests itself in the rotting of her body (the ego/self with which she has been familiar). This process is the alchemical *putreficatio*, which the patient experiences as terrible suffering that must somehow be both endured and worshiped, for it is part of god's (Ereshkigal's) order. Suffering grounds the patient in life.

Just as the patient must accept the death of the hero, so the therapist must let go and submit to the therapeutic process rather than try to run it. We need to recognize our helplessness and focus not on how to *do* the work but on how to *let* the work happen, how to restrain our impulses to block the process, how to find the courage to sit still to receive the emotional experiences that a descent of any significance unleashes. We are called upon to accept a far humbler (and more difficult) role than our academic training prepared us for. We must witness rather than guide, enter into the patient's pain rather than cure it. We must accept the disorienting *participation mystique* generated in the therapeutic container and relinquish the Apollonian, analytic separateness that offered only the illusion of understanding our experiences. We must be willing to be confused and lost if we are to accompany someone into the chaotic, uncharted areas of his or her soul.

When Ereshkigal's deadly negativity is resisted, it becomes stuck, demanding an opportunity to exist in the material world; accepted, it leads to rebirth. But what is the nature of that rebirth? We can be sure that the cure will not be the one imaged by the old ego, for that ego denied the demands of Ereshkigal. The reborn initiate has learned, to one extent or another, to honor life's darkness as well as its light. Inanna is surrounded by demons when she first emerges from the underworld. The "cured" patient no longer seeks a happily-ever-after ending. There will be those who are not thrilled with the transformation, for the reborn individual is one who "can be obnoxious, but she speaks her own word, and looks deep inside to find it" (1981, p. 41). Patients, losing their old adaptation to collective norms, will be clumsy and difficult in the struggle to integrate the dark forces—Ereshkigal's eyes of death—that have been contacted. They will *not* meet society's expectations but will each be his or her own true self: not a static self, but a developing individual who can be unpleasant as well as nice. They will be less amenable than previously, but more vital, more real, and more exciting to know.

Roughly half way through our survey of analytic descriptions of the archetypal layer of the therapeutic process, I wish to note the central role that regression has played in each of the theorist's conceptions. Jung's patient-therapist pair immersed themselves in an alchemical bath and returned "to the chaotic beginnings" (Jung 1946, p. 247). Sandner's patient surrendered to the transference experience—identified with the symbol—and returned to his origins. Perera's analysand descended into preverbal depths. As we study these three Jungians' work, the pattern of analysis which is emerging centers on a regressive experience. The death and rebirth of the therapeutic process occur for the patient in an infantile, disoriented state. In a letter to Jung, John Perry asked if the birth of the self necessarily involves a return to the personal infantile complexes. Jung replied that in general "patients revive their infantile reminiscences. . . . It is an unavoidable mechanism . . . a teleological attempt to grow up again" (1984, p. 123).

Perera's work has been helpful in sketching what we might experience in the clinical situation as the archetypal process mapped out by Jung and Sandner unfolds. Non-Jungians have worked extensively in this area—the manifestation of the archetype in reality. They have been less able to imagine the archetype *an sich* but are more fascinated with the forms of its concrete emergence in the analytic process than Jungians have been. As we turn now to neo-Freudian work, we will be looking through the clinical reality toward its archetypal foundation. Where Jung and Sandner described the archetypal basis of the work, and largely left us to intuit what it might be like to live the archetype out, the neo-Freudians will help us get a firmer grasp on how Jung's "chaotic beginnings" will feel for the analyst/patient couple immersed together in the bath.

Michael Balint: *The Basic Fault*

Unlike Winnicott or Kohut, whose work I shall look at later, Michael Balint did not offer a major perspective on the nature of the psyche; but he explored at length both the potentialities and the dangers of the deep regression that occur in a successful analysis. He describes what I would consider the universal—i.e., archetypal—human wound that fuels all analytic work: The analysand's initial environment failed, in one way or another, consistently over time, adequately to meet all needs. Out of this initial failure arose a basic fault, a pattern of adapting to an inadequate environment which enabled the individual to cope at the cost of distorting his or her essential nature. To the extent that an analysis is successful, it will enable the patient "to go back to the pre-traumatic period . . . to relive the trauma . . . in order that he may mobilize his 'fixated' libido and find new possibilities [for life]" (Balint 1968, p. 82). The patient regresses in order to make a "new beginning" (ibid., pp. 131–32).

The analyst knows the patient has reached the level of the basic fault (often called the preoedipal level) when words no longer serve their ordinary purpose of communicating content. Interpretations are experienced as "an attack, a demand, a base insinuation . . . [or] as something highly pleasing and gratifying, exciting or soothing, or as a seduction. . . ." The analyst's every "gesture . . . assume[s] an importance far beyond anything that could be realistically intended" (Balint 1968, p. 18). The analyst knows subjectively that the patient has regressed to this formative layer when the analyst begins to feel a wish to rescue the patient, to *make* his or her environment behave properly, to provide the love and concern that parents failed to offer (ibid., p. 184). When the analyst feels a yearning to bypass the analytic task of *experiencing* the patient's suffering, the analyst knows that they have reached a point where interpretations are no longer a useful tool in the work.

How, then, is the therapist to work? Balint suggests that the therapeutic task at this stage centers on creating and maintaining an object relationship that can hold the regressed patient. Whereas an effective interpretation will lead to insight, "the creation of a proper relationship results in a 'feeling'; while 'insight' correlates with seeing, 'feeling' correlates with touching . . ." (1968, p. 161). The therapist must touch the patient at the level of his soul. The analyst must be a "primary object" for the patient, consenting "to sustain and carry the patient like the earth or the water sustains and carries a man who entrusts his weight to them. . . . [T]he analyst . . . must prove more or less indestructible, must not insist on maintaining harsh boundaries, but must allow the development of a kind of mix-up between the patient and himself" (ibid., p. 145). Out of this "*unio mystica,* . . . [this] harmonious interpenetrating mix-up" (ibid., p. 74), the patient's true self can be born.

Balint meticulously sorts through the dangers that a therapeutic regression can unleash: the infinitely spiraling demands for one special gratification after another, culminating at its worst in a psychotic reaction when the analyst's limits must eventually be faced. He suggests that we differentiate between regressive demands that seek to gratify the individual's cravings and those that seek a witness to the depth of the patient's needs. When the patient's demands fall into the latter category, *or when the therapist can stay centered in a willingness to witness but not to gratify*, an object relationship may be established within which the patient can experience regressive needs fully, by letting go of the adapted false ego and becoming centered in the true self waiting to be born.

Like Perera, Balint urges us to recognize the value of the patient's complaining rather than attempting to soothe the complaints away (1968, pp. 108–9). He tries to "tolerate" the patient's pain, to "bear with it" (*ibid.*, p. 184), to accept the experiences of darkness and death which emerge as the patient's psyche slowly unravels in the therapeutic container. Like Jung, Balint focused on the value of "entering in" to the patient's suffering as the key healing factor rather than attempting to operate from the outside.

Balint's therapeutic goal is Jungian in nature. He does not hope to cure but rather to "enable the patient to experience a kind of regret or mourning about . . . the unalterable fact of a defect or fault in [him]self which . . . has cast its shadow over [his] whole life, and the unfortunate effects of which can never fully be made good" (1968, p. 183). The goal is wholeness, not perfection.

D. W. Winnicott

Balint and Winnicott were mutually influenced colleagues. Balint suggested that by regressing to the site of the primary wound, the individual could reconnect with a "true self." This conception of a true self and of a false, caretaker self is Winnicott's (1960). The false self shields the true self from the impinging toxic environment. To the extent that the individual lives out of a false self, his or her life is based on complying with the demands of external reality; the result is a sense of futility, a pervasive doubt about the value of living. Cut off from life by the false self, the true self cannot develop; but its existence can be preserved, along with the hope that some day a more nourishing environment will present itself within which it may emerge and begin to grow.

Winnicott's image of an effective analysis centers on providing that adequately nourishing environment for the patient. As one comes to trust the analyst's reliability and good-enough-ness, the patient will regress to *need*—meaning, to that infantile level where the split between the true and false selves began to entrench itself. At this level, the patient reconnects with the true self and redevelops to a new maturity based on creative living rather than on complying with the demands of the outer world.

The true self, which can live creatively, is both the beginning and the goal of the work. (We see in this paradox one example of Winnicott's delightfully alchemical approach.) Psychotherapy consists of a search for the self, and "it is only in being creative that the individual discovers the self" (Winnicott 1971, p. 54). In the experience of *playing,* which is the basis of all creativity, the individual discovers his or her existence as a center of initiative rather than as a reaction to outer impingements. The spontaneous, playful gesture, which can only originate in the true self, becomes the thread that leads the patient to the self.

> Psychotherapy takes place in the overlap of two areas of playing, that of the patient and that of the therapist. . . . Psychotherapy has to do with two people playing together. . . . [It is] a highly specialized form of playing in the service of communication with oneself and others. . . . When a patient cannot play, the therapist must attend to this major symptom before interpreting fragments of behavior. . . . Playing is itself a therapy . . . a creative experience. (*Ibid.,* 1971, pp. 38, 41, 47, 50)

In Jungian terms, Winnicott is suggesting that we treat the analytic interaction as an exercise in active imagination. Jung describes active imagination as a procedure in which "an unconscious *a priori* precipitates itself into plastic form . . ." (Jung 1954, p. 204). By experiencing the "unconscious *a priori*" in the material world, one encounters the tangible reality of the unconscious psyche. Rather than encouraging the patient to attempt this focused playing alone, Winnicott invites him or her to deintegrate in the consulting room and to surprise both patient and analyst with the spontaneous, creative movement that emerges from the patient's own depths. By gradually falling backwards in time into a state of unintegrated formlessness, the patient opens the way for a creative gesture to emerge from the true self; and the analyst has the opportunity to mirror this creative movement back. If it is seen and reflected back, it can be integrated by the conscious personality. The unplanned, mutual experience that develops is the "plastic form," the sensual creation that makes the self real.

Winnicott suggests there is a normal infantile developmental process that can be constellated anew in the analytic situation. Navigating this process heals the crippling that resulted from the ways the individual's initial environment blocked on authentic unfolding:

> When I look I am seen, so I exist.
> I can now afford to look and see.
> I now look creatively and what I apperceive I also perceive. (Winnicott 1971, p. 114)

Winnicott explicitly states that psychotherapy involves redoing development (see, e.g., 1971, p. 137). The crucial element the analyst offers is a specialized setting within which the patient can descend into "a nonpurposive state" (*ibid.*, p. 55). The patient gradually hands over to the analyst the caretaking functions of the false self and begins to live out of a breathtakingly vulnerable center, the true self.

Interpretive work is of minimal significance. "[T]he significant moment is that at which [the patient] *surprises himself or herself*" (Winnicott 1971, p. 41, italics in original). Winnicott voices "a plea to every therapist to allow for the patient's capacity to play . . . to be creative in the analytic work. The patient's creativity can be only too easily stolen by a therapist who knows too much" (*ibid.*, p. 57).

> Psychotherapy is not making clever and apt interpretations; by and large it is a long-term giving the patient back what the patient brings. . . . [I]f I do this well enough the patient will find his or her own self and will be able to exist and to feel real. . . .
> But I would not like to give the impression that I think this task of reflecting what the patient brings is easy. It is not easy, it is emotionally exhausting. (1971, p. 117)

Winnicott offers a particularly lovely image of the essence of the regressive experience on which therapy is based. All of the clinicians discussed in this paper see analysis as recapitulating development. Winnicott is especially adept at describing how the tiny interactions of each analytic moment can work to bring the patient back to the center he or she started from, where the self can be found.

Heinz Kohut

Heinz Kohut founded a new branch of psychoanalysis, Self Psychology. Unbeknownst to himself, this neo-Freudian became involved in an attempt to describe the archetypal patterns underlying the analytic encounter. He has been a thinker of considerable influence in American Jungian Institutes: What does Kohut offer beyond (or beside) the work of Jung and the post-Jungians?

The basis of Kohut's ultimate break with Freud was similar to that of Jung's: both men rejected Freud's libido theory. Using different termino-

logical systems, both Kohut and Jung turned their attention to the individual's wholeness—to one's self—and both men postulate that issues of
selfhood rather than drives are paramount in human motivation. Jung described the central human attempt as the urge to individuation, the attempt to become the whole person one is meant to be. Kohut believed
that successful analysis will enable the patient "to devote himself to the
realization of the nuclear program laid down in the center of his self"
(Kohut 1984, p. 152). Where Jung focused on the intrapsychic ramifications of the drive to individuate, Kohut studied the manifestations of that
drive in the analytic situation. His relative comfort with entanglement
(relative to Jung, at least, and perhaps to analysts in general) enabled him
to penetrate deeply into the analysand's personal experience of an archetypal core.

He postulated a universal transference pattern within which the patient experiences the therapist as a "selfobject," as an extension of the patient's own being. Kohut identified three varieties of this experience,
each revolving around a particular set of defects in the self, each healing
the injuries of the ego-self axis from a different angle.

One pole of Kohut's "self" involves the individual's creative ambitions. To the extent that the patient's psyche focuses on healing the self
from the vantage point of the creative pole, a "mirror transference" to the
analyst will develop. The patient will need and demand unbroken mirroring from the therapist/selfobject, who, by seeing the patient as an
intact unit with a consistent wellspring of initiative emanating from the
center, can enable the patient to connect with that wellspring and to actualize an increasing proportion of creative energies.

The other pole of Kohut's "self" involves ideals. When trying to heal
the self by attending to the wounds of this pole, an "idealizing transference" emerges. In this pattern the therapist is seen, perhaps unconsciously, as omnipotent and omniscient. The patient unconsciously
merges with the therapist and enters into a godlike state, introjecting the
idealized strength and solidity of the therapist, and transforming them
into psychic structure. In Kleinian language, the patient eats and digests
the therapist.

Between the poles of ambitions and ideals lies the area of the individual's native talents and capacities. Work in this area causes a "twinship
transference" to develop, and the patient imagines that he or she and the
selfobject/therapist are identical. The healing potential of this experience
is rooted in the need to be a human being among other human beings.
The disorder this process eases is imaged in Kafka's *Metamorphosis*.
Where a mirror transference functions to "vitalize via emotional partici-

pation and reflection what the patient [experiences] but [is] unable to feel as real" (Kohut 1984, p. 196), a twinship transference enables someone who feels real to feel human.

These three varieties of selfobject transferences are universal—archetypal—rather than personal in nature. Kohut is not looking at the way the patient reexperiences idiosyncratic original objects. Instead he is studying the instinctual energies that initially fueled the individual's attachment to those original objects, and he is describing the way those instinctual energies re-emerge and shape the individual's new attachment to the analyst. The energies of Kohut's focus are *psychologically* rather than *biologically* instinctual in nature. Where Freud began with the body and postulated the psyche as a secondary phenomenon, Kohut, like Jung, postulated the psyche as the primary reality of the work. We cannot consider Kohut a Jungian, for there is too much of Jung that Kohut missed; but Kohut's work can be comfortably contained in Jung's, and its clinical depth enriches the relative scarcity of Jung's writings about clinical work.

Regardless of which particular form of the transference is operating at any moment—for in practice all three always operate to one extent or another—Kohut describes a consistent underlying pattern for analytic work. In one way or another the patient has managed to keep alive some hope that a satisfactory, empathic selfobject exists, despite the ways in which the parents failed to fill that function. The patient's hope is activated by the inherent nature of the psychotherapeutic situation, in which the patient experiences himself or herself as "the focus of the empathetically listening analyst" (1984, p. 202). If the analyst does not interfere too much, "selfobject transferences arise spontaneously and without any active encouragement from the side of the analyst . . ." (*ibid.*, p. 201). Given the space to operate in, the patient will regress to the site of the original childhood traumata and will attempt to redo development. "[T]he progression of the therapeutic process . . . essentially repeats (though not in all details) the steps of normal childhood maturation" (*ibid.*, p. 186).

Kohut suggests a particular conception of the healing process in this central stage of the treatment, where the analyst holds the regressed patient through his or her dark night of the soul. Time and again, the selfobject transference is disturbed by the analyst's imperfectly empathic behavior. Each time, the analyst will optimally respond to the patient's distress by understanding it, by recognizing (often with the patient's help) how his equilibrium was upset, and, when the patient's self has become strong enough to tolerate it, by tying the upset to its genetic roots in the patient's childhood. Each time this process occurs, a potential trauma is transformed into a structure-building experience that Kohut calls "transmuting internalization" and which I described earlier as the patient's eating and digesting the therapist. As these experiences accumulate over the years of analysis, the patient's self grows in strength and integrity. Dependence on the analyst as an *archaic* selfobject lessens as the patient becomes increasingly able to find *mature* selfobjects in outer life; and the analysis comes to a natural end.

"Transmuting internalizations" is Kohut's particular fantasy of how the growth process works. It is a useful fantasy for it provides a container to hold the therapist through the process that must be allowed to unfold in its own way. The fantasy functions as a rationale for the therapist's continuing support of the patient and the process, until the process more or less completes itself and the patient emerges from it a more solid and authentic adult than the one who entered treatment. Whether one accepts or rejects this fantasy is peripheral to our interest here. Kohut has described a pattern for the work that, regardless of *how* it works, meshes well with the other descriptions of this pattern that we have been examining.

Discussion

I have looked at the work of Jungian analysts, of British Object Relations analysts, and of the founder of American Self Psychology. While we must assume that these three groups of clinicians have some familiarity with each other, they almost never cite each other's work. We can therefore also assume that each school's work is relatively independent. Before underlining the striking similarity in the vision of analysis *qua* analysis which we have seen in their work, I wish to deal with an area of ambiguity.

Perhaps because they do have available the concept of archetypes, the Jungians are comfortable suggesting that the patterns of analysis they describe are universal. Both Balint and Winnicott hedge on this issue; and it was only at the very end of his career that Kohut allowed himself to assert that his work was about mankind rather than about a particular diagnostic segment of humanity. It is always clear in reading these analysts and their followers that *their interest* was in those patients who immersed themselves in a deeply healing, regressive experience, but they do maintain they are talking about "patients *in a certain classification category*" (Winnicott 1971, p. 86, italics in original). Other patients presumably live out a different analytic pattern. Contemporary depth psychological work increasingly centers on patients in this "classification category," the category called "borderline" in America and "schizoid" in Britain. The distinction that Winnicott and Balint made (fuzzily and in passing) between "borderline" cases and true neurotics is now made quite adamantly by such leading theoreticians of borderline pathology as James Masterson.

I believe this division is itself an important example of borderline pathology, of splitting. Let me quote Winnicott's description of the borderline case:

> [T]he kind of case in which the core of the patient's disturbance is psychotic, but the patient has enough psychoneurotic organization always to be able to present psychoneurosis or psychosomatic disorder when the central psychotic anxiety threatens to break through in crude form. (1971, p. 87)

In my very ordinary outpatient practice, among my close friends and family, in my intimate dealings with colleagues, and certainly in my exploration of myself, I have yet to find a human being to whom this description does not apply. I do not wish to suggest that there are not profound differences between people in ego strength, in their abilities to experience and contain the underlying psychotic anxieties. But I do believe that the psyche always contains a borderline layer where islands of madness emerge and recede in inchoate forms. Whose dreamscape does not include the manwoman locked in the attic, the rabid dog, the homicidal maniac, the suicidal anorexic? The individual therapist's ability to experience this psychotic layer of himself or herself and to allow patients to bring it into their analyses is often a sign of ego strength, not fragility.

Talking about "this kind of case"—which I would call "non-psychotic human beings"—Winnicott continues:

> [T]he psychoanalyst may collude for years with the patient's need to be psychoneurotic (as opposed to mad) . . . the analysis goes well, and everyone is pleased. The only drawback is that the analysis never ends. It can be terminated, and the patient may even mobilize a psychoneurotic false self for the purpose of finishing and expressing gratitude. But . . . there has been no change in the underlying (psychotic) state and . . . the analyst and the patient have succeeded in colluding to bring about a failure. (1971, p. 87)

In very different ways, these six major thinkers offer congruent pictures of the psychic place where healing occurs. It is a place of deep regression or descent, where the primary process holds sway, and unreasonable, infantile emotional experiences are the norm. Bit by bit, the patient sheds defenses, and character armor, held in the secure container created by the relationship with the analyst. The patient regresses to the wounded center where the archetypal forces ruling his or her existence are experienced as directly as possible. The defensive fantasy that human beings construct, in which the individual is imagined in control of his psyche, is dropped, and a recognition emerges that the psyche contains and dominates the ego which must, willingly or otherwise, follow the dictates of its human nature. The individual is reborn, centered in the self rather than the ego. From this place the patient constructs a new maturational line along which a second journey to adulthood can be undertaken. Where early development was distorted by various wounding splits that alienated the patient from the self, this second development can integrate sophisticated ego skills with a more authentic connection to his or her true nature.

In different ways, all six of these thinkers emphasize the fact that this regressive experience involves a deep and disorienting merger between analyst and patient. Jung's *coniunctio* grows out of a state of *participation mystique* between the two individuals. He compares the transference experience to a chemical combination which alters both the analyst and the analysand. "It is inevitable that the doctor should be influenced . . . and even that his nervous health should suffer. He quite literally 'takes over' the sufferings of his patient and shares them with him" (Jung 1946, pp. 171–72). Sandner's shaman "symbolically becomes the supernatural power" (Sandner 1979, p. 21), thus embodying the patient's unconscious psyche. The patient finds his or her depths in the other. Perera discusses the therapeutic merger at length: "On the deep levels of the transference-countertransference . . . two individuals share one psychic reality. . . . [I]t is often hard to discern what affect or image belongs to whom" (Perera 1981, p. 60). Balint describes this crucial loss of boundaries as a "harmonious interpenetrating mix-up" and surveys some of the terms that other Freudian analysts have used when referring to it:

> Anna Freud: the need-satisfying object
> Heinz Hartmann: the average expectable environment
> W. R. Bion: the container and the contained
> Margaret Little: the basic unit
> Masud Khan: the protective shield
> R. Spitz: mediator of the environment
> Margaret Mahler: extra-uterine matrix. (Balint 1968, p. 168)

Some terms are more explicit than others, but all call up an image of two individuals losing their edges and mingling with each other at the level of their souls. Winnicott, as Balint notes, coined images of this merger prolifically: the good-enough analyst/mother, the environment analyst/mother, primary maternal preoccupation, the facilitating environment, etc. Kohut's core concept of "selfobject" emphasizes in its spelling as well as its definition the merger on which successful therapy rests.

In Jungian circles, a regressive experience is sometimes contrasted with an archetypal one. I am suggesting that an immediate experience of the archetype can occur only in a regressed state. It is in infancy that we are in direct contact with the transpersonal psyche, and only by shedding the complicated defensive shields that make up "adults" can we experience these primary energies again. We can talk *about* them as adults. But if we are to *experience* even the most spiritualized aspect of the living numen which *is* the archetype, we must come, like Inanna, "crouched and stripped bare" (Perera 1981, p. 9), in all our smallness before the greatness of the forces from which we come. Paradoxically, we find the archetypal layer of the psyche in our most deeply personal and private self.

The Jungian world has been divided along an axis that has been called the London-Zurich split. Where the London school can be seen as placing the transference at the center of the work, Zurich Jungians put the dream at the center. The image of analysis I offer here might represent a step toward reconciling those positions, for it would be a misunderstanding of my view to imagine that I think the analysis of the transference is the central element in the work. I am rather suggesting that the analysand's *experience of the living reality of the psyche* is the crucial therapeutic agent. In analysis, that experience occurs in the interpersonal container called "the transference relationship," and it is therefore natural to expect that relationship to capture some significant amount of the participants' attention. Outside the analysis, the individual may experience the reality of the psyche in dreams or in life. Unfortunately, many people, lacking a vision of existence that values suffering or an intimate relationship to support them in their suffering, are afraid to wake up. It is only by the intensification of aliveness that analysis provides that they can develop the capacity to experience their dreams and their lives. Jung suggests that the heat of the "strong compulsive tie" of the transference bond enables the individual to "rediscover the force of [his inner, archetypal world]" (Jung 1946, p. 256).

In analysis, the *content* of the conversation between patient and analyst is of secondary importance. The nature of the object relationship between them is the primary issue, for this is the medium within which the reality of the patient's psyche may become manifest, where a volatile inner world can become as real as the couch or chair that holds the material body. For some people, at some points in the work, talking *about* that object relationship can destroy its nourishing potential, especially if the discussion tends toward "analyzing" the bond. Similarly, talking about a dream may undermine the person's potential living connection to that part of his psyche the dream is imaging—especially if the dream is analyzed rather than played with. What matters is the essence of the underlying process between the two individuals, not the manifest content of their exchange. The regressive unraveling may be partially, perhaps even largely, unconscious; but it is that dissolution of distorting adult structures and the subsequent development of new, more supple and authentic ones, that form the core of the work.

References

Balint, M. 1968. *The basic fault: Therapeutic aspects of regression.* New York: Brunner/Mazel.
Campbell, J. 1949. *The hero with a thousand faces.* New York: Pantheon Books.
Jung, C. G. 1921. *Psychological types.* In *Collected works,* vol. 6. Princeton: Princeton University Press, 1971.
———. 1946. *The Psychology of the transference.* In *Collected works,* 16:163–323. Princeton: Princeton University Press, 1954, 1966.
———. 1954. On the nature of the psyche. In *Collected works,* 8:159–236. Princeton: Princeton University Press, 1960, 1969, 1981.
———. 1984. *Selected letters of C. G. Jung, 1901–1961.* Adler, ed., with A. Jaffe. Princeton: Princeton University Press.
Kohut, H. 1984. *How does analysis cure?* A. Goldberg, ed., with P. Stepansky. Chicago: University of Chicago Press.
Perera, S. B. 1981. *Descent to the goddess: A way of initiation for women.* Toronto, Canada: Inner City Books.
Sandner, D. 1979. *Navaho symbols of healing.* New York: Harcourt Brace Jovanovich.
Winnicott, D. W. 1971. *Playing and reality.* London: Tavistock Publications Ltd.
———. 1960. Ego distortion in terms of true and false self. In *The maturational processes and the facilitating environment.* New York: International Universities Press, Inc. 1965

Looking Backward: Archetypes in Reconstruction

Murray Stein

It is a commonplace view among Jungian analysts that archetypes are to be found and to some degree experienced in the transference. In one of his greatest papers, "On the psychology of the transference," Jung himself emphasized this understanding and showed how the complex relationship between analyst and analysand is fundamentally conditioned and informed by archetypal processes (1946). The archetypal process he described, the *coniunctio*, accounts for the healing that occurs in those analyses that show evidence of its constellation. Many other analyst-authors have followed this lead, and most Jungian discussions of the transference/countertransference process rely heavily on an archetypal perspective, whether they focus on the *coniunctio* or on a different constellation (cf. Schwartz-Salant and Stein, eds. 1984).

In vivid contrast to this, it has *not* been widely published that archetypes play an essential role in the theapeutic use of reconstruction. It is

Murray Stein, Ph.D., is former president of the Chicago Society of Jungian Analysts and has a private practice in Wilmette, Illinois. A graduate of Yale College, Yale Divinity School, the C. G. Jung Institute of Zurich, and the University of Chicago, he is editor of *Jungian Analysis* (1982), co-editor of *Jung's Challenge to Contemporary Religion* (Chiron Publications 1987), and the author of *In Midlife* (1983) and *Jung's Treatment of Christianity: The Psychotherapy of a Religious Tradition* (Chiron Publications 1985).

my contention that remembering and reconstructing the past, as this takes place within the context of analysis, can be as transformative and as deeply a part of the whole transformational process of therapy as the transference/countertransference process is, because reconstruction also rests upon and is informed by archetypal processes and factors.

A preliminary point needs to be made and underscored. Reconstruction can truly be done only within the transference, because the transference both makes the past deeply accessible and allows for the transformation of the analysand in the bipersonal field. Reconstruction, it should be noted, is essentially different from anemnesis or simple recollection of the past. It occurs piecemeal over the course of a long analysis and is put together bit by bit from emerging memories and interpretations. One might say that the analysand's personal history is constellated in the course of an analysis, and this constellation depends upon the energy of the transference/countertransference process. At the beginning of analysis, the full scope of the final picture is largely unknown by both analyst and analysand. An early anamnesis often leaves out the most essential parts of the history, the repressed and overlooked pieces, which will "pop out" and become prominent as the analysis proceeds.

Furthermore, an essential factor in the healing power of reconstruction is the role of the witness, the analyst. The story that is told and pieced together in analysis is told to, and partly by, a particular audience, the attentive analyst. The analyst is generically important as the constellator of the atmosphere in which the story emerges, and as the assistant in the task of reconstructing and understanding, but he or she is particularly important for bringing the most personal ingredients of this other psyche into the intimacy of analysis. Reconstruction of personal history in analysis emerges within the context of this relationship and the transference. Thus it is importantly different from writing an autobiography or relating a personal account of life to a neutral party, a biographer. The analyst hears and gets to know what the biographer rarely does, not only factually but also feelingly. The values and personal meanings assigned to specific persons and events are fully disclosed. The tone of each history is unique; the accents on persons and events are special; the details constantly shift in value until they find a resting place in the firmly woven tapestry of a life.

Analysis is continuous history-making, which calls for the active participation of both analyst and analysand. In the Jungian literature, however, there has been little rigorous discussion of the technique and place of reconstruction in analysis. Jung himself rarely uses the term. (Para-

graph 595 in *Collected Works*, volume 4, is the only instance noted in the
General Index.) Occasionally he speaks of "recollection" in a vague and
nontechnical way. Neither have later Jungian authors focused on reconstruction in analysis. Such standard texts as Edward Whitmont's *The Symbolic Quest*, June Singer's *Boundaries of the Soul*, Hans Dieckmann's
Methoden der Analytischen Psychologie, and my own (edited) *Jungian
Analysis* skirt this subject. Instead, the center of Jungian discussions of analytic practice has been occupied by consideration of various methods of
interpretation and (lately) of the transference/countertransference process. Educational tools in therapy, such as amplification from myth
and religion, and the various means available for evoking symbolic
material—active imagination, sandplay, dance/movement, bodywork,
painting—have found a place in the standard texts. Reconstruction,
however, has been largely ignored. Only the English authors of the de-
velopmentalist orientation, particularly Michael Fordham and Kenneth
Lambert, have given it more than passing attention.

This general neglect originated in Jung's divergence from Freudian
technique and in his own differing theoretical interests. One of Jung's
criticisms of Freud's early psychoanalysis was that it ran the risk—and often succumbed to it—of paying too much attention to patients' stories
about childhood. In Jung's Fordham University lectures (1913) he criti-
cised psychoanalysts for sometimes following their patients endlessly
into the maze of their dubious meanderings and ruminations about
childhood, thus getting lost in the neurosis themselves. By focusing so
much on childhood and on the reconstruction of repressed "scenes from
childhood," psychoanalysis was in danger of coming to resemble the
neurotic diseases it was intended to cure. In this period, Jung regarded
the most important cause of neurosis to be a person's unwillingness to
face up to the emotional demands of the present. Analysis, therefore,
should keep a careful eye on what the patient is shirking in the present
and should interpret the patient's flights into childhood memory or into
incestuous transference fantasies as evasions of the task at hand. Unless
the patient manages to surmount this obstacle, neurosis will continue
(1913, pars. 291–313). Jung here supported Freud in his movement away
from the childhood trauma theory of neurosis.

With this attitude it was unlikely that he would give himself with
great enthusiasm to the work of reconstruction. It was seen as a clever
trap laid by the neurotic mind to divert attention from the real problem.
To become caught up in endless rememberances of things past, not to
mention the intensely intriguing possibility of "screen memories," would

play into the crafty patient's already too-well-developed tendency to evade the responsibilities of the present. Analysis would become mere woolgathering.

A second early trend in Jung's thinking that led him to look away from the role and value of reconstruction in analysis was his fascination with myth and symbol. In *The Psychology of the Unconscious*, written in 1912–13, Jung's overwhelming fascination with myth and symbol is apparent. This tendency was emphasized by many of Jung's followers. When archetypal themes are rendered in the literature of analytical psychology, one often hears little about a patient's "personal history." We are then in the territory of impersonal, or transpersonal, or archetypal psychology, where personal matters are not significant. The distinction between "personal" and "archetypal" has been used to create a breach between a person's history and the psyche, by dividing them into two separated realms of mental life. On the clinical level, then, the personal transference has sometimes been looked upon as a mere recapitulation of the childhood relationship with parents, whereas the archetypal transference has been considered as having to do with a relationship to the gods and grander meanings.

When put this starkly, of course, it becomes obvious that one is speaking of a complex and not a truth. The polarization between personal and archetypal elements of experience has been created by careless usage and thinking, but it has also been used for defensive purposes. To claim archetypicality avoids the hazard of claiming personal responsibility. Jung himself does not actually polarize these dimensions either clinically or theoretically, nor do most practicing Jungian analysts, but the theory of analytical psychology can provide a handy means by which this kind of "complex thinking" can be fostered. As I will show later, Jung himself actually used a method of reconstruction in his clinical practice, and he certainly assumed it in his general discussions of the therapeutic process (cf. Stein 1985, ch. 2).

As a result of these two features of Jung's early thinking, the conscious utilization of reconstruction in analysis by Jungian analysts and the discussion of this method in the literature of analytical psychology have been badly neglected. While many, if not all, Jungian analysts actually practice some form of reconstruction—wittingly or unwittingly—every day and in almost every analytical hour, we have not reflected enough on this aspect of clinical work in our literature.

This may be so much the case that I should go no further without defining what I mean by the term "reconstruction." In the broadest and simplest sense, I am referring to the activity in analysis of telling and hearing the life story of the analysand. In the more precise sense, this term refers to piecing together the *inner* history, the emotional life of the analysand, often with particular emphasis on childhood and on repressed memories, by using the means of dream interpretation, interpretation of the transference/countertransference dynamics, emerging memory images, and general theoretical understandings of development and psychodynamics.

Etymologically, reconstruction means to rebuild something by fitting the parts together. In the context of analysis, this means taking the bits of history as they emerge in the general course of analytic uncovering and piecing them together to show the shape of a coherent story.

When a person enters analysis and begins to speak personally about the present, it is not long before the historical antecedents come to the fore. Certain memories are associated; images of earlier times and places come to mind; dreams and experiences from childhood and adolescence are related to the analyst; the stories of relationships, work, significant moments are told. The person who comes to analysis today is prepared by our culture to begin to tell a personal story. This happens more or less automatically and without much prompting from the analyst. Then there are the dream figures who are embedded in earlier periods, and these bring associations from other, often long-forgotten, periods in the analysand's life. As time goes on and session follows session, the analyst gets an increasingly sharp picture of the analysand's psychological patterns and of how they have grown and developed in the past, as well as of how they operate in the present. The analyst's interpretations often take on an historical cast: This dream image or that transference reaction bears an uncanny resemblance to an earlier scene or relationship. In this fashion the present comes to be seen as a continuation, sometimes a repetition, of the past. When these kinds of continuity and repetition have been established such that even the subtlest feelings and emotional reactions and images, as they are experienced in the present, can be related to older, established themes, the work of reconstruction has been undertaken and to some extent completed. Lambert quotes Novey as saying that reconstruction is "an attempt . . . to see the patient and have him see himself in some continuing context in which his present modes of experiencing and dealing with himself and others are a logical outgrowth" (Lambert 1981, p. 115).

The reaction of Jungian analysts to this possible outcome of analysis has not been altogether receptive. In fact, they have raised still another objection to reconstruction, which might not have surfaced otherwise. Tying the present to the past in this way has seemed to some to be too reductive. It has been argued that the psyche is not and should not be bound to history, any more than to logic or rationality or to the interpersonal field, for this would fetter its operations. Any such final connections of psyche to anything beyond itself and its ultimate freedom is too confining. By tying the psyche to history and to the patterns of thought and feeling that come about in the course of development, one places Psyche in Procrustes' bed. Reconstruction, it is felt, hampers the freedom of the psyche to soar, to create, to resurrect and begin again. History chains the soul to a corpse. The psyche is discontinuous, illogical, and free, as much as it is continuous, logical, and bound to the past. Therefore any attempt to create linkages between the operations of the autonomous psyche and its surroundings—interpersonal, cultural, historical—have been vehemently resisted by some. To these analysts, the possibilities of deconstruction in analysis are more appealing than the potentialities of reconstruction. For them the aim of analysis should be to free the soul from history, not to bind it further. This objection needs to be answered, for Jungian analysts still continue to practice reconstruction, often unwillingly or unwittingly—perhaps also rather poorly—simply because analysands take the lead or because this method has become a somewhat unconscious complex in the professional psyche of every practicing therapist.

My purpose in writing this paper is to bring this topic of reconstruction in analysis into focus and to reflect upon it from a Jungian viewpoint. By "Jungian viewpoint" I mean the theoretical apparatus of complex and archetypal theory, as well as current clinical views regarding interpretation and the role of the transference/countertransference relationship in analysis, all of which should be brought to bear upon the process of reconstruction. My view is that the activity of reconstruction in analysis has an archetypal basis in the healing process and that "personal history" is infiltrated by archetypal elements. The Jungian contribution to reconstruction lies precisely in this sense of the deeper background processes active both in the activity of analytical reconstruction and in the lineaments of personal fate as they appear in the story that is gathered and told in analysis.

I want to acknowledge Kenneth Lambert's sensitively balanced account of reconstruction in his book *Analysis, Repair and Individuation*, in which he reviews the literature of psychoanalysis and analytical psychology on this subject and makes judicious comments. His work helped me gain the courage to write this paper, for reconstruction is not exactly a "Jungian topic." The term is used largely only in classical psychoanalysis, and yet, as Lambert points out, Jung himself produced "what amounts

to a massive reconstruction of the Hebrew-Christian psycho-cultural tradition" in the last two decades of his life (p. 117). Independently I have
argued this same point and detailed it in my book *Jung's Treatment of
Christianity: The Psychotherapy of a Religious Tradition*. My examination
of reconstruction here fills in more detail by focusing particularly on the
archetypal elements of reconstruction. Lambert does not emphasize
these, but I do not believe he would object to my specification of them.

Lambert raises a question that needs to be considered. He points out
that reconstruction is generally done by analysts of a particular temperament (p. 113). He does not name which temperament it might be, but
one supposes he is referring to analysts who work largely with the thinking and/or feeling functions. These are analysts, he says, with "a sense of
history" and an interest in the social and cultural background of their patients. I would like to carry this a step further by noting that it may also be
the analyst's countertransference attitude, not only or primarily his temperament, that plays a role in the activity of reconstruction.

This "attitude," which I have described (1984 pp. 85–87) as a persistent set of perspectives, ideas and feelings already in place at the beginning of analysis and continuing throughout the course of it, perhaps
being interrupted occasionally by countertransference "reactions" or
longer-lasting "phases," is itself archetypally based; it reflects an archetypal pattern. In considering the role of archetypes in reconstruction,
therefore, we need to consider also the archetypal constellation that underlies the countertransference attitude that is involved in the very act of
doing this activity. Is there an aspect of the healing archetype that, in the
case of psychotherapy, leads to the activity of reconstruction? Or do various archetypal patterns influence the analyst's consciousness as the task
of reconstruction is performed? Perhaps both situations obtain. In the
first instance, the idea of history has come to hold a firm and established
place in the therapist's attitude: There is the predisposition to see bits of
data as embedded in patterns of historical evolution and development. In
the second instance, there are more specific features, such as fantasies of
mothering and feeding in the countertransference, which govern the way
in which historical patterns are divulged and experienced by the analyst
(cf. Fordham 1978, pp. 125–28), or an erotic father-daughter incest pattern, which occurs in the countertransference and is used for reconstructive purposes (Schwartz-Salant, 1986, pp. 41ff).

In speaking about archetypal dimensions of reconstruction, therefore, I am speaking of several different things: the archetypal basis of processing data historically, archetypal features of the act of remembering,
archetypal elements within the remembered events of one's personal

history, and archetypal elements in countertransference feeling and imagery that can be used for reconstruction. All of these dimensions have a place in reconstruction. The remainder of this article will examine them, with the caveat that these four aspects cannot be cleanly separated and held distinct.

On the Archetypal Basis of Thinking Historically

Is there an archetypal basis for the activity of reconstruction in analysis? If so, what is it, and what is the evidence for its existence?

One basis for claiming archetypicality for any human activity is its ubiquity. Historical thinking is ancient and, so far as I can discover, universal. Every human group seems to have a story of its origins and history. Generally the origin is situated *in illo tempore* (Eliade), in a mythical creation event, a "big bang" from which history unfolds (for examples, see von Franz's *Creation Myths*). In the Biblical tradition, prehistory is occupied by God and His brooding over the waters of chaos; He creates the heavens and the earth, humans, the garden, and history begins from there. Rome's history begins with the myth of being founded by the orphans, Romulus and Remus. American history begins in a myth of revolution against the parent country. The story of the nation or of the tribe then follows, and the various significant human and divine figures are recalled by the historian in detail as they appear on the stage of history and influence the historical process. Historians remember the story.

"History" derives from the Greek adjective *histor*, meaning "knowing, hence erudite, itself an agent . . . from *eidenai* . . . to know" (Partridge 1966, p. 289). At the root is *weid-*, "connoting vision, which subserves knowledge; cf. Gr *eidos*, form . . . akin to Skt *vedas-*, knowledge" (*ibid.*). The knowing, erudite ones, the original historians, were poets and storytellers who could remember history back to the very walls of Troy or to the days of the patriarchs, all the way back to the mythic source of history itself, and could then come forward into the present—if one could stay awake long enough to hear the whole account. This was not scientific history in the modern sense, but it was equally based on the human urge to know a history. The "idea of history" was at work in an archaic way in the minds of these early historians.

After the storytellers came the historians proper—Biblical, Greek, and Indian. Every nation and tribe, including our own American nation, our own Jungian tribe, as well as our individual families, has a history. It is a broken group indeed that has lost its story. The same is true of individuals.

There is another type of evidence of the archetypicality of thinking historically. It appears that a historical record is kept by the unconscious quite independently of conscious intent. One of the original insights of psychoanalysis was that the mind does not simply erase the past. One may repress a memory trace or temporarily forget or screen it out of awareness, but events are not normally lost. They are deposited in the unconscious. The "memory bank" is only partially conscious; much of it is unconscious.

There is a strand of thinking in Jung's work that holds that the unconscious is not bound to the Kantian categories of space and time. In the unconscious, Jung often said, time does not exist as it does in consciousness. Past and future are not arranged sequentially, and therefore it is possible to have "precognitive dreams," for example, which are messages from the unconscious that indicate knowledge of events ahead of time. Beside this description of unconscious processes, however, is the equally important (though less developed in relation to clinical practice) idea that the unconscious keeps a historical record and anticipates events because it has a time-keeping device within it. This time-keeper in the unconscious has a sense of historical pattern and duration, a sense of how long things should take. This may be similar to the notion of circadian rhythms or bio-rhythms, but it is more "cognitive" than those concepts. It is time-consciousness folded into the unconscious.

Jung gives an example of this in reference to a case that he alludes to in "The Psychology of the Transference." He says that when the transference is initiated, "a queer unconscious time-reckoning, lasting for months or even longer" begins (1946, par. 376). The example he cites is from the dreams of a sixty-year-old woman patient who was having dreams of a baby, "a child hero or divine child" (par. 378). At the time of the dreams, this child was six months old. Upon investigation, it turned out that six months earlier the analysand had had a birth dream. Nine months before that she had painted a picture of "a naked female figure from whose genital region [a serpent] rears up towards the heart, where it burst into a five-pointed, gorgeously flashing golden star" (par. 380). Jung comments:

> The serpent represents the hissing ascent of Kundalini, and in the corresponding yoga this marks the first moment in a process which ends with deification in the divine Self the syzygy of Shiva and Shakti. It is obviously the moment of symbolical conception. . . . (par. 380)

This whole sequence of conception, birth, and growth had occurred spontaneously in the unconscious and had unfolded in a time frame that matched that of actual historical time. The unconscious was keeping time.

A similar example of unconscious time-reckoning occurred recently in my practice, though not directly in my analysand's psyche. The sixteen-year-old daughter of my analysand had a secret abortion in early summer, which she confessed to her parents in August. In September she returned to school and was doing quite well until late October, when she developed a peculiar and undiagnosable malady. She consistently ran a temperature of 100° F., which did not respond to medical treatment. As a result she could not go to school. The parents took her to the best diagnosticians in the city, and none could find evidence of disease. Everything was tried, to no avail, and she was forced to stay at home, mostly in bed. The theory was that the fever was caused by a pelvic infection and that it was located in the reproductive organs, but no evidence could be found. She stayed in bed from October onward. In mid-February a new doctor decided it was time for exploratory surgery. This was done, and the girl responded poorly, having to be hospitalized for two days rather than overnight. She came home, took a week to recover, but then developed a case of common flu. This disappeared in a week, and with it all signs of illness. There was no more fever, and she returned to school. The doctors had found no evidence of disease in the exploratory surgery. The peculiar coincidence was that the operation and hospitalization took place exactly nine months after the conception of her baby, just when she would have been going into the hospital to give birth. It was as though the unconscious had kept time, knew it was now time to release her from her pelvic distress, and recognized the surgery as equivalent to birth.

Anecdotes such as these do not prove the existence of a time-keeping function in the unconscious, but they do strongly suggest this to be the case. It is this psychic factor, I would guess, that is at the root of the pervasive human tendency to think historically in a conscious way.

It is important to make this point about the archetypal basis of reconstruction, because otherwise it could appear that it is merely the "times," and the peculiar modern bent toward historicism, that has captured the minds of therapists as well as of educated persons in our culture generally. Historical thinking in academic life has certainly flowered in the last several centuries. The 19th century saw a great burgeoning of it, and our own century has continued the tradition. This tendency toward historicism in the intellectual community has produced great stress and conflict because of the ways in which secular historians have interpreted history and the kinds of "facts" they will accept as valid. The basic conflict has been joined between the mythic, religious thinkers on the one side and the scientific, empirical thinkers on the other. For the former, history is grounded in and profoundly shaped by divine interventions; for the latter, such mythic elements need to be ferreted out of the historical record. The debate has not been so much about whether or not history is important or should be pursued as an intellectual discipline, but what can be counted as a "fact." The same argument can be transposed to the psychological and clinical level. Almost everyone would agree that history and development are molar ideas in psychology and in the practice of psychotherapy, but not all would agree on what counts as valid data. Should important dreams be included in the developmental story? Or synchronistic events? Or should one count only the normal unfolding of a developmental sequence and the influences of the environment? The conflict between views of history and what makes history could be as intense in psychological circles as it has been in philosophical and theological ones.

Jung broadened the idea of history in its application to clinical practice. Included in the analysand's history are not only childhood and the immediate family, but also the much larger matrix of culture, of generational patterns, and of archaic history as this is embedded in the collective unconscious. Jung's interpretation of history and his account of psychological development includes the personal dynamics of identification, introjection, *participation mystique*, complex formation, and also the archetypal dynamics of constellation, synchronicity, and spontaneous influences from beyond the horizon of external factors. If anything, Jung is a more rigorous and consistent historian than most other clinical theorists, because he recognizes the individual's life to be deeply formed by these many factors, all of which play a part in development. Jung's inclusion of archetypes within the historical nexus leads to the realization that the influence of history upon the individual is ubiquitous, rooted in culture and the unconscious, pervasive through all segments of emotional and mental functioning, and fundamental to identity. For this reason he warns of the danger of departing too far from one's personal and cultural roots.

This understanding of the importance of history in the life of the individual would seem to give the Jungian analyst a particularly keen appreciation of the importance of reconstruction in clinical work. Reconstruction would seem to be a key part of becoming conscious of oneself. But this has not always been the case, because the value of archetypal depth in the healing process has sometimes been contrasted to the superficiality or intellectuality of historical understanding. It has not been clearly enough stated that historical consciousness rests upon an archetypal base, and that the clinical work of reconstruction functions to connect the analysand to that archetypal process within. Reconstruction is truly healing because it restores consciousness to an archetypal base. Its healing power derives not only from the benefit of attaining a sense of one's own history, and thereby gaining an identity, but equally from the healing effects of historical reflection, of re-membering one's wholeness.

On Jung's Use of Reconstruction in Clinical Practice

One reason many readers come away from Jung's *Collected Works* with the impression that he did little reconstruction in analysis and that he preferred to amplify archetypal aspects of his patient's dreams and unconscious contents is that he spends so few pages actually detailing his analytic cases. I am convinced that if he had written up his cases, the surprise would be the importance of personal history in them. One reason I am confident of this is that in the several cases he does describe, the personal historical details that are uncovered are *always* critical for understanding the "case" and its outcome. I will cite only three such instances.

The earliest case (1961, pp. 115–17; 1935, pars. 107–108) derives from the time of his residency at the Burghölzli Klinik in Zürich. A woman was admitted to the hospital and diagnosed as schizophrenic. Jung disagreed and thought it was a reactive depression. By using the word-association test and analyzing her dreams, he discovered her story: She had unconsciously, but willfully nonetheless, killed her child by giving it unclean water to drink. The reconstruction of this piece of repressed personal history led to a full recovery, according to Jung, and constituted the whole of her treatment.

The second case is of a young Jewish woman with an anxiety neurosis (1939, pars. 635–36). Jung recounts that she had been in analysis before, and the analyst had fallen in love with her. The treatment had failed to relieve her symptoms or to cure her mental anguish. Jung says that he dreamed of her the night before he met her and realized in the dream that she had a "father complex." When he interviewed her, however, he could find little evidence of this problem, so he dug further into her history and found that she was the granddaughter of a Hasidic wonder-working rabbi. This bit of personal history proved to be the key to a cure. Jung told her, "Look here . . . you have been untrue to your God. Your grandfather led the right life, but you are worse than a heretic; you have forsaken the mystery of your race. You belong to holy people." Upon hearing this she was able to accept her Jewishness and her religious identity, and within one week the anxiety neurosis was cured (par. 636).

In this instance, the reconstruction of family history led not only to a stronger sense of personal identity but also to realizing the symbolic, religious proclivity and need of the psyche. The appropriation of personal history and admission to the archetypal psyche happened in one and the same psychic event. Again, reconstruction represented the key to therapeutic healing.

A third case reported by Jung is more extensive. He refers to it several times in the *Collected Works* (1942, par. 189; 1950, pars. 656ff.; 1937, pars. 546–63; 1935, pars. 334–337), as well as in the Kundalini Seminar (Autumn 1932, pp. 91ff.). This is the case of a young woman who spent her childhood in Java. She was 25 years old when Jung began to see her. Jung was her third analyst, the former two treatments having ended in impasse and failure. In the course of his treatment of her, Jung reports, he was at first put off by her vulgar persona and then extremely puzzled by the physical symptoms she developed in the course of their work together. He was ultimately able to amplify these physical maladies by using kundalini yoga's chakra system, which he discovered independently in the course of this treatment. His extensive knowledge of the historical details of this person's life and his evaluation of their central importance in her psychology (cf. 1937, pars. 546–63) make it extremely evident that he did a great deal of reconstruction of her early years, particularly of her childhood in Java and the relationship she developed with a Javanese *ayah*, a nanny or native nurse. Jung was able to understand her bizarre dream images and physical symptoms, and to explain their meaning to her, because he could relate her Javanese childhood to the symbol system of tantric yoga. Treatment broke off, he says, when she reached the manipura center and experienced a bird descending and piercing through the fontanelle to the diaphragm. At this point she realized she wanted to have a child, literally, and gave up psychological treatment without explanation. A year later she returned to Jung and explained why she had abruptly stopped treatment; he, in turn, was able to amplify her motives by using tantric philosophy.

> This little bit of Tantric philosophy helped that patient to make an ordinary human life for herself, as a wife and mother, out of the local demonology she had sucked in with her *ayah*'s milk, and to do so without losing touch with the inner, psychic figures which had been called awake by the long-forgotten influences of her childhood. What she experienced as a child, and what later estranged her from the European consciousness and entangled her in a neurosis, was, with the help of analysis, transformed not into nebulous fantasies but into a lasting spiritual possession in no way incompatible with an ordinary human existence, a husband, children, and housewifely duties. (Jung 1937, par. 563)

This paragraph, as clearly as any single passage in Jung's written works, illustrates the intimate blending of personal and archetypal factors in his method of reconstruction. The personal elements and the archetypal ones are seen as making up a whole, and they are held closely together in the fabric of a person's history.

Others of Jung's cases could be cited to make the same point. In practice, the line of demarcation between personal and archetypal aspects in the personality is much less straight than it sometimes is made to seem in theory. And historical reconstruction is deeply woven into the process of analysis, alongside the other aspects of treatment. More than that, the product of reconstruction—the history—often occupies the center of clinical treatment, forming a kind of center pole that supports the whole analytic edifice.

Clinical Applications

It is sometimes supposed that the strength of Jungian analysts lies in our ability to see things archetypally. Give us a grain of sand and we'll find a world in it. Indeed, one of the current understandings of what the term "archetypal" means is that it has to do with a way of seeing: "archetypal" is an attribute of the eye of the beholder (Samuels 1985), or a term used to indicate the great importance of something (Hillman 1983). Jungians are supposed to have archetypally oriented eyes. The problem with this usage of the term archetypal is that it sacrifices the connection to the underlying reality of archetypes, like paper money that is no longer related to real property. Consequently the term can become inflated, devalued, and meaningless.

The more usual Jungian usage is that "archetypal" means that a psychic fact—an image, a dream, an idea, a perception, or a pattern of behavior—reflects an archetype, which is a structure that is deeply rooted in the psychic matrix that can be regarded as generally human and innate, and that is basic to human *qua* human functioning. Archetypes, Jung would say, are the basic bulding blocks of the psyche. The trained clinical eye can see these elemental forms in the welter of facts presented by a patient, can see the basic patterns and the deeper than manifest meanings. The truly trained eye, the true clinical imagination, can see that "all events are echoes" of universal themes (Davenport 1984), but that which recognized is not a resident solely of the trained eye. Beyond the surface, the eye is *seeing something.*

The surface behind which one sees in analysis may be the analysand's life story. The clinician with an eye trained to perceive archetypal factors at work in the analysand's history may reverse the background/foreground fields, perhaps thus missing some detail but looking more deeply into the underlying patterns that have organized the details in a person's life. In the background one can see evidence of archetypal dynamic/developmental themes, individuation phases and their typical movements through time: the constellation of the puer, the hero, the romance with the father, the *coniunctio*, the death and rebirth motif. One can also find the typical archetypal "figures" in personal history: mother, father, child, hero, witch, trickster, clown, anima/animus, wise old ones. Gazing into "background" has the feeling of studying life's fate.

The activity of reconstructing history in analysis can be carried out on a completely personal basis: this mother, this father, this set of siblings, this school, etc. The result will be a complete set of facts, a story, but it will not include the fatedness of this life to be this way and not that. It is recollection, but it has little therapeutic value. It will miss the spiritual purpose of this life and its meaning. It will also miss its deepest suffering, such as was experienced by a 50-year-old woman who, racked with sobs and outrage, whispered through her hot tears: "When I was seven years old and my mother gave me that doll with my sister's dress on it, I *knew* I would never have children and she would. This is my *fate*." The therapist feels inclined to look away from such finality, but a chord of truth is struck.

The sensitive therapist shudders at the thought of such finality and limitation. Are we not in the business of helping people to change, to grow, to become what they are not and want to be? If we look for archetypal patterns, though, we come upon limits, sometimes cruel destinies, but also sometimes inexplicable charm and good luck. It doesn't always seem fair. "The doctor knows that always, wherever he turns, man is dogged by his fate," writes Jung in his seventies (1946, par. 463).

I once worked in analysis with a young man whose presenting problem was intense jealousy. He felt that his beautiful girlfriend was always looking at other young men in their high school class and secretly hoped he would get lost. Despite much reassurance from her, his gloomy thoughts persisted. We began by looking at his dreams and putting together his history and trying to understand his thinking, which he often confessed was bizarre and out of his rational control.

After a few months we had assembled the main features of his story. He was the only child of a couple in which the mother felt far superior to the father, a common worker. The mother doted on her son, and he grew up feeling special. At an early age, however, he had been sent to the country to live with grandparents because his mother had to return to work and didn't have time to care for a small child. So until he was old enough to enter primary school, he lived several hours away and saw his parents on weekends when they came to visit him. This absence increased the intensity of the bond, but also created feelings of abandonment and lack of worth. As he grew, he became much more closely identified with his mother than his father. She was musical, poetic, artistic, as he was, while his father was seen by them both as gross and uneducated. His father favored rough sports like football and wished the son were more athletic. By the time I saw him, he had decided to become a high school teacher. He enjoyed writing and painting; his particular pleasure was sculpture.

At one point he had written a poem in which he expressed his feelings of inferiority by depicting himself as a hunchback who lived underground. He was despised by passers-by, and occasionally they would spit on him. He felt that his body was "too thick" and often wished that he were more slender and small in build. He felt particularly oversized in his chest, upper torso, and hips. He felt womanish and unmasculine, rejected by "real men" like his father.

One night as he was sitting at the desk in his atelier dwelling on his jealous thoughts, he tooked at his leg and noticed it had turned blue from the foot to an area above the ankle. Greatly upset, he got up and went over to his bed. As he sat there he saw footprints moving across the carpet and thought they might be his father's. Then the vision passed and his foot returned to normal. This highly disturbing experience brought him into therapy with me. He had no other such experiences, and a physical examination had revealed nothing of concern.

Some months after therapy began, he took a brief holiday in the mountains by himself. His girlfriend had gone on a school trip to another city. While camping out, he dreamed that she was having an affair with a young man in the city she was visiting. This dream, which was a nightmare, occurred during a thunderstorm, and he awoke in a panic.

After all of these details had been set out, it occurred to me one day in a session that there were elements of his story that reminded me of the Greek god Hephaestus. He was cast out of heaven shortly after birth, and crippled in the foot. He was a craftsman and sculptor, scoffed at by the other gods for his physical awkwardness, and betrayed by his beautiful wife Aphrodite, who went to bed with his half-brother Ares. I mentioned this association and told him I didn't know much about Hephaestus, which was true at the time, but since he was interested in myth he could look it up and get some more information on his own.

In the next session he told me that he had indeed looked up everything he could on Hephaestus, and that he was stangely moved by this figure. In fact, he had been so taken by the stories about this god that he had shared some of them with his girlfriend over the weekend. When he came to the story of Hephaestus discovering Aphrodite in bed with Ares, he began to weep. Surprisingly, his girlfriend also began to cry, and she confessed that she had indeed had a sexual encounter with a young man during her school holidays. As it turned out, the timing of it coincided precisely with his dream during the thunderstorm on the mountain. This confession had actually relieved him a great deal, because he now knew he wasn't just crazy. His girlfriend was unreliable sexually, and it was better to know this than to keep wondering about it.

It would be preposterous to claim that this amplification of certain facts in his life history and experience with the Hephaestus myth cured him completely of his jealousy. The roots of his jealousy were fed by deep and persistent forces in his psyche. His self-esteem was certainly improved by this association however, and the wider context of meaning supplied by the myth helped him place his life experience into the context of an archetypal pattern. The sense of deeper pattern for the crippled craftsman that he was provided a redeeming frame of reference. It also gave us a direction to work toward in therapy. There is a good deal of strength and potential for life in the Hephaestian character, but this sense of archetypal pattern also brings awareness of limitations: Hephaestus will never be Hermes, or Zeus, or Apollo. He will always have to struggle with lameness, with fears of rejection, with vulnerability to threats of abandonment. Reflecting later on this case, and eventually writing a paper about it (1980), it occurred to me that this pattern is fairly typical of young men who are innately introverted, who become artistic and creative, and who have suffered an early experience of parental abandonment. Their salvation lies in staying true to their introversion, to their creative vocation, and to their capacity for eventually filling themselves out as husbands and fathers, as Hephaestus does after his failure with Aphrodite.

The discovery of a mythic pattern in this case was important as an orientation device. It also reassured us that beneath all the facts of this particular history an archetype was operative. This meant we could have faith in history's unfolding.

If Jungian analysts are reputed to be able to find worlds in a grain of sand and to perceive archetypal patterns in the data of a person's history, they are less well known for doing the reverse of this, i.e., finding the personal, historical element in an obviously archetypal image or fantasy. Yet, clinically, this is at least as crucial as the other skill.

Satinover (1985) made the astute observation that archetypal figures are often presented when psychic compensation is taking place in areas of failed adaptation or unresolved trauma. He compared the activation of an archetypal fantasy image and its role in restoring a person to quasi-healthy functioning to the way a weak heart compensates for its malfunctioning: It becomes enlarged and thereby manages to keep blood flowing. But this is not a healthy heart. So, he argued, archetypal figures move into consciousness when the ego is impaired inherently or by circumstance and otherwise would not be able to continue functioning adaptively. Satinover's advice is always to look for personal complexes where archetypal images or behaviors appear.

Jung himself made a similar point in 1946 with regard to his theory of complexes and archetypes. Jung observed that when experiences and familiar figures become enveloped in a fold of unconsciousness, they are assimilated by the complexes. If they are kept unconscious long enough, they eventually come into contact with the archetypes. When this happens, the complexes

> assume, by self-amplification, an archaic and mythological character and hence a certain numinosity, as is perfectly clear in schizophrenic dissociations. Numinosity, however, is wholly outside conscious volition, for it transports the subject into the state of rapture, which is a state of will-less surrender. . . . These peculiarities of the unconscious state contrast very strongly with the way complexes behave in the conscious mind. Here they can be corrected: they lose their automatic character and can be substantially transformed. They slough off their mythological envelope, and, by entering into the adaptive process going forward in consciousness, they personalize and rationalize themselves to the point where a dialectical discussion becomes possible. (1954, pars. 383–84)

In a footnote he adds: "In schizophrenic dissociation there is no such change in the conscious state, because the complexes are received not into a complete but into a fragmentary consciousness. That is why they so often appear in the original archaic state" (Ibid., p. 187, n. 48).

From this it follows that the clinical picture presented by the analysand who seems to have little sense of personal history but comes fully packed with big dreams and archetypal images should alert the analyst to rather severe trauma and damage in the area of personal history. Instead of speaking about father and mother, this analysand speaks of the king and queen; instead of presenting a continuous narrative of personal history and development, this person tells of radical transformations and a disjunctive series of vaguely perceived happenings; instead of identity, there is protean change among a number of stereotypes and personas.

The task of analysis here is to find the grains of sand in these archetypal worlds.

For this kind of an analysand, the painstaking work of careful reconstruction of personal history is particularly essential. The greatest obstacle lies in the astonishing lack of a continuous memory. Much of the detail must be collected, therefore, through transference interpretations, and this always leaves things a bit speculative. The work of finding an inner history, which tells the emotional story of this person's life experience, is slow and tenuous. If successful, the "mythological envelope" is gradually opened and the personal story, along with the feelings, come forth.

I once began treating a woman of this type. Her father had just died, and there was no relevant affect. Instead I was presented with many ideas and images. The dreams, too, were immense, archetypal, otherwordly. This woman could exist in a psychic wonderland while her personal life was a disaster. She was not schizophrenic, but was perhaps occasionally a bit psychotic, in the sense of being flooded and overwhelmed with archetypal contents. She did not hallucinate, but she had a vivid imagination and minimal impulse control. While she could speak fluently and easily about her dreams and ideas, she spoke about her personal life and history only haltingly, surprised that anyone would care to talk about that. Philosophy, ideas, myths and images—that's where the action was. We made little headway in the brief time I saw her, and I had to refer her elsewhere when I moved to another city. She continued in therapy with a psychoanalytically oriented psychotherapist, and when I met her again some eight years later I could scarcely recognize her, psychologically speaking. She was emotionally connected, she was personal, she could speak of her feelings for her family and her children, she was a devoted mother. She was completely transformed. I asked about her analysis, and she told me that it had been entirely based on transference interpretation and reconstruction of early childhood. Dreams had hardly been discussed, archetypes never mentioned, philosophy shunned as a defense against personal feelings in the present. She was grounded; she had a history; she had an identity as a woman. I was impressed.

I did not say, but nonetheless thought: This whole development was promised in the earlier dreams, but symbolically. The archetypal dreams showed that potential intactness, wholeness, and identity were there, but personal history was all shadow, all unconsciousness, and only after this had been integrated into consciousness could wholeness shine through. Integrating personal history in the transference had grounded her and provided a conscious identity. The archetypal dreams had indicated this possibility, while at the same time they had covered and hidden the very detail of history she needed to become a person.

If one tries to live the "symbolic life" before personal history has been woven tightly and intractably into consciousness, it is likely to be a false life. The archetypal end of the psychic spectrum crowds out both the instinctual and the personal aspects, and the ego uses these symbolic contents defensively, to block the rest out. This type of ego-consciousness tends to fear the pain of "reductionism" and of thereby losing the sense of specialness. For the narcissistic character, the symbolic life is a defense and not a real possibility. The symbolic dimension can be contained adequately only by an ego-consciousness that is itself personally integrated. The personal must precede the impersonal.

Jung's point that what falls out of consciousness becomes assimilated to unconscious content and re-appears as archetypal image leads us clinically to look for historical reality in archetypal idea and image. When the historical figure is retrieved from the archetype—a personal mother from the witch archetype, for example, or a father from the bull—personal relationships become unburdened of the weight of archetypal projections and the ego is freed to experience life less delusionally. The archetypes too are freed of the burden of the personal, and this allows these "psychic organs" (Jung 1940, par. 271) to function in a new way. The pathway to the symbolic is cleared.

I will turn now to a third analytic move. The first is finding an archetypal pattern beneath the welter of historical detail. Here we feel we are studying the outlines of personal fate. The second is finding historical detail in a welter of archetypal images and helping consciousness to integrate and to consolidate personal identity. The third move is to see where the personal/historical and the archetypal elements are joined, either because of an archetypal "intervention" in history (synchronicity), or through the effective union of personal and archetypal data and figures such that personal history takes on the feeling of religious meaning and destiny. This is a level of reconstruction that attempts to hold the personal and the archetypal dimensions of history together in a single vision. This is a *mysterium coniunctionis* at the level of history.

Jung quotes the *Rosarium*:

Whiten the lato and rend the books lest your hearts be rent asunder. For this is the synthesis of the wise and third part of the whole *opus*. Join therefore, as is said in the *Turba*, the dry to the moist, the black earth with its water, and cook till it whitens. In this manner you will have the essence of water and earth, having whitened the earth with water: but that whiteness is called air. (1946, par. 484)

This summarizes, symbolically, the operation I am speaking of here, where the personal aspects of one's history (the "lato," a black substance) are given the fullness of analytic attention (the "water," which is the divine gift of illumination) until that history lifts from the concrete to the symbolic (the "whiteness," the "air") and personal and archetypal elements become united. This is the stage of the *opus* referred to by Jung as "Purification," and is accompanied by the lines:

> Here falls the heavenly dew to lave
> The soiled black body in the grave. (1946, p. 273)

Religious thinkers have developed the idea of a "sacred history," a *Heilsgeschichte* ("salvation-history"), to speak about the inner story of how a people has been chosen, formed, given a vocation and a meaning on the stage of world history received a sense of destiny. This is the "inner history" of religious communities (Niebuhr 1960), the story of how God has guided, intervened, tended, driven, criticized, and blessed them. It is quite different from the "outer history" as written by noninvolved, dispassionate, objective or academic historians. An inner history is the story of meaning, in which time and eternity, consciousness and unconsciousness, specific historical and archetypal forces all together perform their roles and produce a particular configuration in time. To be totally inside such a history is to be quite unconscious and ignorant of other historical trends, of objective history. To be totally outside of any such history, however, is to be unconscious and ignorant of transcendent factors at play within the historical process. Traditional persons live wholly inside such a sacred history; modern persons live wholly outside; postmodern persons, such as Jung was, dwell both inside and outside, carrying the tension of these opposing perspectives in a single paradoxical vision (cf. Harvey 1966).

In analysis these three stages may also be traversed, at least to some extent. The psychological beginner is wholly enclosed in conscious subjectivity, and the objectivity of the unconscious and its influence is completely unknown. Analysis brings about some measure of awareness of this "other" within, an objective psychic reality made up of complexes and archetypes, which dwells alongside conscious subjectivity and impinges on it in innumerable ways. Analysis seeks to achieve some detachment from one's own biases and perspectives and limited history. This is generally what it means to be "analyzed." But can analysis also take the third step? This would occur when in the course of reconstruction and remembering the personal and impersonal past, subjective and objective elements would fuse in such a way that both remained in consciousness.

Archetypal elements would not be used to obliterate personal ones or get placed in the service of the ego-defenses, nor would the personal elements obscure and hide the archetypal ones. Both would appear and be held in consciousness simultaneously. In this instance, the symbolic becomes personal, and the personal is symbolic.

The brief but extremely powerful and far-reaching experience of a particular man illustrates this. He was in his early 40s. His father, a minister, had died some years previously. In church one Sunday he became extremely emotional and felt the memory of his father pressing in on him. For the first time, the presence of God and the presence of his father-image were joined consciously in his mind. Suddenly he had the vivid thought/image that when he died and went to heaven and looked into the face of God, he would look into the face of his father.

In this experience we find the marriage of the personal and the archetypal. This man was otherwise well-grounded in a personal history and had done a good bit of reconstructive work in analysis. His father had been a present and immediate figure in his life, and the two of them had gone through the usual oedipal struggles. After the death of his father he had both assimilated him to his ego and had allowed his image to fall into the unconscious, where it became assimilated to the father archetype. In this moment of religious experience and insight, the image of his father reappeared as a fused personal/archetypal figure, and this would provide the key for reinterpreting his history. Now, looking back, he could see that the father archetype had been embodied and had acted in his personal history through his own actual father. For this man now to say that God acts in history was to say that he could understand the relationship with his father in archetypal terms.

It also happened that his father was a Yahweh-like, emotional, claim-making figure (Jung 1952, par. 568) and also the self-sacrificing God of love. This confluence of personal and archetypal father elements allowed this man to *feel* the action of the Biblical God in his own life, through the person of his father. A part of his "inner history" would have to be perceived in this way. At the same time, he retained a clear grasp of the actuality of the man who was his father. The two images remained in consciousness side-by-side.

Jung's woman patient with the Javanese childhood runs along similar lines. There is a synchronistic confluence between an archetypal process and a personal history, and this is uncovered and understood and accepted in the reconstructive work of analysis.

The final psychic product of the stage of reconstruction I am describing here is *amor fati*: not only knowledge about one's history, nor even the more intimate knowledge *of* it, but a full embrace and love of it, as that which has been archetypally meant to be.

References

Davenport, G. 1984. *Apples and pears*. San Francisco: North Point Press.
Dieckmann, H. 1979. *Methoden der analytischen Psychologie*. Olten: Walter Verlag.
Eliade, M. 1959. *Cosmos and history. The myth of the eternal return*. New York and Evanston: Harper and Row.
Fordham, M. 1978. *Jungian psychotherapy*. Chichester, New York, Brisbane, Toronto: John Wiley & Sons.
Franz, M.-L. von 1972. *Creation myths*. Dallas: Spring Publications.
Harvey, Van A. 1966. *The historian and the believer*. New York: MacMillan.
Hillman, J. 1983. *Archetypal psychology: A brief account*. Dallas: Spring Publications.
Jung, C. G. 1913. The theory of psychoanalysis. In *Collected works*, 4:83–226. Princeton: Princeton University Press, 1961.
———. 1916. *Psychology of the unconscious*. New York: Moffat, Yard and Company.
———. 1932. Psychological Commentary on Kundalini Yoga. Unpublished seminar notes.
———. 1935. The Tavistock lectures. In *Collected works,* 18:267–90. Princeton: Princeton University Press, 1976.
———1937. The realities of practical psychotherapy. In *Collected works*, 16:327–38. New York: Pantheon, second edition, 1966.
———. 1939. The symbolic life. In *Collected works,* 18:267–90. Princeton: Princeton University Press, 1976.
———. 1940. The psychology of the child archetype. In *Collected works*, 9/1:151–81. Princeton: Princeton University Press, second edition, 1968.
———. 1942. On the psychology of the unconscious. In *Collected works*, 7:3–119. New York: Random House, second edition, 1966.
———. 1946. On the psychology of the transference. In *Collected works*, 16:163–324. New York: Pantheon Books, second edition, 1966.
———. 1950. Concerning mandala symbolism. In *Collected works*, 9/i:355–84. Princeton: Princeton University Press second edition, 1968.
———. 1952. Answer to Job. In *Collected works*, 11:355–472. Princeton: Princeton University Press, second edition, 1969.
———. 1954. On the nature of the psyche. In *Collected works*, 8:159–234. Princeton: Princeton University Press, second edition, 1969.
———. 1961. *Memories, dreams, reflections*. New York: Random House.
———. 1966. *The practice of psychotherapy*. In *Collected works*, vol. 16. Princeton: Princeton University Press, 1966.
Lambert, K. 1981. *Analysis, repair and individuation*. London, New York, Toronto, Sydney, San Francisco: Academic Press
Niebuhr, H. R. 1960. *The meaning of revelation*. New York: The Macmillan Company.
Partridge, E. 1966. *Origins*. New York: The Macmillan Company.
Samuels, A. 1985. *Jung and the post-Jungians*. London, Boston, Melbourne and Henley: Routledge & Kegan Paul.
Satinover, J. 1985. At the mercy of another: Abandonment and restitution in psychosis and psychotic character. *Chiron: A Review of Jungian Analysis* 1985:47–86.
Schwartz-Salant, N. 1986. On the subtle-body concept in clinical practice. In *The body in analysis*, N. Schwartz-Salant & M. Stein, eds., pp. 19–58. Wilmette, Ill.: Chiron Publications.

Schwartz-Salant, N., & M. Stein (eds.), 1984. Transference and Countertransference Processes in Analysis, *Chiron: A Review of Jungian Analysis.*

Singer, J. 1972. *Boundaries of the soul.* Garden City, N.Y.: Doubleday.

Stein, M. 1980. Hephaistos: A pattern of introversion. In *Facing the gods*, J. Hillman, ed. Dallas: Spring Publications.

———— (ed.). 1982. *Jungian analysis.* La Salle & London: Open Court.

————. 1984. Power, shamanism, and maieutics in the countertransference. *Chiron: A Review of Jungian Analysis* 1984:67–88.

————. 1985. *Jung's treatment of Christianity: The psychotherapy of a religious tradition.* Wilmette, Ill.: Chiron Publications.

Whitmont, E. 1969. *The symbolic quest.* New York: G. P. Putnam.

Emerging Concepts of the Self: Clinical Considerations

Charles H. Klaif

In this article I will offer the conjecture that the ego personality in dreams and in life experience can and does at certain times stand as symbol for and representation of the self.

These views are supported by

1) developments and modifications of the concept of the self put forth in recent years by both analytical psychologists and psychoanalysts,

2) extensions of certain of Jung's theoretical postulates,

3) clinical findings.

The past several years have seen a wide-ranging, at times scholarly, at times heated, personal, and affect-laden discussion of the ego-self question in the Jungian literature. The debate has turned on terminology, definitions, points of overlap, and points of difference between these two concepts. Despite strenuous efforts to clarify the distinctions between ego and self, these efforts have in the minds of some authors ended in varying degrees of "muddle" (Jacoby 1983, p. 109; Redfearn 1983b, p. 115). This present paper may serve to create more of a muddle, but I present it with two thoughts in mind. First, from the clinical point of

Charles H. Klaif, M.D., is a member of the Northern California Society of Jungian Analysts. He has a private practice in San Francisco and teaches at the Jung Institute of San Francisco.

view, the ideas presented here may be helpful in introducing a more vivid and immediate sense of the self into analyses where that aspect is deficient. Secondly, from the theoretical viewpoint, the position taken here is that the muddle may reflect something of the true nature of the two entities, i.e., that they are not separate and distinct but have an area of overlap. This area of overlap provides the theoretical background for the clinical observations explored herein.

I. Some Jungian Views of Ego-Self

At the present time some grouping of the various viewpoints regarding ego and self among Jungians is possible. The classical school (as defined by Samuels 1983) holds to sharper distinctions between ego and self and to the view that the self is an archetypal phenomenon having to do with totality, wholeness, and integration. On the other hand, both the developmental school and the archetypal school (again using Samuels's classification) seem to have become strange bedfellows engaged in a process Samuels calls "dethroning the self."

> Fordham and Hillman are each proposing a situationist, relativized, pluralistic Self in which clusters of experience carry the feeling of 'being myself' rather than that of being or feeling 'whole.' If the part self or psychic fragment is lived out fully, then wholeness will take care of itself. It should not be forgotten that the feeling of being oneself is often extremely uncomfortable and thus fulfills Guggenbuhl-Craig's objections to the idealized, perfect Self. (1982, p. 49)

Rosemary Gordon (1985) offers an innovative and useful resolution here by suggesting that the word self can be used to describe three different, though related, concepts and groups of phenomena. The first of these she calls "Jung's self, the big self," which is a metapsychological construct referring to the wholeness of the psyche and its totality. She sees this "big self" as the source of those symbols that convey wholeness and the eternal, i.e., mandalas, magic circles, and numerical sequences. The second division, the primary self (based on Fordham's definition), is that self found in the baby at the beginning of life. It is a primitive form of the self, a simple totality with very little differentiation and refers to the potential faculties of the organism. The third, and most interesting concept, is the "little self." "It refers to the experience of one's self and to the awareness of one's own personal identity. It is this self that psychoanalysts like Kohut and Kernberg, et al. seem to refer to in their writings" (*ibid.,* p. 267). The little self is "the self that refers principally to the idea of one's self, the self that observes and creates the experience of images, emotions, and feelings as they concern oneself" (*ibid.*). It is intimately related, Gordon says, to "what Jung has described as the endopsychic system of consciousness" (*ibid.,* p. 267).

Her definitions of the little self seem to edge into, and begin to merge with, definitions of the ego and, in fact, in one passage she seems to equate the two: "the development of a relatively appropriate and realistic body image is one of the first signs that an ego—the 'little self'—is becoming established."

The self that Kohut refers to in his writing is, however, seen differently by Redfearn. In his efforts to clarify the distinction between ego and self in the Jungian world, Redfearn suggests that "Jung's 'ego' is almost exactly the same as . . . the Hartman-Kohut 'self'" (Redfearn 1983, p. 98). This view met with disagreement from both Jacoby and Schwartz-Salant in their comments on Redfearn's article. Schwartz-Salant presents a useful mathematical model of two slightly overlapping circles representing self and ego in whose area of overlap "the self is a content of the ego as much as the ego is a content of the self" (1983, p. 112). This model is similar to Edinger's important contribution regarding the ego's origin in, and gradual emergence from, the self and the consequent formation of the ego-self axis.

II. Psychoanalytic Views of Ego-Self

In the psychoanalytic literature there is a similar lack of clarity regarding the distinctions between the self and the ego—an unclarity that has become more profound and more problematic to psychoanalysts during the past two decades. As a result of the rapidly growing interest in so-called self-psychology, the self has supplanted the ego for many theorists as the central focus of psychoanalytic thinking, writing, and investigation. In a kind of uncanny mirror-imaging of the ongoing efforts among Jungians to understand ego and self distinctions, a debate rages between those psychoanalysts who adhere to Freud's classical metapsychological theories in which an id-derived, conflict-ridden ego accounts for all psychic phenomena (Rangel 1982) and those, foremost among them Kohut, who propose, if not an enthroning, at least a position of central importance be afforded to the self.

There is also an effort by some psychoanalysts to reclaim the self, legitimatize it, and return it to the psychoanalytic mainstream by attributing to Freud's translator the error of constraining Freud's use of the word "Ich" to mean only ego rather than including the other possibility—self (Kernberg 1982, pp. 894–97; Richards 1982, pp. 942–43). These theorists

generally adhere to the basic tenets of Freudian metapsychology and follow Hartman's revered contribution to the topic as well as Jacobson's extension of his line of thought. One, for example, concludes that "the introduction of a supraordinant self-construct really offers no theoretical or
clinical advantages over traditional psychoanalytic formulations; indeed
such consideration reveals that the new self-psychologies are actually regressive in their tendency to gloss over Hartman's meaningful distinction
between the domains of ego and self." (Richards, pp. 944–45). Kernberg,
in turn, proposes defining the self as "an intrapsychic structure that originates from the ego and is clearly embedded in the ego. To conceptualize
the self in this way is to remain close to Freud's implicit insistence that
self and ego are indissolubly linked" (Kernberg, p. 900).

Kernberg goes on to state that the self is "an ego function and structure that evolves gradually from the integration of its component self-
representations into a supraordinant structure that incorporates other
ego functions—such as memory and cognitive structure—and leads to
the dual characteristics implied in Freud's Ich" (p. 905).

In previous papers (Klaif 1985a, 1985b) I have presented my views
regarding the relevance for analytical psychologists of the development
of theories of the self by non-Jungian theoreticians. I will briefly summarize in the next section some of these previously mentioned, non-Jungian
views of the self and also add an additional view of the self that has come
to my attention since the previous publications.

Samuels points out that "analytical psychologists from all schools are
actively modifying Jung's original statements about the self" (1982, p. 43).
These modifications in some instances bring them, I believe unknow-
ingly on both sides, very close to some of the theories and modifications
being advanced by psychoanalysts. I will therefore additionally note
where appropriate in the following section, some of the areas of concor-
dance between analytical psychologists' and psychoanalysts' writings.

III. The Convergence of Psychoanalytic and Jungian Views

In a previous paper (Klaif 1985a) I noted the shift away from the traditional Freudian metapsychological viewpoint in the work of certain
Freudian writers and the expanded importance and centrality given to
the concept of the self in psychoanalytic theories. I examined the work of
several modern theoreticians and suggested that there was a significance
to the diminishing importance of the metapsychological view and the
concurrent elaboration of increasingly broad and encompassing concep-

tualizations of the self. I saw the recognition of the importance and centrality of the self by non-Jungian therapists as consistent with, and indeed confirming of, Jung's theories regarding the archetypal structure of the psyche. When people from widely differing backgrounds and with different approaches evolve similar theories, one begins to think that the archetypes are leading the way. I speculated that this was the case on the part of the investigators I studied and I concluded that each had encountered the archetype of the self, and that his or her theories reflected the influence of that entity. This influence I perceived in three psychoanalytic treatments I previously reviewed: George Klein; Sampson and Weiss; and Heinz Kohut. It is now seen in a fourth, one not previously mentioned, Mardi Horowitz.

George Klein

George Klein, in his work in the mid- and late 1960s reported: "I had to begin with the assumption of a single apparatus of control which exhibits a variety of dynamic tendencies, the focus of which is either an integration experienced in terms of a sense of continuity, coherence, and integrity, or its impairment experienced as cleavages or dissonance. I call this central apparatus the 'self'" (Klein 1976, p. 8). The self, according to Klein, had to do with a sense of "continuity, coherence, and integrity at every stage of life." Continuity refers to the sense one has that "one is continuously evolving in the face of change: that what I am today is continuous with even though different from what I was yesterday and what I will be tomorrow" (*ibid.*, p. 180). Coherence refers to a sense that one's actions and relationships are compatible with both the autonomous—that is, separate and individual—as well as the social aspects of one's selfhood. "Integrity refers to a sense of moral truth concerning what one does and feels." Klein refers to the self at various times as a "central apparatus" or "controlling center" (*ibid.*, p. 183) or "integrating apparatus" or "ego center beyond the ego" (*ibid.*, p. 171). He seems to be attempting to define something central and encompassing which he understands to be neither ego nor id and which can best be apprehended subjectively and experientially.

Klein speaks further of a "capacity for experiencing messages of the meaning of actions" as they relate to the self. When these messages lead to a sense of continuity, "a sense of coherence and a sense of integrity, there is then an experience of integration of the self." Klein's reference to the experiencing of "messages of the meaning of actions" is significant here in that it accords well with a frequently quoted statement by Elie

Humbert: "If you were to ask what the self signifies for me I should reply that it is above all the inner voice which tells me frequently and precisely how I am to live. . . . It is not a matter of specific words, but of a 'thought,' though not a reasoned one, offering itself like evidence, with a quite particular intensity, and a call to do what it proposes. It is the revealing of an unconscious source of knowledge . . ." (1980, p. 238).

Harold Sampson and Joseph Weiss

These two clinical investigators, after scrupulous examination of hundreds of hours of psychoanalytic interviews, have proposed that independent activity of the patient's unconscious can lead to warded-off (repressed) unconscious material coming into consciousness without interpretative activity on the part of the analyst. They found in their studies that this new material came into consciousness without anxiety and was readily worked with and assimilated by the patient. This is in contrast to traditional psychoanalytic theory which holds that previously repressed material can come into consciousness only through interpretive activity of the analyst. Should it break through without being properly interpreted, the result predicted by the theory would be considerably increased anxiety. They postulate therefore an unconscious which is capable of "higher mental functioning." In their view the patient "thinks, plans, and decides unconsciously and carries out methods of working in the analysis to bring forth and master the impulses, affects and ideas . . . which he has warded off and with which he is in conflict" (Weiss 1977, p. 4). They determined that in contrast to the traditional theory, which holds that the patient unconsciously wishes to gratify certain infantile impulses, that the patient, in fact, "unconsciously wishes to solve his problems by making conscious and mastering the mental contents which he has warded off and with which he is in conflict" (Weiss 1977, p. 7). Their concept of higher mental functioning of the unconscious thus includes the capacity of the unconscious to act autonomously in highly sophisticated ways and to effect healing within the analytic situation independent of the classical methodology of interpreting defenses traditionally used by psychoanalysts. Their view accords well with a Jungian view of the unconscious as having homeostatic tendencies. It comes close to Whitmont's statement that "Jung credits the psyche with a potentiality towards self-healing. The idea that the unconscious contains also a healing potential and not only the disturbing elements was one of Jung's unique and revolutionary discoveries" (1969, p. 295). Whitmont's view that "there is an inherent tendency in the psyche to bring forth the other side" and that "transformation postulates a change in the drives themselves, [through which] they cease to be threatening and disruptive and are converted into helpful elements" also accords well with the Sampson and Weiss view of higher mental functioning of the unconscious. Sampson and Weiss, it should be noted, make no specific reference to the self. It is, however, this author's view that their findings allow a conceptualization of the self based on their findings.

Heinz Kohut

Kohut's views of the self have been subjected to careful and thoughtful comparisons with those of Jung, and these articles are no doubt familiar to this audience. (Jacoby 1981, 1983; Schwartz-Salant 1980). In Kohut's view (1977), the self is the original and continuing "center of the psychological universe." The self is constituted of "innate potentialities" that are to be found in the baby. These, converging with the expectations of the self object, are "the point of origin of the infant's primal rudimentary self" (*ibid.,* p. 99). Michael Fordham also uses the term "primal self" or "original self" and both authors seem to be referring to "those simple and primitive states of the self which one finds in babies at the beginning of life when their reactions and view of the world which surrounds them are global and still comparatively undifferentiated" (Gordon 1985, p. 2263).

Mardi Horowitz

Although using somewhat unfamiliar terminology (which he, however, defines with great clarity), Horowitz (1983) seems to be drawing near to some familiar (to Jungians) conceptualizations of the self. He presents first the idea of "multiple self-concepts," each one the "I" of a particular state of mind. These are characteristic, familiar, and recognizable to the individual and are associated with typical mood, affect, and behavior. He next introduces the concept of a "supraordinant self organization." This is a kind of overarching container which gives rise to another kind of "I" experience. The "I" experience that derives from the supraordinate self organization "provides for a continuity between the various subsidiary self schemata" (*ibid.,* p. 286) and points to "a larger structure that patterns interconnections between various self-concepts" (*ibid.,* p. 286). Horowitz's purpose in the use of this somewhat cumbersome terminology is to give "the useful implication of a whole greater than the sum of its parts" while curiously making a clearly stated effort to avoid sounding "too transcendental" (p. 286).

Jung, of course, was not the least bit uneasy about sounding transcendental. In fact, as Samuels points out, he emphasized "that the self is
a special transcendental concept" (1982, p. 44) a totality, a unity, "a special . . . transcendental archetype" (K. Newton, cited in Samuels). Samuels
goes on to point out that there is a "trend" among post-Jungians away
from an "exclusive consideration of integration . . . toward conceiving the
self as a system composed of relating subsystems, partial states, representations of parts of the self" (p. 45). It certainly seems odd that Horowitz, a
distinguished psychoanalyst researcher, although a little uneasy about
the risk of being seen as too transcendental, seems to move comfortably
toward a unifying concept of the self at the exact moment when some
post-Jungians are seemingly deserting this traditional Jungian "transcendental" viewpoint.

We are reminded by some of Horowitz's statements, of the previously cited work by Rosemary Gordon (1985) in which she states:

> It is clear that the more an individual recognizes the cohesion and inter-
> relatedness of his several selves, [Horowitz's multiple self-concepts?] the
> closer does he approach an experience of the big self [the supraordinate self
> organization experience?]. And this is increased further if he can also get a
> feel of those little selves that seem diametrically opposed, alien or even dis-
> tasteful to those he can experience and recognize as his. In other words, his
> capacity to be in ever better and closer touch with more and more aspects of
> his shadow puts him also in better and closer touch with the big self. (*Ibid.*,
> p. 266)

It is intriguing to compare Gordon's explanation with this passage from
Horowitz:

> When this supraordinant self organization is actively functional . . . [a person]
> organizes thought by the knowledge that he has different states of mind and
> that he may behave in ways that seem like opposites as he cycles through
> these states. For example, he knows that he is mean in some states of mind
> and kindly in others. He knows that these character traits are complementary
> halves of a conflict in attitudes. . . . In a similar manner, he knows that others
> shift their own attitudes toward him as they also pass through varied states of
> mind." (Horowitz, p. 286)

From Gordon's side, she closes her paragraph by saying, "The closer
a person can get to a feeling of rapport with the big self, the greater,
deeper, and the wider is likely to become his capacity for understanding
and compassion, both of others and of himself" (p. 266).

IV. Jung's Theoretical Postulates

Jung himself was not unaware of the difficulty in separating ego from
part selves from big self. He clearly stressed the importance of avoiding

concretization or rigidity in making definitions and differentiations between ego and self.

Jung asserted the "supreme importance of the ego in bringing reality to light." In his discussion of Sol and Luna as symbols of the opposites in the psyche, he goes on to say, "One could even define it [the ego] as a *relatively constant personification of the unconscious itself* or as a Schopenhauerian mirror in which the unconscious becomes aware of its own face" (1963, p. 107). And he then states:

> The conviction of the West [is] that God and the ego are worlds apart. In India, on the other hand, their identity was taken as self-evident. It was the nature of the Indian mind to become aware of the world-creating significance of the consciousness as manifested in man. The West, on the contrary, has always emphasized the littleness, weakness, and sinfulness of the ego, despite the fact that it elevated one man to the status of divinity. The alchemists at least suspected man's hidden godlikeness. (*Ibid.,* p. 109)

In *Mysterium Coniunctionis,* his final major work, Jung was perhaps endeavoring to correct an unfortunate misapprehension that the study of the activities of the ego was in some way less important than a study of the symbols of the self. These references suggest a new respect was being granted the ego in Jung's thinking. His suggestion that the ego can be used *pars pro toto* and the enhanced significance given the ego in these passages seems to suggest that Jung was inviting a kind of ego psychology, but a profoundly different kind of ego psychology. The ego is recognized by Jung as the living manifestation of the self, the latter a psychic entity which is a potential and is ultimately an unknowable. Jung even seems to overstate the case when he suggests that the main purpose of the concept of the self as a pre-existent personality, out of which are derived the ego and the shadow, is that this concept "serves to put the empirical material in order." "The empiricist has nothing to say about the concepts self and God in themselves and how they are related to one another" (Jung 1963, p. 108).

The alchemists, Jung felt, came very close to realizing that the ego was the mysteriously elusive arcane substance and the longed-for lapis. The sun symbol of the alchemists, he felt, established an intimate connection between God and the ego, a connection "nature herself" expressed through the involuntary projection of this identity by the alchemists. He goes on to say that:

> The East resolves these confusing and contradictory aspects by merging the ego, the personal atman, with the universal atman and thus explaining the ego as the veil of Maya. The Western alchemist was not consciously aware of these problems. But when his unspoken assumptions and his symbols reached the plane of conscious gnosis, it was precisely the littleness and low-

liness of the ego that impelled him to recognize its identity with its extreme opposite. It was not the arbitrary opinions of deranged minds that gave rise to such insights, but rather the nature of the psyche itself, which, in East and West alike, expresses these truths either directly or clothed in transparent metaphors. This is understandable when we realize that a world-creating quality attaches to human consciousness as such. In saying this we violate no religious convictions, for the religious believer is at liberty to regard man's consciousness (through which, as it were, a second world-creation was enacted) as a divine instrument. (1963, p. 109)

The crucial point for purposes of the present discussion, however, is made in the next paragraph:

I must point out to the reader that these remarks on the significance of the ego might easily prompt him to charge me with grossly contradicting myself. He will perhaps remember that he has come across a very similar argument in my other writings. Only there it was not a question of ego but of the self, or rather of the personal atman in contradistinction and in relation to the suprapersonal atman. I have defined the self as the totality of the conscious and the unconscious psyche, and the ego as the central reference point of consciousness. *It is an essential part of the self, and can be used* pars pro toto *when the significance of consciousness is borne in mind.* But when he wants to lay emphasis on the psychic totality it is better to use the term "self." There is no question of a contradictory definition, but merely of a difference of standpoint (1963, p. 110; italics added).[1]

V. Ego and Self: Ego as Self

In Jung's extensive descriptions of the various symbols of the self in *Aion,* he points out that, after geometric and arithmetic images, the most common symbolic form in which the self appears in dreams is the human figure. It (the self) takes the form, Jung says, of "a God or a Godlike human being, a prince, a priest, a great man, an historical personality, a dearly loved father, an admired example, the successful older brother—in short, a figure that transcends the ego personality of the dreamer" (1959, p. 225).

It is my view that there are instances in which (no doubt through the influence of the self) the ego personality, i.e. the individual himself, or his physical representation in a dream or memory "transcends the ego personality" and becomes a "Godlike human being," or one of the other "beautiful, good, admirable, and lovable human figures" Jung mentions in the above passage (*ibid.*). Alternatively, noting Guggenbuhl-Craig's brief for their inclusion, representations may also appear of "the deficiency, the invalidism of the self" (1980, p. 25).

Although subject to other interpretations, I believe that the ego personality of the dreamer may, at times, appear in dreams (through the homeostatic and compensatory influence of the self) as a symbol of the self. These dreams, themselves, are particularly moving, often having an invigorating or stimulating effect on the dreamer, although they are often told with some hesitation and perhaps embarrassment. These dreams often seem not to need interpretation. Their message seems clear to the dreamer and seems to be well understood in its own terms. The embarrassment in telling the dreams might reflect the anticipation of the same criticisms and prohibitions that eventuated in these aspects of the self being inhibited and banished from consciousness in the first place.

These appearances of the ego may be thought of as perhaps the adult version of "self-representations"—a term used by Fordham to refer, in infants and children, to "any experience felt by the infant and growing child as perceived and felt to be separate from his ordinary field of consciousness and yet referable directly or indirectly to himself" (Fordham 1976, p. 13).

The ego as symbol in dreams and in life makes manifest the self or aspects of the self. Undiscovered or barely known aspects of the self present themselves to the dreamer in the form of the ego personality, that is, in the person of the dreamer. These potentialities can in this way become known to the dreamer and thereby accessible for integration.[2]

The question of why these aspects of the self are not already available to the ego is pertinent here. Why must the potentialities appear in dreams rather than simply be lived out? Stevens (1983) suggests that the superego censors aspects of the self which are unacceptable to ego consciousness. Superego development, he feels, does not arise because of fear of castration but out of fear that exposure of certain parts of the self would evoke abandonment by the mother (*ibid.,* p. 210).

Stevens seems to be on the right track here, although the addition of the intrapsychic structure superego to the discussion may perhaps be superfluous. The ego may be considered to serve as the representative and intermediary of the self, and in that capacity titrates the expression of the self in life to the exact degree that it (the ego) judges to be safe and possible in a given situation. The ego's judgments are imperfect and almost inevitably result in painful woundings and in the elaboration by the ego of defenses against further wounding. Among these defenses are the elaboration, creatively and ingeniously, of so-called false selves. These are perhaps better understood to be "as-true-as-they-can-be-selves" in that they allow a partial, perhaps muted, expression of the self's potential and at the same time serve to protectively conceal those not welcomed aspects of the true self. The emergence in dreams of more true-to-the-self forms of the ego personality reflects, I believe, the capacity of the psyche to "bring forth the other side" and is an expression of the psyche's homeostatic tendency as well as of the self's unceasing efforts to become manifest in the world.

It can be moving indeed to see, in the course of analytic work, a false to the self ego adaptation give way to an appreciation of one's own self and a more unrestricted expression of it. In dreams and upon reflecting on its own history, the ego personality obtains glimpses of itself living up to its potential selfhood.

A consultee reports her patient's dream. The consultee's patient is also a therapist and is very admiring of my consultee's manner of working, her intelligence, and her poise. The patient under discussion dreams she is going to see her therapist (my consultee), but the setting is different, more like her own (the patient's) office. She enters the consulting room and looks up to find that she is looking at her therapist but the face is her own (the patient's) face. "I am looking at myself," she says. "It is me standing there."

A highly successful businesswoman who had serious conflicts and uncertainty about remaining "feminine" while competing successfully and advancing rapidly in the business world had the following dream:

I am at a very large meeting—many hundreds of people—one which I had arranged and orchestrated. It had gone very well and I was feeling pleased and proud. I meet a woman friend who has an equally demanding and responsible position with another firm. We are talking to each other. I become aware that we both have the complete sexual organs of each sex and it seems perfectly ordinary.

In contrast to her day ego's uneasiness and uncertainty about her androgeny, her dream ego is perfectly comfortable with it and is aware that hers is not a unique or shameful situation.

For some, what the images provide are those darker aspects of the psyche that have been kept hidden or have been unknown, barely known, or not at all lived out. These are the aspects which Guggenbuhl-Craig (1980) feels are missing from Jung's view of the self—the psychopathy, the immorality, and the invalidism.

A successful, mid-fortyish, professional man presented with doubts about his career goals. He was a devoted family man, a good provider, a church goer. He was troubled that he wasn't sufficiently socially responsible. He had for years considered leaving his current employment, which paid him amply, to strike out on his own in a more risky but potentially more fulfilling endeavor. At the critical moment, however, his nerve always failed him. There were also problems at home with his inability to either conform to his wife's many demands and expectations of him, or, alternatively, to openly disagree with her. He dreams:

I am struggling across some rough terrain, hilly. I cross a deep ravine and then have to cross a rushing river. I somehow get across, cold and exhausted, and see a house. I enter the house, go through it into another house. An older friendly man is there. He gives me some dry clothes to put on and some hot tea. There is a sharp pointed file lying on the table. I pick it up and kill him with it.

He wakened from the cream in a highly excited, very emotional state, with tears—but not of sadness or distress about the dream. He was eager to come to the next hour to talk about the dream, having a sense that it was important. He wasn't certain about who the victim in the dream might be. He thought perhaps it resembled his father, but, then, perhaps it was the analyst. He wasn't really sure. He was filled with strong emotion when he told the dream and reported that this had happened each time he'd thought about the dream in the past several days.

In the days that followed the dream he felt himself to be freed somehow. He had an angry, mildly physical confrontation with his wife when she attempted to interfere with an activity he had arranged with his son. He reported that he was able for the first time to tell her how much he resented her intrusion and her managerial bullying and he was able for the first time to tell me how much he disliked therapy—the resentment and humiliation he felt about having to reveal things about himself to me that no one else knew.

Although one might consider this dream to simply reflect the emergence of shadow aspects, there is a striking absence of any moral concern either in the dream or on reflection upon the dream. Guggenbuhl-Craig (1980) raises the question of whether there is an immoral self. The dream presented seems to suggest a heretofore unlived, unavailable, immoral aspect of this individual's self. This view is also suggested by the subsequent behavior of the patient. He became increasingly involved and fascinated with rather risky "wheeler dealer" business transactions involving large sums of money. He showed a considerable flair for these activities and considerable success.

It is hypothesized here that in addition to appearing in dreams in the form of the ego personality, aspects of the self can be glimpsed by the ego in the recalling of its own history. Upon reflection, the ego personality recognizes that it has, at certain moments in life, lived out the potentialities of the self. These are deeply moving moments and, I believe, recognizable in part by the strong affect in both the individual and in those who hear or witness the recounting of the events.

A colleague at a recent meeting spoke of her adolescent devotion to dance and of the ardors of her rigorous training. She then recalled the ·endless difficulty and frustration at one point in her training of learning to do turns *en point.* She at last learned to do two consecutive turns and she recounted then the moment of breakthrough, when, setting out yet one more time to attempt two consecutive turns, she found herself, most unexpectedly, doing four, then five, then six consecutive turns. Though 25 years had passed since the occurrence, the intensity and the power of the experience was clearly evident in her face and body as she described it, and it was resonant in, and appreciated by, the audience.

A more clinical example of the ego sensing, becoming aware that it had somehow fulfilled a piece of its potential, occurred with a rather rigid, middle-aged professional man. He recalled an experience from many years before as a coach of a Little League team. He had coached a team of nine and ten year olds, all beginners to the sport, for an entire season. By the end of the season, they had lost every game they played. Quite unexpectedly to him, at the start of the following season—and here in a rare display of feeling my patient became choked up and tears filled his eyes—every one of the boys he'd coached turned out to rejoin the team he would be coaching. My own reaction, to my surprise, was to find myself also very moved. My thoughts initially were that there had become established in our work the positive father transference and countertransference that had been so painfully absent in his youth, so that he could take pride in recounting to me his successes and feel assured by my mirroring approval. However, another perhaps complementary view occurred to me later. It seemed possible that my patient had momentarily seen himself—by glimpsing the reflection of it in his youthful players' eyes—as possessing qualities that made him a "good, admirable, and lovable human figure."

A second clinical example highlights again the effect on those who are witness to them of accounts of those moments in which an aspect of the self is realized.

A thirtyish computer expert with a keen appreciation for new technological developments frequently discussed in his hours his enthusiasms for "state of the art" sound equipment, video equipment, and the like. He had, after extensive and painstaking research and investigation purchased a new sports car. He had devoted a great deal of time and energy to refining its performance and had recently test-driven it at a local race track to fully evaluate the car's performance under extreme conditions. He had installed a special suspension system, but during his test drives he concluded that some further refinements were possible and he was conflicted as to whether he was being "silly and unreasonable" or perhaps "neurotic" to want to spend even more time and money on slight improvements for a car that would only be driven for pleasure and never in competition. With his therapist's affirming and non-critical assistance, he explored his longstanding love for, and fascination with, advanced technology and his equally longstanding sense of having to conceal, or at best strongly mute, his devotion to it. He experienced a realization that he was at last free to fully pursue this passionate interest of his, and this realization was accompanied, as in the first clinical example, by quite unaccustomed tears on the part of both the patient and his therapist. It seemed as if the patient was at last free to fulfill that which he had for years felt himself to be, but which by reason of circumstances he could not be. Those aspects of the self not validated are unlikely to develop fully and are expressed hesitantly, if at all. That the therapist was so deeply moved by his participation in this hour was no mystery when, in discussing the case, his own passionate but somewhat muted and restrained interest in technological advances was revealed.

I believe that the ego can recognize that it has at certain times been influenced by something "other," with the result that the ego was in some way made fuller, larger, wider than it had been or had believed itself capable of becoming. This recognition is often accompanied by strong affect—delight, exhilaration, tears, sometimes awe, perhaps even reverence—affects which are often shared by those who witness the recounting of the event. The subjective sense of having achieved, if even for a moment, that which seemed unobtainable, a level of being or of accomplishment that was a hoped for, sought after, seemingly unobtainable goal or state of being—this is what the individual's ego transiently experiences when it manifests in life the potentialities of the self. The intense response of those who are audience to these moments lends credence, I believe, to the hypothesis that it is the self that is moving among the players in the scene.

That the analyst is also moved by these intense moments may suggest a syntonic (or concordant) countertransference response. The analyst himself is of course subject to experiences analogous to those of his patient. One can thus suppose that another component of the analyst's reactions to his patient's moments of realization of the self derives from the analyst's own analytic self being realized.

To put it another way, these moving patient experiences bear witness to the fact that the analyst has provided the facilitating environment and the healing presence in which transcendent experiences can, and have in fact, occurred. He is thus informed that his own much-sought-after analytic self—the healer of souls—has been, at least for a moment, realized. This might be thought of in psychoanalytic terms as the achievement of the analytic ego ideal—the ego's image of what the analyst might optimally be. In Jungian terms we might call this the analyst's fulfilling a potential of his self. When this occurs during the analysis, there are at these moments synchronous self experiences occurring in the transference/countertransference field.

Conclusions

Rosemary Gordon raises an important question when she says, "We have asked ourselves at various times how we can understand and explain the fact that the images and phantasies produced by our patients lack the grandeur of the symbols which Jung has described as characteristic of the self" (Gordon 1985, p. 267). It is Jung's self, the big self, to use Gordon's helpful terminology, which no doubt gives rise to the more familiar, more grand symbols of the self. But what of the little self—what are its images? We suspect that the little self occupies that liminal, overlapping, shared space of egoself and that its images are of the nature of those we have observed above. They take the form of the ego personality enriched and expanded by the influence of self.

The images that we are referring to here are not of course images of totality but are rather in that category of symbols that express parts of the self. They are related to the whole in and of themselves but perhaps more importantly the whole is made known by the fact of their appearance, i.e., their appearance offers evidence of the workings of forces in the unconscious that are impelling us in the direction of wholeness through the creation of the images which promote this journey.

Fordham a decade ago postulated two forms of the self—the whole self and part selves (Fordham 1976, 1979). He offers (1979, p. 25) the possibility that the subjective experience of the various archetypes may be considered to be part selves. By doing this he feels,

> We have moved a long way from the grand archetypal forms that were said to influence the course of history, and from the mystical indefinable self, descending to a pedestrian level quite out of keeping with the conception of the self that has little to do with less complex personalities. But the notion of parts of the self felt to be "myself" are essential in an ordinary person living an ordinary life. . . . In varying ways the parts of the self can cohere and then a sense of identity or wholeness and unity with the cosmos can emerge. (*Ibid.*, p. 247).

We have here another view of the now-familiar notion of part selves (Horowitz's multiple self concepts, Gordon's little selves) cohering to form a wholeness (Horowitz's supraordinate self concept, Gordon's big self) and perhaps even as Fordham suggests, a sense of a unity with the cosmos. The part self experiences described above—those derived from the ego's observing itself in dreams and in life as a symbolic manifestation of (parts of) the self are, I feel, a part of this wholeness-seeking process.

Notes

1. Schwartz-Salant (1983) also employs this series of excerpts to argue the absence of rigidity in Jung's distinction between ego and self.
2. Dr. John Beebe, after reading the manuscript of this talk at the Ghost Ranch Conference, kindly called my attention to his review of James Hillman's *The Dream and the Underworld* in which he embraces a similar proposition (Beebe 1979).

References

Edinger, E. 1972. *Ego and archetype*. G. P. Putnam's Sons, New York.
Fordham, M. 1976. *The self and autism*. London, Heinemann.
———. 1979. The self as an imaginative construct. *Journal of Analytical Psychology* 24:1.
Gordon, R. 1985. Big self and little self: Some reflections. *Journal of Analytical Psychology* 30:3.
Guggenbuhl-Craig, A. 1980. *Eros on crutches: Reflections on psychopathy and amorality*. Dallas: Spring Publications.
Horowitz, M. J., and Zilberg, N. 1983. Regressive alterations of the self concept, *American Journal of Psychiatry* 140:3.
Humbert, E. 1980. The self and narcissism. *Journal of Analytical Psychology* 25:3.
Jacoby, M. 1981. Reflections on Heinz Kohut's concept of narcissism. *Journal of Analytical Psychology* 26:1.
———. 1983. Comment on J. W. T. Redfearn's paper. *Journal of Analytical Psychology* 28:2.
Jung, C. G. 1959. *Aion: Researches into the phenomenology of the self. In Collected works*, 9/ii. Princeton: Princeton University Press.
———. 1963. *Mysterium coniunctionis. In Collected works*, vol. 14. Princeton: Princeton University Press.
Kernberg, O. 1982. Self, ego, affects and drives, *Journal of American Psychoanalytic* 30:4.
Klaif, C. H. 1985a. Emerging concepts of the self: A Jungian view, *Quadrant* 18:1.
———. 1985b. Developments in the Psychoanalytic Concept of the Self. *Journal of Analytical Psychology* 30:3.
Klein, G. S. 1976. *Psychoanalytic theory: An exploration of essentials*. New York: International Universities Press.
Kohut, H. 1977. *The restoration of the self*. New York: International Universities Press.
Rangel, L. 1982. The self in psychoanalytic theory. *Journal of American Psychoanalytic* 30:4.
Redfearn, J. W. T. 1983a. Ego and self: Terminology. *Journal of Analytical Psychology* 28:2.
———. 1983b. Reply to comments *Journal of Analytical Psychology* 28:2.
Richards, Arnold D. 1982. The supraordinate self in psychoanalytic theory and in the self psychologies. *Journal of American Psychoanalytic* 30:4.
Samuels, A. 1982. *Dethroning the self*. Dallas: Spring Publications 1982.

————. 1983. The emergence of schools of analytical psychology. *Journal of Analytical Psychology* 29:4.

Schwartz-Salant, N. 1982. *Narcissism and character transformation: The psychology of narcissistic character disorders.* Toronto: Inner City Books.

————. 1983. Comment on J. W. T. Redfearn's Paper. *Journal of Analytical Psychology* 28:2.

Stevens, A. 1982. *Archetypes: A natural history of the self.* New York: William Morrow and Co., Inc.

Weiss, J., *et al.* 1977. Research on the psychoanalytic process. Bulletin No. 3, The Psychotherapy Research Group, Department of Psychiatry, Mt. Zion Hospital and Medical Center, San Francisco.

Whitmont, E. C. 1969. *The Symbolic Quest.* New York: G. P. Putnam's Sons.

Archetypes on the Couch

Rosemary Gordon

I want to start my paper with some theoretical assumptions and reflections, for it will give an idea of where I stand and how I think. The problem of bringing together theory and practice is a thorny one, and I cannot claim that I am anywhere near to having firmly and finally grasped that nettle.

I have entitled this paper archetypes *on* the couch; not *from* the couch nor *for* the couch but archetypes *on* the couch. In other words I want to explore the nature of the concept "archetype," look at it as one might look at a patient, listening and receptive to what is overt or covert, and explore its meaning, its function and the mood, feelings, and fantasies communicated by it, what experience of the subject, the patient, may characterize it as archetypal, and what reaction does such an archetypal experience evoke in the object, the observer, the therapist. Thus such an exploration will concern itself both with the nature of the experiences coming from the patient and with the responses and the interpretations given by the observing participant, the therapist.

The concept of the archetypes itself was born—or at least was con-

Rosemary Gordon, Ph.D., is a member of the Society of Analytical Psychology (London) and editor of the *Journal of Analytical Psychology.* She is the author of numerous books and papers and is a training analyst in the Jung Institute of London.

ceived—as a result of that archetypal transference/countertransference clash, the war of the two giants, Freud and Jung. Jef Dehing, a colleague in Belgium, has made a fascinating study of their relationship, their love and their hate for each other, by analyzing the letters that passed between them. For instance, in February 1910 Freud writes to Jung:

> True, what you write about it [symbolism] now is only a hint, but in a direction where I too am searching, namely *archaic repression*, which I hope to master through mythology and the development of language. It would be wonderful if you could do a piece on the subject for the *Jahrbuch*.

Or in June 1910 he writes:

> Don't be surprised if you recognize certain of your own statements in a paper of mine that I am hoping to revise in the first few weeks of the holidays, and don't accuse me of plagiarism, though there may be some temptation to. . . . I conceived and wrote it two days before the arrival of your "Symbolism"; it is of course a formulation of ideas that were long present in my mind.

In January 1911 he ends a letter to Jung with:

> I don't know why you are so afraid of my criticism in matters of mythology. I shall be very happy when you plant the flag of libido and repression in that field and return as a victorious conqueror to our medical motherland.

And in August of the same year:

> . . . I have been working in a field where you will be surprised to meet me. I have unearthed strange and uncanny things and will almost feel obliged not to discuss them with you.

This is an allusion to the work prepared secretly that would become *Totem and Taboo*. Even as late as 1918 in his paper on the "Wolfman," Freud writes:

> I have come to the end of what I had to say about this case. . . . The first relates to the phylogenetically inherited schemata, which, like the categories of philosophy, are concerned with the business of "placing" the impressions derived from actual experience. I am inclined to take the view that they are precipitates from the history of human civilisation.

The concepts of innate ideas and of "typical mythological forms" are obviously precursors of the notion of the "archetype." That this word should have become part of the exclusively Jungian nomenclature is one of the results of the "Great War," the war of the two giants.

"The archetype" is, of course, a concept, not a datum. It is a mental construction. It is a metapsychological model to account for the recurrence and apparent universality in humans of certain experiences and images, the archetypal images. Models are *ad hoc* provisional devices;

they are attempts to order or to assemble together a number of phenomena which have certain characteristics in common or which collect into an easily perceived pattern what is actually beyond our sensory grasp. We make, for instance, models of sub-atomic particles, or of astronomic, that is, stellar or planetary, constellations. Geographical maps are models; they allow us to catch in one glimpse a vast, extensive land mass, and inform us through agreed conventions of the political or the geological features involved. Where a model is a tangible object, like a map, there is little risk of confusing the model with actual reality. But when we are dealing with functions and qualities, as we do in psychology, the danger of confusing model and fact—the signifier and the signified—is very great indeed.

When one deals with a model, the question to ask is not, Is this true? Is this correct? Instead it is appropropriate to ask: Is this model useful? Is it still useful? I will return to this question later.

Jung, being ever aware of the danger of confusing model and reality, insisted again and again that the archetypes are devoid of form and content; that they are non-perceptual and irrepresentable. He described them as psychosomatic or psychoid factors that cannot "as such reach consciousness until personal experience as rendered them visible" (Jung 1935, para. 846).

The word "archetype" thus denotes an abstract idea, pointing to the existence in man of the potential to have images, drives, fantasies, and emotions that are "archetypal" because they possess four principal characteristics:

1. universality across space and time, that is, across different cultures and epochs;
2. bipolarity, that is, they each carry both positive and negative complementary qualities;
3. powerful affects, such as fascination or feeling possessed, or experiencing something awesome—awesomely terrible or awesomely beautiful or awesomely significant, that is, spiritual, divine, numinous, and beyond conscious, rational comprehension;
4. an "all-or-nothing" quality; thus whatever is archetypal is experienced as stark, powerful, and absolute, as absolutely good or absolutely bad, as "bigger than big" or "smaller than small," as "always" or "never."

Archetypal processes, the commanding drives and the affectful images and fantasies that they release, ensure the survival, the maturation, and the development of the organism by acquainting it on the one hand with its needs and, on the other, with the objects around it that can satisfy those needs.

Michael Fordham's work and formulations have, I think, increased our understanding of the possible roots, origin, and nature of the archetypal processes as they emerge and develop in the course of an individual's life. He has postulated the existence, at the beginning of life of an "original self," which is the primitive and therefore simple and relatively undifferentiated form of Jung's self. Both the "original self" as well as the "big self," that is, Jung's self, can be thought of as the storehouse of the archetypal images, themes, and drives. They lie, so Fordham has suggested, in readiness to be activated and to emerge through the spontaneous process that he has called "deintegration." It is through this process of deintegration that the original self differentiates and gives birth to the archetypal forms or, as Fordham has called them, the deintegrates, which then, like the scintillae in Jung's terminology, make up the nuclei of consciousness.

I see the relationship of Fordham's "original self" to Jung's big self as analogous to the simple fertilized cell, which, after innumerable divisions, becomes a living organism, composed of innumerable diverse cells and diverse functions.

Deintegration is a lifelong process. The various archetypal themes have each a "critical time" when their emergence is right and appropriate in terms of the stage an individual has reached in the life-cycle.

Through the process of deintegration the ego, defined by Jung as the center of consciousness, becomes differentiated out of the original self. For deintegration involves the development of specific modes of perception, imagery, drives, emotions, fantasies, etc., which search out and, if all goes well, discover in the environment the objects appropriate to them; this then makes experience, and even conscious experience, possible.

The organism is, as it were, programmed to develop deintegrative processes, just as the acorn is programmed to develop into an oak, given a good enough environment. The importance and the reality of this proviso—the good-enough environment—implies that there is inevitably mutual interaction and interdependence between the environment on the one hand and the individual's inherent and constitutionally determined programming on the other.

This interdependence of the objects external to the individual and the deintegrates, evolving from within the individual, makes possible the eventual humanizing of the archetypal themes and figures. This then links the individual's world of fantasy and imagination to his phenomenal, personal, and real world. Fordham made it clear that he has regarded the concept of the deintegrates and the concept of the archetype as being more or less identical when he wrote:

> In so saying he [Jung] implies that the origin of consciousness lies in the archetypes, and so we can conclude that deintegrates, if not identical with, are at least closely related to, them. (1955)

There is clearly some connection between Jung's concept of the archetypal and the ethologist's concept of the "patterns of behavior" and the "innate release mechanism." In fact, Elie Humbert has discovered that Jung himself, as early as 1938, had already observed an evident kinship between these two concepts, his own and that of the ethologists. Fordham also by 1955 had come to recognize the coincidence of these two concepts. He was intrigued, stimulated by it, and seemed to find it illuminating. He did indeed reflect upon it and pursued it further, particularly when he developed his concept of the process of deintegration.

My own study has led me to find an interesting parallel in the religions, particularly in Africa, to Fordham's triad—original self, deintegrate (or archetype), and ego. For I found that there is indeed an almost universal belief in the existence of what I would call a "cosmological triad": a great God who is unknowable, ineffable, and hence unworshipped; and his sons, or messengers, or what the Ashanti of Ghana have named "the pieces of God." Through these the Great God manifests himself in a form that can be intelligible and relatively familiar to men; and lastly there are the men themselves with their more or less conscious awareness. Jung had already explored the relationship between the psychological concept of the self and the religious ideas of God. My discovery of a cosmological triad in religious beliefs paralleling Fordham's triad in his concept of the structure of the psyche seems to make his thesis even more convincing, because it provides a mythological equivalent. Moreover, the parallel or equivalence between archetype-deintegrate and the messengers, "sons," or "pieces" of the Great God, could help us to understand better why archetypal experience is so often marked by a sense of containing and carrying something numinous. For each is liable to express wholeness; each is, as it were, a messenger, a piece of the wholeness—God or self—and so it can act as an agent of the synthetic and integrative process.

The term "deintegrate" is valuable, so it seems to me, because it reminds one of the origin and the process that brings them into being. In the early stages of their emergence they seem indeed to be as simple as are the IRM. However, as a deintegrate becomes admixed with what has been learned and experienced in the world of objects, persons, and cultural artefacts, and as it moves towards consciousness and the ego position, so it becomes much more rich and complex. When this more evolved state has been reached, then, I would now suggest, it is really more appropriate to speak in terms of an archetypal process and an archetypal content.

The relationship between deintegrate and archetype has troubled me for quite a long time, for they evoke somewhat different moods and associations; yet they are obviously very closely related. It is by going back to my reflections which I described in a paper "Losing and Finding: The Location of Archetypal Experience" (Gordon 1985) that I reached the idea that archetypal forms and processes, being rich, enriching, and potentially numinous, are in fact hybrids, hybrids of, on the one hand, the simple deintegrate, which is primarily innate and intrapsychic in origin, and, on the other, of experienced and remembered objects and events. It is, I would now suggest, only those hybrids which have evolved beyond the character and status of a deintegrate that truly deserve to be acknowledged and named "archetypal"; while the deintegrates can be thought of as identical with the alchemists' "scintillae," those germs of consciousness, those "seeds of light," as Jung described them (Jung 1947, para. 388).

The interdependence of objects external to the organism and the deintegrate-archetype differentiating within the organism add another rationale to Jung's theory that when archetypal images detach themselves from the unconscious matrix, they can at first be experienced only—and so take the way to potential consciousness—in and through projection. While they are projected, they are perceived as if they existed only "out there," attached to something or somebody in the external world. They can of course also be identified with and be incorporated in a delusionary manner into the self-image, but in that case it may prove to be more difficult for them to become recognizable as being archetypal contents.

When archetypal figures and images are either identified with or projected, they clearly distort the character of the actual objects or persons involved and so tend to endow them with the stark, absolute, and all-or-nothing qualities that mark them out as characteristically archetypal. Naturally this tends to vitiate relationships. It is probably because of this negative consequence that many analytical psychologists tend to think of "the archetypal" as being a primitive force from which we must free ourselves and which we must outgrow if we are to develop, assume our personal responsibilities, and enter into good, realistic, and mature relationships that are reciprocal and mutually satisfying.

However, although archetypal projections in the course of maturation need to be withdrawn from actual objects and persons, yet to escape altogether from their impact on our experience—even if this were possible—would undoubtedly make life flat, dull, monotonous, stereotyped, and without sparkle, lustre, or adventure. For the archetypal processes do have a very important function. But they can fulfil this only if, instead of distorting objects and persons, they move into that part of the psyche that Winnicott called the "area of experience" or the "area of illusion."

He has postulated that this third area develops out of the infant's experience of a transitional object. This is in fact its first creative act, because in relation to the transitional object the question, "Have you found it or have you made it?" is inappropriate, for the child has both found it and has made it into whatever meaningful object he or she needs and wants it to be. This area, so Winnicott has suggested, is then the source and bedrock of play, creativity, symbolism, and of the symbolic and hence of all art, religion, ethics, aesthetics, and so on. It is the crucible where fantasy and reality meet, fuse, de-fuse, and re-fuse. This third area, I would now argue, is the locus in the psyche appropriate for the functioning and experiencing of the archetypal processes. For these can enrich our inner world, enliven it, activate imagination, and restore to us a sense of the wondrous, the awesome, the mysterious, the poetic.

I mentioned above that Jung himself had recognized a "kinship" between his concept of the archetype and the ethologist's innate behavior and innate "release mechanisms." Fordham conceived and elaborated further on this parallel. I, too, have felt impressed by it.

However, the archetypal imagery and the archetypal motifs that we meet with in our clinical practice are often much more intricate and complex than are the "releaser" and "behavior patterns" described and discussed by ethologists.

Some of these puzzles and confusions can perhaps be lessened or even resolved if we restrict the concept of "deintegrate" to the immediate products of the process of deintegration, for it is these that parallel the ethologist's "innate release mechanism." The deintegrates emerge from the original self as appetites and instincts; consequently they search out and relate to part objects only like—at the beginning of life—breasts, nipple, eyes, warm holding arms, and to specific stimuli like milk, smells, the fearsome situation of falling; that is, to those objects and situations that either protect or else threaten survival. Fordham has described the deintegrate as

a readiness for experience, a readiness to perceive and act. . . . Only when the object fits the deintegrate can a correct perception occur (Fordham 1955).

But when the deintegrate or patterns of deintegrates on the one hand and the objects in the external world on the other have met and have begun to affect and modify each other, then we begin to deal with the hybrids, that is the archetypal contents, images, forms, feelings, and processes. Fordham has been particularly interested in what happens when object and deintegrate do not fit exactly, which is the condition that brings a dawning of consciousness and an awareness of a distinction between subject and object. And then, so he suggests, images no longer mirror precisely the objects they are supposed to represent; instead they change or recombine in various ways and so reflect both the internal psychic processes and the natural as well as cultural objects and events encountered.

It is in Winnicott's "area of illusion" that the hybrids, the archetypal processes, interact with those psychological functions — sensing, perceiving, remembering, thinking, etc. — through which we get to know reality. Here then is the source of the genuine and valid creativity which produces neither idiosyncratic, fanciful hallucinations nor mere copies of reality. Thus the rich and elaborate images we find in our clinical work, whether they occur as fantasies in dreams or in wakefulness, derive from the interaction and the interpenetration of processes from both the archetypal and the cognitive sources.

This thesis, so it seems to me, underpins Jung's belief, as I have already quoted above, that the archetypes themselves are devoid of content until "personal experience has rendered them visible" (Jung 1935, para. 846). It also makes sense of the fact that although many themes in dreams and myths are universal, the actual form they assume are distinct and vary from person to person, from culture to culture, and from epoch to epoch.

I use my own feelings, my sense of familiarity, and my associations to either myths, legends, and fairy tales, or to particular persons or events that the patient has previously talked to me about in order to assess the relative importance of the archetypal as against the personal-historical factors in the material a patient lives and brings to me. This "material" may be in the nature, character, and quality of our transference/countertransference interrelationship; it may be the patient's behavior and actions either inside or outside the consulting room; it may lie in his or her imagined themes, stories, figures, or personages.

Case History: Carolyn

I take as my first example of how this works out in clinical practice a young woman, Carolyn. She was 23 when she started an analysis that lasted 7 years. She had been referred to me because she was haunted by compulsive thoughts that she would, and that she wanted to, kill those nearest and dearest to her if left alone with one of them.

Carolyn, born second, and Mary were fraternal twins. There were two brothers, one four years and one six years younger. The twins had been born six weeks prematurely. The parents were farmers, rather puritanical and perfectionist. As incubators were not near to hand, the twins were kept warm in an airing cupboard. Both were weak and delicate. Carolyn believed that at the start she was the weaker of the two; but, whichever of the two was thought to be at any given time the more delicate or the most endangered twin, that twin was put first to the breast. The one who had become the healthier had to wait. Mother feared that she would not be able to handle the babies all by herself, so there was also a nanny who helped to look after the twins. In this family it was the father who was the more maternal one. When the twins were six years old, the nanny was dismissed. Carolyn was never told why, but she remembers the nanny as a warm, affectionate person able to give the twins bodily comfort and affection. The parents would later talk about the nanny as sloppy and sentimental who, they feared, was spoiling the children.

One incident which Carolyn was told of but could barely remember herself happened when she was about four years old. It seems that she slipped into a pond that was on the farm; she could not yet swim and was actually in danger of drowning. Mary, it is said, gave the alert, the nanny rushed out, saved Carolyn, and revived her. I am sure that this traumatic experience expressed itself and was relived in many of her hypochrondriacal and psychosomatic symptoms, such as her fear of fainting or choking, and her compulsion to stay awake at night in order to monitor her breathing and heart beat, which led to severe insomnia.

Soon after the beginning of her analysis, Mother told Carolyn that she had been expected to be the first born but that at the last moment the twin babies shifted position, so Mary was born first, and Carolyn was born half an hour later. The story—probably the myth—was told that Mary, the firstborn, did not breathe for half an hour, as if she had refused to enter into life until Carolyn also was born. On hearing this account of her birth, Carolyn was swept by a wave of resentment; she had been, she felt, pushed back by Mary and deprived of her birthright—to be the first born. This released in her, and led her to express, violent feelings of rivalry, though she would also try to contain and counter them: "Actually I am proud of Mary; I am glad she was the firstborn." This weak and unconvincing denial was a response not only to defend herself against guilt, but there was also considerable closeness between the twins who often combined as a united front against the parents and could give one another some of the physical tenderness and affection that the parents failed to provide. When they were nine years old, the parents sent them to different boarding schools. Not only were the twins then separated, but their two schools each had a different ethos and educational theory.

When Carolyn first came to see me, I saw a hunched-up person "enveloped" in a large coat of indeterminate color. She looked crumpled up and bent over like a little old woman or like an embryo, as yet unborn. All her colors were gray or dull beige. She wore no make-up and had no particular hairstyle.

She would come into the room, quickly glance around, then look at me furtively as if she needed to reassure herself that I was really there. She often stared into space, her mouth hanging open; I felt that she had dropped into a "thought-hole." She spoke with a little voice, which made it difficult to hear her. This was undoubtedly significant because her mother had become very deaf at an early age; Carolyn had never known her otherwise. Was the soft voice in my room her attempt to prevent the transference on to me of her own mother? Carolyn was in fact a good musician, sang in a choir, played the cello and was an active member of an amateur orchestra that gave public performances.

The compulsive thoughts of killing someone—later referred to by her simply as "the thoughts"—had started suddenly one evening while she was making lampshades with her twin sister. The idea suddenly came to her. It struck her that the scissors she was using could turn into a weapon with which she could kill Mary. After the first appearance of "the thoughts," they stopped for about three months; but then they reappeared and stayed on. They used to come—almost punctually—at about 7:00 P.M. and stayed until late in the evening. They were directed mainly against her twin sister, Mary, but could sometimes be aimed at her mother and sometimes against anybody with whom she found herself alone, except her father, because, as she tried to explain, "He is stronger than I." Her fear of killing others was often turned also against herself; the method of killing was strangling or the use of a metallic weapons.

These killing fantasies, we soon discovered, also expressed omnipotent and omniscient fantasies: "You don't know that this is the last time that you brush your hair." "You don't know that in a few minutes you will be dead." She also fantasied that she was the worst, the most evil of murderers, and how the next day this would be proclaimed in the headlines in all the papers everywhere.

About one month after she started analysis, I felt, for the first time, the presence of "the thoughts" in my consulting room in relation to me. I sensed that Carolyn wanted to attack me, probably with a knife.

But—and this is strange—I did not experience any fear. It did not feel in the least eerie. Instead I felt that even if she attacked me, I would experience love and tenderness for her. As I am not particularly brave or heroic, my reaction was significant. It suggests to me that her "killing" was not just a sadistic-destructive act but was also an expression of a wish for fusion; a love-fight. I made no interpretations and I did not mention my own suspicions. However, almost immediately at the beginning of the next session my suspicious feelings were confirmed. Carolyn told me that she had had "the thoughts" with me and against me during the previous session, but after that she did not have them as usual in the evening. This was a relief, but she was sad and very anxious because she had experienced my room as a refuge and now it had become contaminated by "the thoughts."

Only a week later Mary, her sister, was offered a job as an *au pair* girl with an English family abroad. This meant renewed separation of the twins. Immediately "the thoughts" gained in intensity and she experienced them as "stronger than they had ever been." This confirmed my hunch that for Carolyn killing is also an expression of love and a desire for fusion and can be understood like the behavior of a sow who devours her young when danger threatens. Also, later in the analysis, she dreamed that her arms were coiled around Mary, not in order to attack, but as if to hug her. The next few weeks were preoccupied with thoughts that their characteristics, talents, and qualities were divided between them. She described Mary as extravert, sociable, intelligent, adventurous, on good terms with herself, more emancipated from the family, and therefore seemed to have all the advantages; while she, Carolyn, had all the disadvantages, being timid, shy, introverted, hating herself, and actually being disgusted by herself. But, and this was the odd but interesting twist, Mary, she thought, would not be strong enough to live and bear emotions like anger, envy, jealousy, and destructiveness as she, Carolyn, has to experience and battle with. She must protect Mary from them because she, Carolyn, is actually physically enormously strong, more like a man. That is, so she explains, what makes her so dangerous.

However, when, after a few months of analysis, "the thoughts" eased up, she began to feel "empty," "insubstantial," a "nothing."

"It is better to be very, very bad than nothing at all."

"I feel like a vacuum when there are no bad thoughts." And indeed when she did not have to report "the thoughts" there were often long silences: I too had some difficulty in keeping my attention centered on her. And then a fantasy came to me that I must create her body, her person, out of myself.

One day, soon after this, there was the continuous noise of an electric drill just outside my house. I found it almost unbearable and feared its effects on Carolyn's session. But she looked almost happy and said that she really enjoyed it. And then a fantasy took shape in her and she described it:

> You make a hole in order to repair something. It is like making a hole in the earth so that you can plant and put something new into it.

The fantasy developed and grew further:

> I have a ramrod in my hand and with it I make holes into the walls—my walls—till the ceiling collapses on top of me. But that feels really cozy. I often want to make holes into someone's tummy; I would like to make a hole into your tummy then I can lie safely inside it.

A few days later she told me that she had recently seen a friend who is pregnant. "Perhaps the baby inside her has a knife so he can cut his way out of her."

Then she had an important dream: I, the analyst, go to a party with her family, and Mary goes too. But I, the analyst, have a sister who stays with Carolyn because Carolyn does not want to go to the party. My sister allows Carolyn to stay for a while in a very hot bath and then she can go to bed. She feels very lucky. This sister knows how to look after her and is very caring to her. It seemed to me that this dream was about being allowed an experience of being in the maternal womb, this time really on her own, without a twin to share it with. My "sister," who knows how to care, very likely represented the warm nanny.

A few weeks later she brought a dream about a hurt and hungry pack of wolves. She then began to talk also about her insomnia and that one of the reasons is a fear "in case I miss something." To this I added: "Perhaps you are afraid to miss a good feed and then Mary will get it. Each feed seems to you to be a matter of life and death." She received my interpretation with a little conspiratorial smile.

When well into her analysis, after about three years, she dared to become critical of her parents. There was a dream in which a witch, who wore a red dress, pursued her on her parents' farm. The witch had claws and could fly. If she caught Carolyn she would kill her, probably by choking her with her claws. By then Carolyn herself was able to recognize that the witch was her mother whom she now experienced as witch-like because she made Carolyn feel inadequate, inhibited, and the carrier of her mother's "shadow," because her mother needed so much to feel and be "good." Some time later she also became critical of her father. She dreamed that she was in a bar with her father. She wanted him to get her something to drink. But he asked her where he could get this for her. She answered him "with sarcasm in my voice." This hostility and contempt for father was in part a defense against envy—envy of his penis, his phallus, his masculinity, which had been symbolized by her dream of the ramrod with which to make a hole into me, her analyst. She also envied his maternal capacities. Her envy and ambivalence in relation to her father expressed an attempt to make conscious and integrate her own masculinity. But she experienced this masculinity also as evil and destructive. This was made clear to us in a fantasy that developed during an analytic hour:

> There is a box and I put something into it which I do not want to own. It is a lump of evil. There is also a man who goes into the box. It is a sort of self-sacrifice. He is tall but the box is small, so he has to curl up inside it. Somebody throws petrol over the box and sets it alight. Then it is dumped in the sea.

She returned to this fantasy a few sessions later but by then the man had transformed; he had grown fins and she described him as a "merman." This fantasy was followed by experiences of dizziness and a fear and a sensation that she had a lump or a "tumor" in her head. "It is as if I had a baby that was growing in my head instead of in my tummy."

It was only toward the second part of the analysis that she could begin to express her overt fear of death—of natural dying. Her fear of being killed, or of killing herself, or of killing others, and her many hypochondriacal—almost delusionary—experiences had been a constant theme. But only when more of a conscious ego had been formed could she speak directly of her thoughts and feelings about death. She had always resented, she had always been horrified that death must come to each of us. She knew that death is inevitable and believed it to be gruesome. It seemed that the existence of death, of our knowledge of its inevitability, offended her need for control and omnipotence because the uncertainty of when and how it will come was unbearable to her. Here perhaps lay also the reason for her state of apprehension as she improved and grew more mature and conscious, for it meant that the end of analysis was coming within sight. It seemed to bear out the fact to which Jung had drawn our attention when he wrote: "The neurotic who cannot leave his mother has good reason for not doing so. Ultimately it is the fear of death that holds him there" (Jung 1930).

What then are the features in Carolyn's analysis that I would regard as predominantly archetypal?

First and foremost there is the twinship. This recalled for me time and again the story of Esau and Jacob: (1) There too was the importance of being the firstborn—though the second may, as it were, catch a ride from the first one, since Jacob was born holding on to Esau's heel. Mary, it was said, had not dared to start to breathe until Carolyn also had been born; (2) then there is the idea that the second twin will overtake the first one sooner or later; (3) there is their mutual trickery, and rivalry, but in spite of this they remain closely and permanently intertwined, and living and dying, killing and succouring remain forever life-issues between them. All this is recounted in the Biblical story of Esau and Jacob; it was a feature in the relationship between Mary and Carolyn.

The conflict between life and death, between the ambivalent feelings about the pleasures and the struggles involved in staying alive as against the fear, abhorrence but also attraction to "easeful death," these are indeed archetypal forces and themes in all of us. They are particularly marked and intense in twins.

This life and death conflict is also, I think, evinced in our desire for fusion, for de-fusion, and for re-fusion; for here lie the roots of those psychic mechanisms that draw us on the one hand toward uniqueness and separateness, and on the other toward being or becoming part of that which is beyond us.

However, the archetypal process that is quite particularly prominent in Carolyn's case, but which is rarely, if ever, recognized by analytical psychologists as being archetypal, is the presence of splitting. This tends to be thought of as either a defensive or a destructive mechanism, featuring importantly—perhaps even exclusively—in the Kleinian school. And yet this is what Hanna Segal writes about it in 1964:

> One of the achievements of the paranoid-schizoid position is splitting. It is splitting which allows the ego to emerge out of chaos and to order its experiences. This ordering of experience which occurs with the process of splitting into a good and bad object, however excessive and extreme it may be to begin with, nevertheless orders the universe of the child's emotional and sensory impressions and is a precondition of later integration. It is the basis of what is later to become the faculty of discrimination, the origin of which is the early differentiation between good and bad (Segal 1964, p. 22).

This process was quite particularly evident in Carolyn. It is indeed a very essential and necessary process in twins if they are to develop and each to gain their own separate identity in spite of all the pressures and temptations to remain fused. In Carolyn we could of course see splitting in the early and more archaic form which, as described by Segal, makes it inevitably "excessive and extreme." There was thus an enactment, in the case of Carolyn, a living of an archetypal theme, the twinship theme.

Earlier in this and in a previous paper (Gordon 1985), I have suggested that there can be several ways of relating to what is archetypal. One of them is the enactment, the living of an archetypal *theme*. Another way is the identification with an archetypal *figure*. This tends to lead to ego inflation, which we can often observe in patients with a narcissistic character disorder. I have in fact described three such patients in my paper, "Narcissism and the Self: Who am I that I love?" (Gordon 1980).

Case History: Jane

I described there an impressive and glaring example of the patient I had called Jane. She idealized her father, who had died when she was five years old. Her relationship to her mother was decidedly ambivalent: She both admired her as someone who knows the world and is extremely capable at making for herself an important, enviable, and materially and aesthetically successful place in it, but she also accused her of being immature, selfish, self-centered, and unconcerned about her, her daughter. Soon after the father's death her mother had remarried—"an intellectual, successful, and rich" man.

Jane herself was attractive and dressed with taste. She was intelligent and a gifted painter; but her difficulty in personal relationships prevented her from having the sort of success her talents deserved.

When she first started analysis, she would explode with anger; she would rant and rave and pour scorn on colleagues, friends, and lovers. It was easy to recognize them as the carriers of the projection of her own shadow because she described them as ruthless, enraged, enraging, contemptible, and as generally inadequate. She was an accomplished actress and would enact and mime her encounter and struggles with her friends, lovers, and colleagues. At that time she felt compelled to try to entertain me.

When her projections entered into the transference, her rages burst into our relationship. She accused me of being unconcerned about her and above all of being unable to recognize her genius and how really special she was. Such vociferous outbursts and claims were often followed by a total collapse of confidence, when she would appear terribly fragile, helpless, empty, and dependent. But generally her behavior, her postures as well as the content of her apperceptions and fantasies, made it quite clear that Jane was identified much of the time with the archetypal personage of the great mother, both in her positive and negative forms; sometimes she was the goddess, sometimes the witch. There was thus much ego inflation with feelings of being omniscient, omnipotent, and perfect. Only at moments when she felt helpless did I sense the presence of some ego capacity. For then I experienced her, in my own counter-transference, as a small infant that despairs of ever being able to make others take note of its needs, or even of its presence. When I think back on those first few months, I think of them as filled with screams of frustration, of hatred, of resentment, and of terror.

Inevitably there was, as yet in those early months, very little experience of any boundary between us. She would tell me that really we two had the same talents, the same feelings, and really did the same sort of work. In one of her earliest dreams she and I were together somewhere in Europe during the late Middle Ages, two prostitutes in a brothel.

From the way Jane had talked about her mother I gained the impression that her mother had also identified with the archetypal figure of the great mother, and that she also tended to identify now with the witch and now with the goddess. Certainly Jane experienced her as seductive and endowed with magical powers, which only magnified both her envy and admiration of her mother. By feeling herself to be goddess or witch Jane in a way she tried to equal her mother and to compete with her. She was really taken aback and incredulous when she became aware that I was not at all impressed by the goddess, but much more concerned for the helpless infant. After all, nobody seems ever to have paid any attention to this baby, and so she herself had come to detest it, for here was the place of pain.

As Jane had invested the major part of her narcissistic libido in an archetypal figure with which she was identified—or, it would be more accurate to say, by which she was possessed—and as this identification seemed to have been reinforced by her experience of her actual mother, I have seen it as my first and major task to help her displace this narcissistic libido away from the archetypal mother and toward the much more rejected and much neglected baby-self.

The projection of an archetypal figure is often the root-cause of a particularly poisonous, intractible, and intransigent human relationship which one can encounter in, for instance, marital work. In analytic therapy it characterizes many a delusional transference, be this temporary or, in the case of borderline patients, relatively long-term state, which most of us have inevitably met and experienced. Many of us may at times have experienced the temptation to collude, by identifying with what has been projected into us, particularly if it happens to be flattering, as when we are cast into the role of the infinitely wise, or the infinitely understanding and compassionate, or the infinitely omniscient one; or we have experienced hurt or fear, or anger or despair if we find outselves saddled with the projection of something or somebody bad or stupid or evil.

I remember a patient who was a sadomasochistic homosexual. In his fantasies he lived out the theme of Artemis to whom annually the youth adjudged to be the most beautiful and the most intelligent was sacrificed by being beaten to death. He would identify now with this perfect sacrificial youth, now with him, who carried out the immolation. In the transference I was at times the goddess determined in my demand that life be squeezed out of him; at other times I was experienced as more insidiously dangerous and destructive, when, for instance, I was seen as a fish hiding under a stone, shooting out a long tongue to catch its victims.

This patient had been the third illegitimate child, fathered by the same man, of a respectable upper-class woman. She had passed off her three children as having been adopted; this then earned her the reputation of being a generous and socially conscious person.

The patient had slept in his mother's bed until a very late age. He could not remember when and at what age he was "thrown out." But he remembered that he had experienced all sorts of anxieties and fantasies in this close contact with his mysterious mother. And he remembered that at times he would put on all available clothes before he went to bed at night—as if he needed many thick layers of protective clothing.

Here again an archetypal figure was, as it were, incarnated and so confirmed by the personal experience of an actual parent.

Case History

In the case of another patient I felt imprisoned in the role of the devouring, insatiable, and mocking giantess, the woman with such an enormous genital cavity that his own penis would be laughably ineffective. For many months I was held fast in that role, and so was he in his as the hopeless, impotent, the forever-criticized, spurned, and ridiculed youth—although he was in fact a man in his forties.

I have chosen to describe these few patients in order to show the different use we can make and the different functions that archetypal processes can assume in our experience, in our behavior, and in our relationships.

I have up to now spoken mainly of the archetypal processes as they may function in our patients. It is, however, important that we also look at the part they may play in the analyst's countertransference. They may be beneficial to our work as analysts; they may help us to empathize, sympathize, and feel with and for our patients by making us open and receptive to the many themes they bring us. We may have met some of these archetypal constellations ourselves, experienced them and done battle with

them in our personal life and personal analysis. But inevitably there must
be areas in each of us which we have not yet sufficiently explored and
worked through. If the patient's material, or events in our own life, stirs
up these areas, these archetypal constellations, then they could distort
our understanding and our perceptions—perceptions of ourselves, of
our patients, or of the role required of us in relation to them. I am thinking here of, for instance, the temptation that is potentially present in our
work, to identify with such archetypal personages as the great mother,
the great father, the every-ready phallic male, the inquisitor, the wise old
man, the wise old woman, the healer, the magician, and so on. Or we
may be tempted to project on to our patients the archetypal child or the
archetypal patient. Such archetypal identifications and projections are
very likely to halt, arrest, or even reverse the analytic work.

On the other hand if access to archetypal experience is blocked or
avoided—be it in the case of patient or analyst—the results may be stag-
nation, lack of growth and development, rigidity and inability to move or
to adjust to new situations, or even to new dangers. This may happen if
there is an anxious clinging to the rational, or the familiar, the known
and, therefore, the apparently controllable. Such a defensive stand may
indeed prevent further growth and development and twist life to become
increasingly dull, flat, and banal.

The question that seems to me to be important and that I now want
to ask is whether the concept of "an archetype" or an "archetypal process" is in fact valuable, carries some measure of validity, and is actually
useful; and if it is useful, when and to whom is it useful?

As a matter of fact during the last few years interest has been shown
in the possible similarities and connections between some of Jung's theories and the new theoretical formulations in the "hard" sciences like
physics and biology. This really bears out Jung's prophetic belief that

> Sooner or later, nuclear physics and the psychology of the unconscious will
> draw closer together as both of them, independently of one another and
> from opposite directions, push forward into transcendent territory. . . . Psy-
> che cannot be totally different from matter for how otherwise could it move
> matter? . . . Psyche and matter exist in the same world, and each partakes
> of the other, otherwise any reciprocal action would be impossible. (Jung
> 1951)

Indeed Fritjof Capra and June Singer have drawn attention to these
new developments. And Elie Humbert has been much involved in the
conferences organized to facilitate the joint exploration of analytical psychologists and thinkers and researchers in the "hard" sciences. Capra, for
instance, in *The Turning Point* writes of Jung:

In breaking with Freud he [Jung] abandoned the Newtonian models of psychoanalysis and developed a number of concepts that are quite consistent with those of modern physics and with systems theory. . . . The difference between Freud and Jung parallel those between classical and modern physics, between the mechanistic and the holistic paradigm (Capra 1982, pp. 396–97).

I, as well as some other colleagues, have been intrigued by the work of Rupert Sheldrake and David Bohm. Sheldrake, a British biologist, has produced a number of hypotheses to account for the fact that things and creatures attain, maintain, and pass on their physical and behavioral forms and how this might be understood. There is a "morphogenetic field," he suggests, which controls the overall development of an organism; through "motor-fields" are shaped the behavior patterns of creatures that are similar. And with the help of his concepts of "formative causation," the "resonance pattern," and "cognitive resonance" and by accumulating evidence from carefully controlled research, we will probably discover that creatures of a given species will learn more easily and more quickly tasks that have been learned by previous generations of the same species—although there has been no direct communication, demonstration, or teaching. He believes that if his theses were to be confirmed, then it would help to explain such phenomena as the collective unconscious and psychic transmission.

Louis Zinkin in England has drawn our attention to David Bohm in a paper given to The Society of Analytical Psychology in London fairly recently. He is interested in the relevance to analytical psychologists of Bohm's theory about the hologram, the holomovement, and his concept of the "implicate order." In the hologram the information of the whole is contained in a small part, in any and every small part, as we can now all see and enjoy, for instance, on our credit cards. Bohm emphasizes that the whole can no longer be thought of as consisting simply of parts in interaction; rather the whole organizes the parts and the whole is "enfolded" into the parts. Bohm argues further that "For thousands of years science has concentrated only on the explicate orders of the universe," but that "beneath each explicate order lies implicate order" (Zinkin 1987).

To explain the concept of explicate and implicate order Bohm has written:

What appears to be stable, tangible, visible, audible world is an illusion. It is dynamic and kaleidoscopic—not really "there." What we normally see is the explicit, or unfolded, order of things, rather like watching a movie. But there is an underlying order that is mother and father to this second generation reality. He called the other order implicate, or enfolded. The enfolded order harbours our reality, much as the DNA in the nucleus of the cell harbours potential life and directs the nature of its unfolding. (Ferguson 1982)

And Briggs and Peat explain that

Bohm's implicate order neatly accounts for a universe that appears both continuous and discontinuous. It just depends on how the ensembles unfold. If they unfold one after the other very near each other, they look like a simple particle moving continuously from one place to another or even like a particle separating into several other particles and then re-emerging as itself again. . . . In Bohm's implicate universe both the observing apparatus and the observer himself are also unfolding ensembles. (Briggs & Peat 1984)

I have found Bohm's thought so particularly relevant to our understanding of the fact that the archetypal processes are often accompanied by a feeling of numinosity, which seems indeed to suggest that here is an experience of a wholeness that is greater than our consciousness can grasp and be aware of. I myself have already described a religio-mythical triad which helps to anchor and confirm further our conception of the structure of the psyche. To have more support and corroboration for some of our models and observations of psychic events from Bohm, a man working in a hard science, is indeed very satisfying.

But to return now to my question regarding the value, validity, and usefulness of the concept "archetype" and "archetypal," at least at our present stage of knowledge. I do believe that this concept is indeed useful and necessary to the theoretician. It is, after all, a cornerstone in the theoretical edifice of analytical psychology. Freud also seems to have come very near to formulating it and to incorporating it in his model of psychological functioning. It seems furthermore to be related to Piaget's "innate schemata" and to the concepts and discoveries that have emerged in the science of ethology.

We have in fact by now so much evidence that there exists in man innate and inherent ordering mechanisms; this makes it almost impossible to avoid arriving at some theoretical formulation of it, whatever name be chosen. In fact, the name seems to function more often as a sort of declaration of adherence to one school of thought or the other rather than as a valuable descriptive tool.

As regards its value to the practicing analyst: the fact that I have been able to describe here some of the signs that can alert me, the analyst, to the presence in the patient of a predominantly archetypal experience, must indicate that the concept provides a real and potentially very important clue. It will certainly make me watchful and aware that I need to be particularly attentive and mindful when something basic and powerful has happened, or is happening, in the patient. A new and perhaps vital process may be preparing itself for him, in him, and/or between us. Thus here, too, the concept serves a useful and important function.

I am, however, hesitant and doubtful as regards its usefulness to the analysand. I find that in my actual work with a patient I hardly, if ever, refer to anything as being "archetypal." I am anxious lest it might distort or set aside the patient's own personal feelings and experience. I am also anxious that the very naming of it might inflate him and tempt him to idealize whatever is happening to him. Or there may be the opposite danger: it may make him feel possessed, in the grip of forces thought to be beyond him, which will make him feel less responsible and more helpless. For I do indeed believe, as Professor Allport said many years ago, that if a person believes himself to be free, then he can use what equipment he has more flexibly and successfully than he would if he were convinced that he dwells in chains. For such a sense of impotence, hopelessness, despair, and fatalism is surely after all the very condition from which we analysts want to liberate our patients.

Summary

In this paper I have tried to re-examine once more the concepts "archetype" and "archetypal experience." I have done so in the light of Fordham's thesis that there is at the beginning of the development of the psyche an original self which, through the process of deintegration, leads to the emergence of what he has called "the deintegrate." He has tended to assume that the concept "deintegrate" is more or less identical with the concept "archetype," that it is a conceptual construct which parallels the ethologist's innate release mechanism, and that it functions very much like the *scintillae* which Jung regarded as islets of potential consciousness and hence as ego nuclei.

However, the images and fantasies that we encounter in our patients—and in our own dreams and fantasies—are so much more rich and complex than the ethologists' innate release mechanism. To do justice to this discrepancy and to sharpen our theoretical tools and so increase our understanding, it may be necessary—and useful—to recognize a difference between the concept of deintegration and the concept of an archetypal process. I have suggested that the term "deintegrate" be reserved for those processes that issue directly from the process of deintegration. The archetype on the other hand is a hybrid, a hybrid between nature and nurture, between a deintegrate or a pattern of deintegrates on the one hand and the relevant objects met with on the other. This would then also draw attention to the fact that although there are indeed reactions and themes that are universal, yet the actual form they take varies from person to person, from epoch to epoch, and from culture to culture.

I have described in this paper some cases in order to show the different relationships a person may have to the archetypal processes. These may take on the form of myths and themes or of personages. They may be projected, identified with, lived and acted out, or they may appear in sleep or in waking fantasies. The enacting in the real world of archetypal experience can be a danger not only for patients but for the analyst also.

As a final point in this paper, I have explored whether the concept "archetypal" is useful to (a) the theoretician; (b) the analyst-clinician; (c) the patient. More and more evidence has emerged to support the validity of such a concept. Only in the case of the patient do I have some apprehension lest it should prove to be counterproductive to the therapeutic process.

References

Briggs, J. P., and Peat, F. D. 1984. *Looking Glass Universe: The Emerging Science of Wholeness*. London: Fontana.

Capra, F. 1982. *The Turning Point*. London: Wildwood House.

Ferguson, M. 1982. Karl Pribam's changing reality, in K. Wilbur, ed., *The Holographic Paradigm and other Paradoxes*. London: Shambala.

Fordham, M. 1955. *New Developments in Analytical Psychology*. London: Routledge & Kegan Paul.

Freud, S. 1925. From the history of an infantile neurosis. *Standard Edition*, 17.

Gordon, R. 1980. Narcissism and the self: Who am I that I love? *Journal of Analytical Psychology* 30:2.

————. 1985. Losing and finding: The location of archetypal experience. *Journal of Analytical Psychology*, 25,3

Jung, C. G. 1912. *Symbols of Transformation*. In *Collected Works*, vol. 5. Princeton: Princeton University Press.

————. 1935. Psychological commentary on *The Tibetan Book of the Dead*. In *Collected Works*, vol. 11. Princeton: Princeton University Press, 1969.

————. 1947. On the nature of the psyche. In *Collected Works*, vol. 8. Princeton: Princeton University Press, 1969.

————. 1959. *Aion. Researches into the phenomenology of the self*. In *Collected Works*, 9/ii. Princeton: Princeton University Press, 1968.

McGuire, W., ed. 1974. *The Freud/Jung Letters*. Princeton University Press.

Segal, H. 1964. *Introduction to the Works of Melanie Klein*. London. Heinemann Medical Books.

Winnicott, D. W. 1971. The location of cultural experience, in *Playing and Reality*. London. Tavistock Publications.

Zinkin, L. 1987. The hologram as a model for analytical psychology. *Journal of Analytical Psychology* 32:1.

On the Theory of Complexes

Hans Dieckmann

For many years C. G. Jung examined the area of emotionally charged complexes, having discovered them through his association experiment. In several of his early works (1979, 1967c, 1976) he views complexes as the contents of the personal unconscious, in contrast to archetypes, which are the contents of the collective unconscious. These remarks, however, apparently contradict another discussion wherein he explicitly distinguishes two different categories of complexes. The first category includes those acquired in life by personal experience, while the second category is comprised of those complexes which have never been in the consciousness before and which therefore could not have been repressed. These complexes come from the collective unconscious—complexes which in certain threshold situations of psychic life would provide a new attitude of consciousness and which contain irrational contents never before conscious to the individual (1963).

Jung discusses these collective complexes in his work "On Psychic Energy" (1967c), drawing a parallel with the belief in souls and spirits of

Hans Dieckmann, M.D., is currently president of the International Association for Analytical Psychology. He lives and practices as a Jungian analyst in Berlin, West Germany. He is the author of many articles and books, among them the standard textbook, *Methods of Analytical Psychology* (1979), and *Twice-Told Tales: The Psychological Use of Fairy Tales* (Chiron Publications 1986).

the primitive races. Later, in his work about "The Psychological Foundations of Belief in Spirits" (1967*b*). Jung makes a very clear distinction between these two categories of complexes by differentiating "possession by a spirit" from what the primitive races call "loss of soul." Complexes of the personal unconscious, which mainly grow out of early traumatic events or early family relationships, normally become unconscious through repression or a sinking into the unconscious. Such dissociation from the ego-complex, because of its emotional charge, does not lose its activity and is experienced by the ego as a loss of libido, corresponding to the "loss of soul" of primitive peoples. If such a complex is resolved by making its contents again accessible to consciousness, the individual concerned feels considerable relief and, with increasing libido, experiences a strengthening of his psychic forces.

According to Jung, a very different process is involved with complexes which come from the collective unconscious, which have primarily irrational and mythological contents. The eruption of these collective unconscious complexes is a very troublesome, often even dangerous, event for consciousness. They emerge when an external experience has acted on the individual such a shocking manner that the customary approach to life is in danger of collapsing, or when the contents of the collective unconscious for some reason have obtained such energy that they break into the consciousness like an alien spirit or demon. But just as Jung always assumed a healthy organization of the psyche and emphasized the prospective activity of the human unconscious, he did not consider the complexes of the collective unconscious basically pathological. In his opinion, they contained in their mythological symbols the approaches to and potentials for a fundamental change of consciousness.

My practical analytical work has made me doubt (over the years) that it makes sense to maintain this bipartition of the complexes between those belonging to the personal unconscious and those of the collective unconscious. In his preface to Jolande Jacobi's book *Complex, Archetype, Symbol* (1971) Jung himself interrelates the complex of the personal unconscious with the collective unconscious. He states that complexes rest on "typical foundations" which correspond to an emotional preparedness or instinct. These instinct residues have a double expression in the individual, inasmuch as they have both a dynamic aspect—a relatively high charge of instinctual energy—and a formal aspect. This formal—one could say "spiritual"—aspect of instinct finds expression in unreflected, involuntary fantasy images which occupy large areas of the human inner world and which prompt specific attitudes and acts. A direct relation is established between the complex expressing personal experience in the individual unconscious and a deeper basis which is rooted in the archetypes of the collective unconscious. In Jung's later work, the *Mysterium Coniunctionis* (1968) this idea reappears in the relation between the complex and the conscious ego-complex.

The ego-complex, in the shape of the old, weak King Sol, is in need of renewal, of repeated renewal in the course of the individuation process. The ego-complex has an unconscious relation to a complex with archetypical bases, and can bring into conscious reality new spiritual contents and the renewal of dynamic forces. By becoming conscious, a complex is able to dethrone the old king. Complexes, as extraordinarily differentiated structures in the human psyche, suggest the existence of partial personalities—a concept which I will take up again later. Jung attributes certain potentially conscious luminosities to them. In doing so he expresses the idea that the dominant of consciousness can be renewed and reinforced by these secondary luminosities, which contain a kind of consciousness, or at least the potential to become conscious.

Before discussing the structure of a complex and its relationship to the archetypes of the collective unconscious, I would first like to present a case as illustration:

A 26-year-old male patient consulted me because of an intense anxiety neurosis which rendered him unable to practice his profession as a photographer. He suffered from different anxieties which, for the most part, had phobic character. Apart from a diffuse fear that something could happen, he was specifically afraid of using public transportation. Any medical symptom—however minor—caused hypochondriac anxieties about a fatal disease. Any pimple on his skin raised the fear of fatal blood-poisoning; and he was afraid he might poison himself with potassium cyanide in his photographic laboratory. His anxieties had become so intense that six months before therapy he had had himself committed to a hospital. The whole symptomatology became manifest shortly after his marriage, about nine months before therapy began, and was undoubtedly connected to his relationship with his wife.

The patient was born shortly before World War II broke out, and he grew up an only child. Because his father was called up shortly after the child's birth and did not return for five years, the patient spent his early childhood mainly with his mother. Quite threatening events set the scene for a childhood under turbulent circumstances. He suffered through some of the heavy air raids on Berlin. While at times he was evacuated with his mother, he had once been sent into the country alone at a relatively early age. He became so unhappy there that his mother had had to take him home again. She died of pneumonia when he was ten, and his father, who had come home in the mean time, took over the education of the boy. As his father was very much involved in his profession and had quite a good emotional relationship with his son, my patient went through a period of relative freedom until his marriage. He was always encouraged by his father in his education and in professional training. Surprisingly, the patient could not remember his mother at all. Her death as well as all the years he had spent with her in his early childhood up to the age of eleven were split off from consciousness.

At the beginning of the treatment it became evident that the patient projected a negative mother complex heavily onto his wife. He compared his marriage with Sartre's play *Huis Clos* (literally, a "closed circle") and always felt teased and pestered by his wife. Their fights were about trivialities; and he always took the pacifying part. When the tension became too strong, he tried to avoid the situation by escaping, often not coming home for hours. He felt that his wife was superior to him in intellectual as well as material respects, as she came from a higher social stratum and earned much more than he did. He left the financial organization of their household completely to her and gave her virtually all the money he earned.

The first phase of the therapy was completely involved with the description of this marriage. All the associations he had concerning his wife had a negative and threatening character. It became evident that the patient had an underlying, irrational, and extreme fear of this woman—a fear of which he was completely unaware and which, even in small confrontations between them, provoked psychosomatic symptoms such as angina (pectoris), trembling of the hands, sweating, and rapid pulse rate.

In the course of the analysis we succeeded only gradually in coming closer to the figure of the personal mother. It became clear that she had been an extremely compulsive woman who, in addition to a compulsion for cleanliness and neatness, had exactly the same phobic anxieties as her son. Every trifle of life which did not meet common norms caused strong anxieties and, in conjunction with her underlying aggressions, led to strict punishments of the child. The boy felt extremely restricted by these maternal fears and experienced his mother as very severe and cold. Because his mother had actually died of pneumonia when he was 10, and because she herself had been as afraid of diseases as he, the real experience of death (which he vividly relived during analysis) reinforced his own fears of disease.

The key to his overwhelming fear of potassium cyanide poisoning came to the surface in about the 120th session, during a very intense emotional cathexis:

When he was three, the patient went on holiday with his mother into the country where they had relatives who owned a farm. While playing in the barn one day, he found two fresh eggs, which he cracked and ate. When he proudly told his mother about it, she reacted in a manner which was terrible and threatening for him. First, she screamed at him and beat him thoroughly; then she gave him a long scolding, telling him how dangerous it was to drink up unwashed eggs and how he could have poisoned himself. He had to promise her solemnly never again to put anything unwashed into his mouth, much less to eat it.

After reliving this early experience his fear of poisoning by potassium cyanide disappeared. His other anxieties also decreased as we worked through his identity with the compulsive, overfearful mother. But his fear of his wife—and, in extension of the problem, of all other women—had not decreased at all, although the patient had by now become aware of the fact—not only rationally but also emotionally—that he projected his negative personal mother complex onto his wife and all other women. Hence we had only succeeded in removing his identification with the restrictive, poisonous, and fearful mother, but not in removing the projection of the terrible mother onto all women.

During the next sessions the patient was seriously and intensely involved in this problem; and, finally, on his own impulse, he decided to draw this mother figure, although he was not practiced in drawing. The result was the figure of a red-haired witch with immense pointed breasts and an imposing, globular belly, dressed in a very short blue skirt or apron. She had a mighty, giant left hand and threatening features with eyebrows recalling Mephistopheles. This figure did not physically resemble his own mother at all; it obviously was the archetypical shape of a Magna Mater with strong archaic traits like the Venus of Willendorf. She rather reminded me of those aggressive mother goddesses like Ishtar or the Babylonian Tiamat, an impression which was especially suggested by the treatening features, the mighty hand, and, above all, the giant pointed breasts. In his associations he related her to the Magna Mater as a prostitute, the great whore of Babylon. (In this context, I should mention that prostitutes had always fascinated him, though he had never had close contact with them and had never dared to approach one.)

The patient's associations with this picture showed partly collective and partly individual, personal material. Among the objective associations, certain specific traits of the Magna Mater's negative character gained prominence. The woman was characterized as the grasping witch,

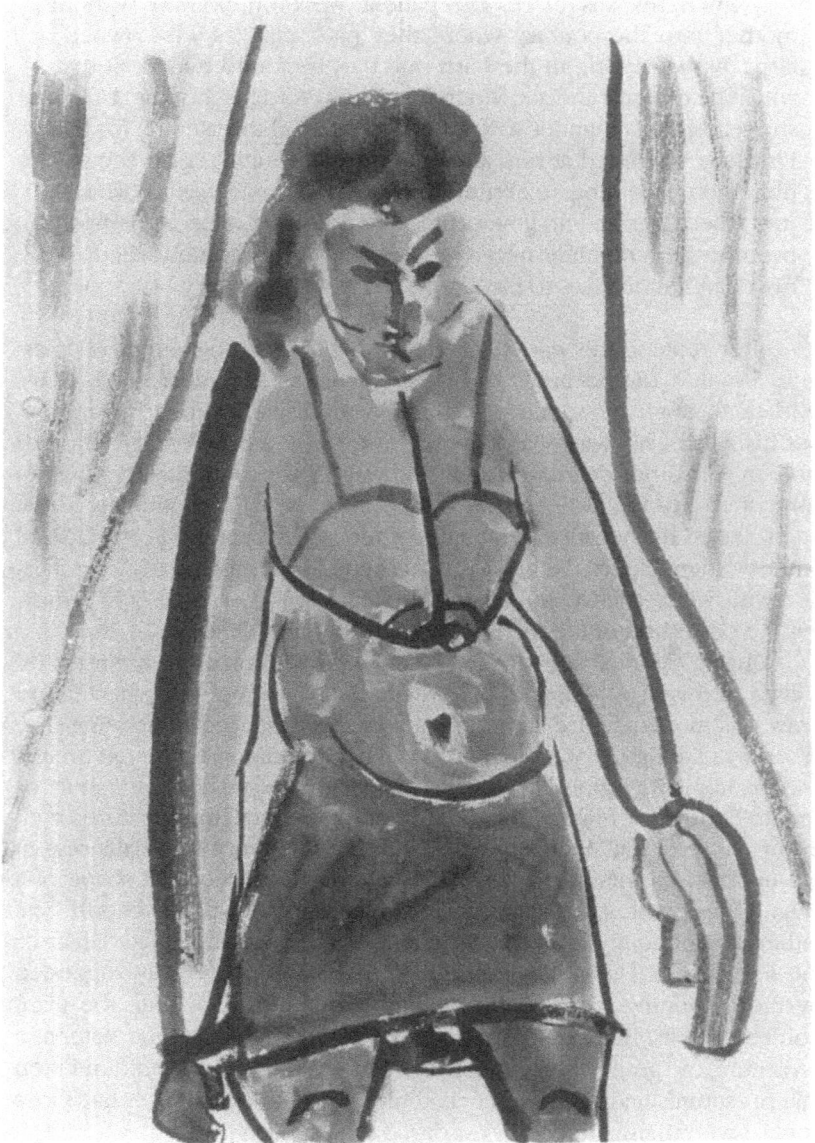

the vile whore, and as the smothering Death Mother. Subjective associations were slaps with the mother's giant hand, in the picture bearing a baseball glove. Notably, the mother had been right-handed, while in the picture it was the left hand which was oversized. The red nipples of the breasts reminded him of his mother correcting his homework with a red pencil; he had been terrified when he had made mistakes. The story of the two eggs (mentioned above) was brought up once again; and he also described another event from the time when he was five:

> He had been given a scooter as a present. When he had made his first attempts to ride, he had fallen down on the street. An arm injury had led to blood poisoning. For several weeks he lay immobilized in bed and was probably kept there much longer than necessary by his overly fearful mother. This memory, repressed up to then, had on the one hand, a subjective individual component and, on the other, an experience of the collective, negative, demoniac side of this world, which can in fact cause diseases and poisonings. The experience had been intensified by the memory of another early event: He once had witnessed the suicide of a neighbor who had jumped out of a fourth-story window.

Some sessions later the patient brought a second picture showing a demonic giant with four arms standing in front of a rock and looking up at a tiny figure who had climbed up to the upper third of this rock. This giant, too, had an oversized hand like the mother figure; but this time it was the right hand. The patient named the giant "Holländermichel" after a figure from Hauff's famous fairy tale, "The Heart of Glass" (Hauff 1896). The story is about an evil magician who exchanges living hearts for hearts of glass. Under his spell, people are able to become unimaginably rich during their life on earth; but, because of the coldness of their hearts of glass they are then condemned to hell. The oversized hand coupled with coldheartedness experienced in his own mother clearly indicates the presence of the animus of the mother or, better, a negative, collective animus of the archetypical Magna Mater.

In therapy the patient projected this figure first onto me. In subsequent sessions he was able to express his aggressions against authority in a personal confrontation. After working through these two images again and again, the patient's fears and anxieties disappeared completely; and he showed very positive development. He gave up the position of photographic assistant, which he had never liked, and began to pursue his real professional goals, getting the necessary training and passing the required exams. Moreover, he was able to normalize his masochistic rela-

tion to his wife in their quarrel-filled marriage. By chance I had the opportunity to meet this patient twenty years later; and it appeared that the success of the treatment had endured so that, from a medical point of view, one could speak of a complete recovery.

I would now like to present a diagram (Fig. 1) of this negative mother complex in order to illustrate the organization of the complex, the relationships between the complex core and complex surface, and the complex's relationships to the ego-complex as the center of consciousness. The diagram, of course, is only a metaphorical, two-dimensional approach to the human psyche, a construct which actually cannot be represented spatially.

The dotted line A represents the boundary between consciousness and the individual unconscious; its relative permeability is marked by interstices. Through this boundary contents from the unconscious can constantly emerge into the consciousness and, conversely, contents from consciousness can sink into the unconscious. In the center of the field of consciousness there is a larger circle—the ego-complex, which partly reaches into the unconscious. The lower area represents the unconscious ego parts, such as the dream ego or the body ego. This part, of course, should actually reach into the collective unconscious, since, even in the collective unconscious and its psychoid layers, there is the possibility of developing the structure of an ego-complex. However, for the sake of simplicity, this was not included in the diagram.

Each of the four smaller circles grouped around the ego-complex in the field of consciousness represents an event which takes place in the here and now, provoking fears and anxieties and therefore complex-mobilizing. Circle 1 represents events that are directly connected with the closest female reference person (in this case, the wife). The emotions which are linked to these circles are all colored by the complex. Circle 2 contains those events which refer to the larger circle of persons onto whom the negative mother is projected (here, the mother in law). Circle 3 indicates male persons, i.e., his authority anxieties (e.g., towards his present superior) which are related to the maternal animus. Finally, Circle 4 corresponds to the experience of a dangerous environmental element which could kill him (e.g., his fear of poisoning by potassium cyanide in his laboratory).

In the layer immediately below the threshold of consciousness are those events which belong to the recent past grouped as points 1' to 4'. They are placed close to the unconscious ego and thus can become conscious at almost any time.

In the next layer down are the events which took place in these

Structure of Complexes
The Negative Mother Complex as Example

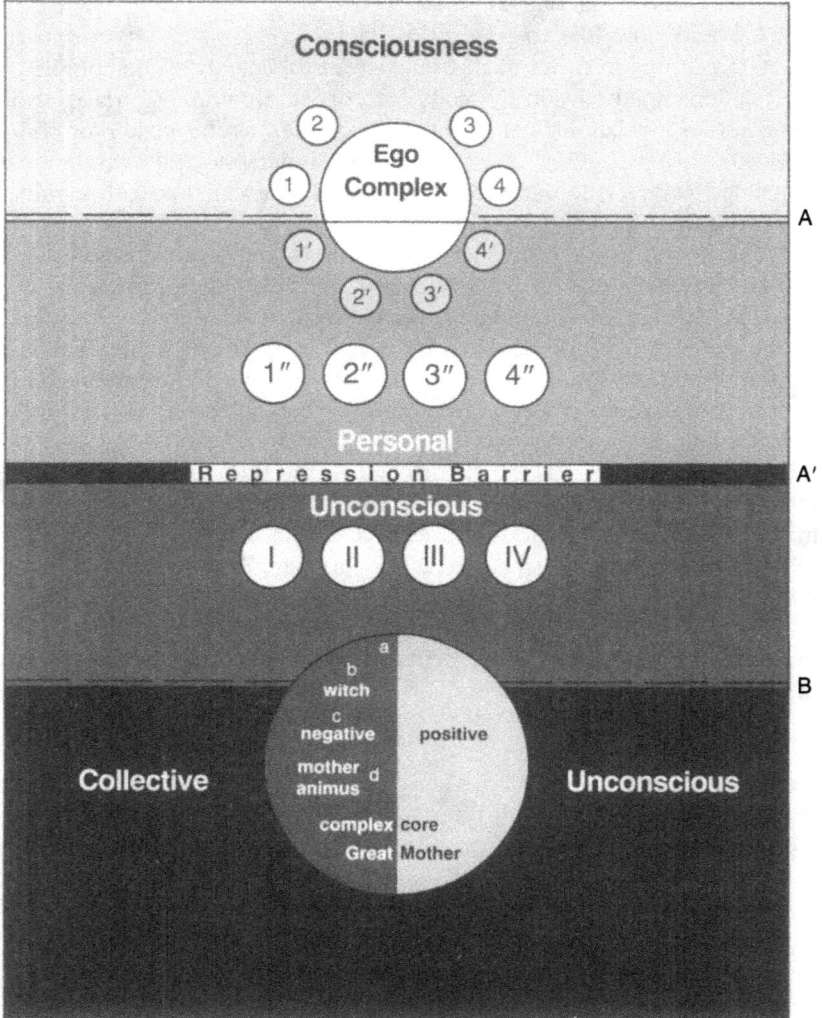

Consciousness

2   3
Ego
1   Complex   4

A

1'   4'
2'   3'

1"   2"   3"   4"

Personal

Repression Barrier   A'

Unconscious

I   II   III   IV

B

a
b
witch
c
negative   positive
mother   d
animus

complex core
Great Mother

Collective   **Unconscious**

Figure 1

gun but ended shortly when she turned away from him, rather coolly he felt, in favor of another boy.

Circle 2″ could indicate a threatening female teacher or an elderly saleswoman who had treated him roughly, against whom he had been unable to defend himself.

Circle 3″ could include early partly latent, partly manifest homosexual experiences in which he always had taken the passive part and which were linked to strong anxieties and the feeling of being overwhelmed. As in all instances of a negative mother complex, latent or partial manifest homosexuality played an important part in the analysis of this patient.

Circle 4″ might then represent early threatening experiences of the world, including, for example, the patient's inability to eat fruits which had not been washed carefully. When he spoke about it, he said that, out of envy and rage, he could still break the neck of everyone who took an apple out of his pocket and bit into it with gusto.

The uninterrupted line A′ in the personal unconscious corresponds to the repression barrier at the age of eleven after the death of his mother. All the complex-related experiences lying beneath this line were repressed and could become conscious again only during the analytical process. These experiences are indicated by the circles I–IV.

Circle I refers to early events when he was beaten or punished by his mother. These would include some scenes which he reported quite vividly—for example, when he had licked a pencil or something else and his mother had dragged him to the sink to scrub his tongue with a brush. On such occasions he was, of course, also beaten (mother's big hand!).

Circle II could deal with what he experienced during an evacuation when he was very young. The female teachers had treated him very badly and had often beaten him, until he finally wrote a letter to his mother asking her to take him back home, which she did.

Circle III might represent a very early memory in which he had had a toy fire engine that he had broken while playing with it. His mother had threatened to tell his father about it, which she in fact did when he came home that night; this time he was beaten by the father.

Circle IV represents the whole experience of the mother's illness and death—an event which, one might assume, he would remember quite vividly, but which, together with the funeral and the following period, was completely wiped out of his consciousness and fully repressed.

The second dotted line B represents the transition between the individual and the collective unconscious. In the center of the collective unconscious there is the core of the mother complex, here drawn in an oval form. In contrast to the arrangement of the ego-complex above, its greater part lies in the collective unconscious while the, smaller part reaches into the personal unconscious. Different fields in different hatchings are drawn in this complex core, representing the activation of the core elements of the mother complex, in this case negative. The upper part (the part of the complex core which reaches into the personal unconscious) includes the experience at the age of two of a paranoid-poisoned world, influenced by the mother's anxieties about his eating the two eggs. (In the figure this is indicated by field a.) In the complex core, field b indicates the incident with the scooter and his actual blood poisoning at the age of five, when he had physically experienced the demoniac force of Mother Earth and her real danger.

Fields c and d are mobilized by very early personal experiences. According to Freud's trauma theory, one can discuss whether these personal experiences actually had occurred as described by the patient, or whether they represent symbol formations which describe the early inner psychic situation of the child symbolically and in a condensed form. During the analysis c and d emerged in the form of the two pictures representing the greater collective background figures of this complex: the mother-witch and -whore, as well as the "Holländermichel" representing the negative animus of the Magna Mater.

Broad fields of the complex core are left blank to indicate that these are areas inside the core of a mother complex which, because of the specific life history, have not been mobilized or filled up with archetypical background images. (I will take up the symbolism of the whole nucleus of a mother complex again in a later paper.)

One has to picture the entire two-dimensional construct not only as three-dimensional and in constant motion, but also as four-dimensional because each of the points has its own subjective time. The whole complex is mobilized—on all levels simultaneously—by a releasing stimulus, such as a quarrel with the wife, differences with a superior, an encounter with a policeman, the touching of a dirty object, or the like.

In analysis this simultaneous coexistence of the different time levels shown here can also be observed empirically when a complex is activated. Things from the past, from puberty and from early childhood, mingle in the facial expression, in the pitch of the voice, and in the way of expressing oneself. Not only can things from the present and the past become evident in the mobilization of a complex, but also from the future in a prospective-final sense. More "mature" parts of the personality which still lie in the unconscious can thus come to the fore. In his dissertation "On the Psychology and Pathology of So-called Occult Phenomena" Jung describes the classical example of a complex which contained large parts of a potentially mature personality.

Two different situations with respect to the strength of the complex in relation to the ego-complex can be distinguished. In the first case, the complex is mobilized; and corresponding phenomena such as tensions, fears, anxieties, and mistakes emerge, while the controlling function of the ego is maintained so that the individual is still able to react to the situation in a relatively rational, adapted manner. With regard to our patient, the situation might be as follows: he meets a policeman in the street; and though he feels tensions and anxieties, he is able to pass by and to continue on his way. In the second case, there is so much energy mobilized in the complex that it blocks the controlling function of the ego; the individual is no longer able to react in an ego-syntonic manner. The ego is eclipsed by the complex, which reacts instead of the ego. Here we have the situation which Jung described in such a striking manner (1966): "it is not me who has the complex but the complex which has me". How strong such a complex reaction can be, was once pointed out to me in an impressive manner by a Jewish patient: Once as she drove to the session, she encountered a motorcyclist who was threading his way through the traffic. She tried to make way for him, doing so in an apparently anxious and nervous manner. The motorcyclist obviously felt somehow hindered by her; and when they arrived side by side at the traffic light, he shouted some angry words at her. As the windows of her car were closed, the patient could not understand what he was saying; but she could see from his face and the movements of his mouth that he was calling out something threatening to her. The patient began to panic, the whole scene became blurred, and she had a violent anxiety attack. She barely succeeded in driving her car past the crossing, where she had to sit for about five or ten minutes, trembling all over, until she had calmed down and could continue driving.

The background for this incident could be reconstructed during the session: the patient had a substantial negative father-complex. During the war both parents had been in concentration camps, which they had survived. They married after the war. From its beginning the marriage had been very unhappy, and the parents divorced when the patient was only three. The patient was brought up by her mother, who villified the father and his family. All that was good came from the mother's side and from the maternal family; all that was bad and evil came from the paternal family, which she completely denigrated and for which she had nothing good to say. The patient spent the first four years of her childhood in Israel—a period which she described as being relatively happy. She then moved to Germany, where her mother kept her imprisoned in a room. For a long time she was not allowed to go out or even to look out of the window, because the mother feared that the child would be kidnapped by the father. Because of this experience, and because of the extremely oppressive concentration camp experience in which only a few members of her family had survived, Germany took on the character of a completely negative, demoniac "fatherland" in the archetypical sense, even though neither parent was German-born. Each time she crossed beyond the German frontier she felt released, and many restraints and anxieties which she felt inside Germany fell away from her. For her, Germany as a whole had the symbolic character of a concentration camp, of confinement in a narrow room where one constantly feared that something awful would happen. The motorcyclist had become an S.S. guard whose annoyance provoked a real fear of death accompanying latent and potent aggressions.

My experience suggests that, in the case where the ego's controlling capacity is maintained, it is not the whole complex which is mobilized, but only those experience formations which pertain to the specific releasing stimulus. The first case described here, in which the patient brought the second picture of the "Holländermichel" to analysis and projected it onto me as part of transference-countertransference, demonstrates this case readily. His associations dealt only with events which were linked to male authorities, involving homoerotic and homosexual tendencies and memories which had to do with the father as mother's animus. With reference to the figure, the system designated as 3, 3', 3", III and, in the complex core, as mother animus was the area mobilized. The mobilization of the "witch" is different because this image, which had frightened him much more, involved associations which were related to all four fields. The energy found in such a case is often surprisingly intense, since it often goes far beyond the psychic libido quantum an individual normally has. Similarly, it can often be observed that individuals in exceptional circumstances have for a brief time amounts of energy which they themselves would not have believed possible enabling them to perform "superhumanly." We obviously have in the collective unconscious a reserve of energy at our disposal which cannot be mobilized deliberately but can only be released by a complex reaction either in a saving, constructive, or destructive manner.

Although it is impossible for us to answer it here, I would finally like to raise an important hypothetical question: is the releasing of a complex due to a causal chain or to real synchronicity in the activation of the experience qualities on different levels? The causal chain would be the linkage of the releasing stimulus,—for example the actual encounter with an authority (circle 3)—first with relatively recent experiences with the same authority (3'), then with the experiences from early puberty up to the age of eleven (3″), and finally with the repressed experiences with the father in early childhood and the mother animus (III) in the complex core. Synchronicity would suggest that there is no causal chain but rather that all fields of experience under point 3 (or in the extreme case, all the interconnected qualities included here) are activated instantaneously.

In modern physics there is a phenomenon which could be used as a metaphor for such a process—the EPR-experiment and the theorem of Bell (in Capra 1984):

Rotating electrons have a so-called "spin". Given an axis of rotation, the elementary particles can rotate in either one or the other direction. It is only when measurement of a chosen axis of rotation is carried out that one can find out in which direction the electron is rotating. The elementary particle at the moment of measurement is given a specific axis of rotation, whereas, before, it only had a tendency or a potential to have one. The EPR experiment consists in putting two electrons into a state where they rotate in opposite directions. They are then removed from each other macroscopically. The distance may be optional; one might be in Berlin and the other one in New York or on the moon. The quantum theory says that, in a system of two elementary particles whose total spin equals zero, the spin of each of the two particles about a given axis is always in correlation to the one spinning in the opposite direction—even though before measurement the spin of each particle exists only as a tendency or a potential. What is paradoxical about this experiment is that each observer is free to choose the measuring axis. As soon as this choice is made, the measurement turns the rotational tendencies of the elementary particles into certainties. We may choose the measuring axis at the last moment, when both particles are already very far away from each other. As soon as we have carried out the measurement for elementary particle 1, elementary particle 2 will take a specific spin even if it is thousands of kilometers away—upwards or downwards if we choose a vertical axis, left or right if we choose a horizontal one. This happens at the very same moment because, according to Bohr, the system of the two particles represents an indivisible whole even if the particles are separated from each other by huge distances. Although they are far away from each other in space, they are connected to one another by direct, non-local correlations. This phenomenon transcends our conventional conception of the transmission of information.

Seen metaphorically, our psychological complex system seems similar. Although the different, condensed experience formations belong to different periods and are in completely different layers of consciousness and the unconscious, they are at the same time an indivisible whole and react as such. This is, of course, only a hypothesis, as we lack the means to measure the transmission of information and the libidinal quantities of psychic processes. Nevertheless, there are some points to be made about the applicability of this hypothesis. In states which are accompanied by intense affectivity, as happens when complexes are released, synchronistic events are often known to occur in the vicinity of the individual concerned. According to Jung's later conclusions involving the Unus-Mundus theory (Jung 1968) and to Erich Neumann's conception of the "unity of reality" (Neumann 1959), the mobilization of archetypical energies calls forth constellations which go beyond the system of the individual.

References

[References in brackets refer to English versions of work cited.]

Capra, F. 1984. *Wendezeit*. Scherz Verlag Bern-München-Wien. [1985. *The Turning Point*. New York: Bantam.]
Dieckmann, H. 1980. Übertragung-Gegenübertragung-Üeziehung. In *Übertragung und Gegenübertragung*, herausgegeben von H. Dieckmann, Gerstenberg Verlag Hildesheim.
Hauff, W. 1896. *Sämtliche Werke*, Bd. 4. Griesbach Verlag Gera.
Jacobi, J. 1971. *Die Psychologie von C. G. Jung*. Walter Verlag Olten. [1968. *The Psychology of C. G. Jung*. New Haven: Yale University Press.]
Jung, C. G. 1963. *Psychologie und Religion. Ges. Werke*, Bd. 11. Rascher Verlag Zürich. [1958, 1969. *Psychology and Religion*. In *Collected Works*, vol. 11. Princeton: Princeton University Press.]
————. 1966. *Zur Psychologie sogenannter okkulter Phänomene. Ges. Werke*, Bd. 1. Rascher Verlag Zürich. [1957, 1970. On the psychology of so-called occult phenomena. In *Collected Works*, vol. 1. Princeton: Princeton University Press.]
————. 1967a. *Allgemeines zur Komplex-Theorie. Ges. Werke*, Bd. 8. Rascher Verlag Zürich. [1960, 1969, 1980. A review of the complex theory, in *Collected Works*, vol. 8. Princeton: Princeton University Press.]
————. 1967b. Die psychologischen Grundlagen des Geisterglaubens. *Ges Werke*, Bd. 8. Rascher Verlag Zürich. [1960, 1969, 1980. The psychological foundations of the belief in spirits. In *Collected Works*, vol. 8. Princeton: Princeton University Press.]
————. 1967c. Über die Energetik der Seele. *Ges. Werke*, Bd. 8. Rascher Verlag Zürich. [1960, 1969, 1980. On psychic energy. In *Collected Works*, vol. 8. Princeton: Princeton University Press.]
————. 1968. *Mysterium Coniunctionis. Ges. Werke*, Bd. 14:2. Rascher Verlag Zürich. [1965, 1970. *Mysterium Coniunctionis*. In *Collected Works*. vol. 14. Princeton: Princeton University Press.]
————. 1976. Über die Archetypen des kollektiven unbewußten. *Ges. Werke*, Bd. 9:1, Walter Verlag Olten. [1959, 1969. The Archetypes and the Collective Unconscious. In *Collected Works*, vol. 9, pt. 1. Princeton: Princeton University Press.]
————. 1979. *Diagnostische Assoziationstudien. Ges. Werke*, Bd. 2. Walter Verlag Olten. [1973. *Experimental Researches*. In *Collected Works*, vol. 2. Princeton: Princeton University Press.]
Neumann, E. 1959. Die Erfahrung der Einheitswirklichkeit. In *Der schöferische Mensch*. Rein Verlag Zürich. [1979. The experience of oneness. In *The Creative Man*. Princeton: Princeton University Press.]

Affect and Archetype in Analysis

Louis H. Stewart

Introduction

For the past few years I have been preoccupied with updating Jung's model of the psyche with reference particularly to the relationship of affect and archetype. Accordingly I shall first summarize some of the salient features of what I now speak of as the "archetypal affective system," as I presently understand it (Stewart 1985, 1986*a*, 1987). Then I shall discuss a case of childhood schizophrenia which appears in *The Body in Analysis* (Allan 1986). I found this case particularly interesting because it illustrates so well the theory of the nature and function of the "archetypal affects." The case material and my interpretations will serve, then, as background for an in-depth discussion of the archetypal affect of shame and its particular role in the psyche, in psychopathology and in analysis.

The Archetypal Affective System

The affects are the life blood of the psyche. Without their ubiquitous presence in the psyche, life would be a pale and drab existence, without

Louis H. Stewart, Ph.D., is a founding member, former president, and training analyst of the C. G. Jung Institute of San Francisco. He practices in Berkeley and in San Francisco. He received his Ph.D. in clinical psychology at the University of California, Berkeley, and is professor of psychology at San Francisco State University, and clinical professor of medical psychology at the University of California, San Francisco.

value: in short, the underworld of death. But life is problematical, as the affects are quick to remind us. The heart rending pangs of loss reduce us to lamentation and weeping; and the icy grip of terror chills our blood, as we quiver and quake. Yet the heart also leaps with joy and pounds with excitement. The emotions, in all their numinous power, plumb the heights and depths of the soul; while, the philosophers have ever sought to reconcile the tranquil goals of reason with these titanic forces.

In analysis the affects can never be ignored. They are always present, whether openly expressed, or felt beneath the surface, or, if seemingly absent, then much in the consciousness of the analyst. In Jung's theory of analytical psychology they are given appropriate attention as energy, value, source of imagery and new consciousness, and, of course, as troublesome, unruly and capable of overwhelming consciousness. Perhaps most significant, the affects are the bridge between body and psyche, instinct and spirit. They reach back into the physiology of the body, to the chemical processes of the hormones, and neurologically to the areas of the "mammalian" brain. Phenomenologically they are an all pervasive presence in the psyche which fluctuates around a steady stream of subliminal awareness of mood, punctuated by intrusions of varying degrees of intensity of the more specific emotions. Developmentally they appear in infancy as eruptions of primal energy of high intensity, normally of short duration, which interrupt a steady state of pleasurable interest and somnolent revery. By adulthood they have been modulated in the crucible of family relationships, and transformed into a complex and sensitive matrix of feelings and emotionally toned complexes. Yet the innate affects never lose their primal autonomy and original mode of expression, which can appear at any time under the proper circumstances. These primal affects have universal forms of facial expression and bodily innervations. They can be recognized in infancy and throughout life in humans everywhere.

The hypothesis I am presenting here as to the nature of the affects has its deep roots in a lifelong interest in the creative imagination; first in art, then, in the archetypal development of the imagination itself, and the transformative function of active imagination in analysis. Its more immediate origins lie in my analytic work with sandplay and active imagination. During recent years while I was writing my papers on sandplay and active imagination I found my interest gravitating to the affects. When I finally took this hint seriously, and looked carefully at the affects and their relationship to play and the imagination, I found that they are intertwined in at least four significant ways as: motivation, transformation, potentiation of imagination, and in the forms of social games.

The four ways in which the affects are enmeshed with play and the imagination exemplify two fundamental and reciprocal aspects of the psyche, namely, *energy* and *transformation*. Children are motivated to play just for the "fun" of it; one can say that play is energized by the affect of Joy. But play is "about" emotion in another way; children play out little dramas involving other affects of a distinctly different flavor, such as sadness, fear, anger, and shame. Careful observation of the day to day experiences of children reveals that they are forever playing out whatever it is in their life that arouses emotion. But in their play, the effects of these emotions are transmuted through compensatory fantasies, liquidating or cathartic experiences, and the like. Thus one must conclude that during the period of development, play and fantasy serve a transformative function in the equilibration of the personality, and this makes it readily apparent why in analysis, active imagination serves an identical transformative function in the "re-creation" of the wholeness of personality.

In the course of this study it also became apparent that the imagination has a twin which finds its expression in the affect of Interest and in the dynamism of "curiosity." Moreover one sees that play (i.e. imagination) and curiosity are inseparably entwined in a dialectical process in which each potentiates the other. With this realization a number of Jung's concepts appeared in a new light. It seemed obvious that his "two kinds of thinking," fantasy/mythical thought and directed/logos thought (Jung 1956, pp. 7–33), were functions which have their origins in play/imagination and curiosity/exploration, and are related to his concepts of Lunar and Solar consciousness, as well as Eros and Logos consciousness. Our findings suggest further that, although Jung never explicitly made any of these connections, it seems inescapable that his two ways of thinking are also related to his concept of the libido as psychic energy, a nonspecific energy which can be directed to any instinct or function of the psyche, (*ibid.*, pp. 132–141). From this perspective the two archetypal affects, Joy and Interest, with their twin dynamisms of play and curiosity, appear as the prototypical energic and dynamic expressions of the libido as Lunar consciousness, i.e. Eros/mythical consciousness and Solar consciousness, i.e., Logos/linguistic consciousness.

At this point my interest turned to two questions: Are other functions of the psyche similarly "energized" by specific affects? And what is the relationship of the affects to Jung's concept of the Self? This inquiry was given an impetus by recent studies of the emotions which have demonstrated their universal modes of expression in all cultures. This idea was originally explored by Darwin; and has been supported by other studies of the evolution of the affects (Ekman 1972, Izard 1977). The subject has been most thoroughly evaluated by Sylvan Tomkins in his two volume work *Affect Imagery Consciousness* (1962, 1963). Further suggestions came from anthropological studies of play and games (Roberts and Sutton-Smith 1962) which consistently demonstrate a fourfold categorization: games of chance, physical skill, strategy and central person, i.e. social games; and from the field of literary criticism in which the imagination is expressed in a tetravalent structure such as Bachelard's four elements and their mythological personifications: the sylph, the gnome, the salamander and the ondine (Stewart 1978). Everything seemed to converge, then, on the hypothesis that the archetypal structure of the Self should be represented in a fourfold affective system structured around a central affect.

Tomkins' studies pointed to a twofold structure of affects which fit the analysis above of the libido, and, also to a specified number of so-called "crisis" affects which seemed referrable to the primal Self. Briefly stated, Tomkins identifies a basic system of innate affects which in his view have evolved in the mammalian species as a twofold structure of "positive" affects of life enhancement, namely Joy and Interest; and a structure of what he terms "negative" affects, namely Sadness, Fear, Anger, Contempt and Shame, which have evolved in response to the major existential crises of life. In addition he identifies Startle as an affect of orientation, the "re-setting" affect.

An evaluation of Tomkins' work led to the following slight modifications of his views and a change in terminology. First as we have said above, the affects of Joy and Interest can be understood as the twin affects of libido, and we speak of them as the archetypal affects of the libido. Second, along with Lynd (1958), we understand the affects Contempt and Shame to be the two faces of a bi-polar affect which is a function of the reflexive nature of consciousness. Whether one experiences Contempt or Shame, is determined by the direction of Contempt toward oneself or toward the other. Consequently we speak of the archetypal affect Contempt/Shame. Finally we consider the affect Startle to be the archetypal affect of orientation and the centering of consciousness. Thus we arrive at a system of seven archetypal affects, which comprise the two archetypal affects of the libido, Joy-Ecstasy and Interest-Excitement; and four archetypal affects of the primal Self, Fear-Terror, Sadness-Anguish, Anger-Rage, and Contempt-Disgust/Shame-Humiliation (Contempt-Humiliation for convenience), structured around a fifth archetypal affect of centering and orientation, Surprise-Startle. (The primal affects have a range of intensity which is represented here now, from lower to higher intensity, as, Joy-Ecstasy, and so on. In most instances for easier readability we shall use the form of lower intensity of the affect, e.g., Joy, and so on. Occasionally, however, to emphasize the intensity potential of the primal, innate state of the affects, we shall use the form of highest intensity, e.g., Ecstasy. It should also be noted, of course, that all of the archetypal affects are contained in the Self as the totality of the psyche. Nevertheless, for purposes of clarification and explication it is useful to discriminate between the affects functioning primarily as libido and those functioning primarily as the centered, fourfold groundplan of other functions of the psyche.)

As for the limited number of affects discussed here, I am fully aware that personal experience, as well as Roget's Thesaurus, impress us with a multiplicity of emotions. This is undeniable. It is my belief, however, that, in the alchemical vessel of the family, the innate primal affects discussed above are transformed into a complex and sensitive matrix of emotional complexes and feelings. With respect to the limited number of primal affects found in Tomkins' work and which I have adopted as appropriate, there are several things to be considered. First, is the fact that in common parlance, as well as in psychological studies, these affects are the ones most commonly mentioned. Second, studies of the affects from Darwin on have identified these as the "universally" observed affects. And third, the most convincing argument, or so I believe, is the nature of the psyche itself, which so far as can be determined appears to have its base in the life instinct, which finds expression in a twofold structure of libido, and further, in its functions of orientation and apperception which find expression through ego and Self, as a fourfold structure around a center. Thus we postulate that:

- 1) The archetypal affective system is an inherited regulatory system of the psyche which functions as an unconscious energic, orienting and apprehension-response system which has evolved to replace an earlier system of programmed instinct.
- 2) It consists of a dynamic system of seven archetypal affects of which two, the affects of Joy-Ecstasy and Interest-Excitement function as twin dynamisms of the life instinct, making it certain that newborn mammals, and particularly humans, will enter the world with joie de vivre and divine curiosity. This assures an active engagement with the world through which the fundamentals for survival are acquired. In addition there are four archetypal affects which are oriented to the existential spiritual crises of life in the world as it is. These are Fear-Terror, Sadness-Anguish, Anger-Rage and the bi-polar affect of Contempt/Humiliation. Each of these primal affects has evolved in relationship to a specific domain of the

world and to the life threatening crises it may evoke. These may be identified through the life experiences, that is the inherent stimuli, which constellate each of the primal affects, namely: *The unknown* (Fear); *loss* (Sadness); *restriction of freedom* (Anger); and *rejection* (Contempt/Shame). The fifth archetypal affect, Surprise-Startle, which has evolved in relation to the crisis of disorientation, has as its inherent stimulus *the unexpected*.

- 3) This archetypal affective system functions roughly in the following fashion. As we have said, each of the archetypal affects is constellated by a particular life experience, i.e., the stimulus, which is a function of the characteristics of the world into which we are born. Thus the four archetypal affects, Fear, Sadness, Anger and Contempt/Shame comprise four basic modes of apprehension of the world and the Self. With respect to the World, these innate affects appear in evolved forms of the psyche as Kant's Categories of Understanding (Intellect), namely time, space, quantitative order and qualitative order. These basic categories may be divided into the implicative; time and space, and the explicative; quantity and quality. As Categories of the Intellect they determine our perceptions of cause and time, and of objects in space, and the explications of such impressions in quantitative-logic and qualitative-organic order. In the psychological functioning of the ego, these categories are experienced as Jung's Ego Functions of Intuition, Sensation, Thinking and Feeling. The fifth archetypal affect of the Self, Startle, appears as a Category of Orientation, and as the function of Ego-consciousness.

As for Joy and Interest, the two archetypal affects of the libido, the instinct of life, it may not be immediately apparent what aspects of the world they correlate with. Here it is necessary to reflect on the two primary ways of experiencing life as expressed, for example, in the philosophical principles of Being and Becoming. Many efforts have been made to characterize these fundamental modes of life experience, as for example, the Tao as the interplay of Yin and Yang, the alchemical images Luna and Sol, or the cosmogonic principles of antiquity, Eros and Logos. All of these concepts and images seek to represent the alternation of life experience through two modes which nevertheless seem to be united within a whole. In so far as the archetypal affects of Joy and Interest may be considered prototypical forms of the expression of these life principles, they have presumably evolved, then, in relation to these two modes of experiencing life. The inherent stimuli of these affects appear to be, respectively, familiarity and novelty. Play and Curiosity are the prototypical dynamic forms of expression of these affects in the psyche.

As we know however, there is another realm in reference to which this system of archetypal affects had evolved, namely the subjective realm of the Self. With respect to the Self, these archetypal affects evoke the age old categories of the Holy, the Beautiful, the True and the Good, Kant's Ideas of Reason. As psychological structures these may be thought of as the fourfold Categories of the Imagination, and are represented in Henderson's Cultural Attitudes: the Religious, The Aesthetic, the Philosophic and the Social (1962, 1984).

- 4) It is not, of course, immediately self evident just how the Ego Functions and the Cultural Attitudes have developed from the primal archetypal affective system of apprehension. Our knowledge of the evolutionary process is very limited, but we can suggest that the distinction between Ego Functions and Cultural Attitudes is related to two basic aspects of the archetypal experience, namely the *noetic* and the *expressive* It would appear that the Ego Functions have evolved from the noetic aspect and the Cultural Attitudes from the expressive.

- 5) This brings us to the realization that there must be both a "stimulus," i.e., a life experience, and an unconscious "image/idea imprint," or the potential for such an "image/idea" with which the stimulus connects; like a key in a lock, or better yet as the half of a broken coin, which reconstitutes a totality, a symbol (Hillman 1961, p. 286). What might these unconscious "image/ideas," be? In as much as they are representative of fundamental domains of life, they must be innate, primal universal images. These we find to be those universal images of pre-creation, the "Abyss," the "Void," "Chaos," and "Alienation." Thus in human experience the archetypal affect of Fear is constellated by confrontation with the "unknown," of which the *Abyss* is the primal innate image/idea; Sadness is constellated by "loss," of which the primal innate image/idea is the *Void*; Anger is constellated by "frustration," that is, restriction of autonomy, of which *Chaos* is the primal innate image/idea; and Contempt/Shame is constellated by "rejection" of self or other, of which *Alienation* is the primal innate image/idea. Finally the affect Startle, is constellated by the "unexpected," of which the primal innate image/idea is *Disorientation*. The nature of the innate image/ideas of the archetypal affects of the libido, Joy and Interest, are not well understood as yet, although it would appear that they are two forms of *illumination*: blissful merger, or focused insight.

- 6) The constellation of an archetypal affect occurs as follows. In response to a symbol, that is, the conjunction of a life experience, the stimulus, with an unconscious primal, innate image/idea, (or the potential for such an innate image/idea) there ensues a rush of feelings of a specific quality which we label as "the emotion." This is accompanied by a specific set of bodily innervations and a typical pattern of behavior. The consequence is an *abaissement du niveau mental* which both heightens and narrows the conscious field to focus primarily on the stimulus situation. This is a total reaction which for a varying period of time transforms the ego. It leads to heightened awareness within a narrowly focussed consciousness, along with a rapid mobilization of energy which takes the form of a stereotyped behavior pattern accompanied by typical vocalizations, facial expressions and body tensions.

- 7) It is important to specify now, as best we can, the prototypical behavior patterns of each of the archetypal/affects. Let us begin with the twin dynamisms of the archetypal/affects of the life instinct, Joy and Interest. All the evidence suggests that the behavior patterns at the most basic level are, for Play, leaping with Joy, and, for Curiosity, reaching for the moon. That is to say the behavior patterns are expressions of the innate rhythms of the life instinct in forms that become in early childhood the function of Play and Curiosity, respectively.

It is somewhat more difficult to specify the behavior patterns of the archetypal affects of the Self (the so-called crisis affects), since they are as yet less well understood. Nevertheless, we are convinced that they have clear and immediate behavior patterns of a stereotyped, and prototypical nature, and that these behavior patterns have evolved into highly differentiated functions of the psyche in the same way that Play and Curiosity have evolved from the primal expressions of the affects of Joy and Interest. Our hypothesis is that the prototypical behavior patterns of Fear, Sadness, Anger, and Contempt/Shame may be characterized in their *expressive* aspects, as: "ritual," "rhythmic harmony", "reason," and "relationship." These are the irreducible elements, respectively, of Religion, Art, Philosophy and Society. And, as we have said, these are the Categories of Imagination, and appear as Henderson's Cultural Attitudes, the Religious, the Aesthetic, the Philosophic and the Social. On the other hand, the prototypical behavior patterns of these same archetypal affects may be characterized in their *noetic* aspects, as an apperceptive focus on fundamental domains of the world: the intangible, the tangible, quantitative ordering and organic ordering. These are the irreducible elements of our experience of the World as Kant's Categories of Understanding (Intellect): time and causality, objects in space, quantitive-logical order, and qualitative-organic order. As psychological functions these are represented in Jung's Ego Functions: Intuition, Sensation, Thinking, and Feeling.

- 8) In this final section of this summary of the Archetypal Affects I shall attempt to briefly characterize three of the affects, Anguish, Terror and Rage, in descriptive and phenomenological terms, using material from various sources. This is a very preliminary effort and does not make any claim to completeness or finality. My purpose is to aid the reader's imagination in bringing these affects to life, and relating them to the differentiated functions of the psyche which have presumably evolved from the affects. A more detailed explication of the affect Contempt/Humiliation will follow further on, and these brief summaries of other affects may prove useful for comparison.

Anguish

At first hand, it may seem a long leap from the sad face, weeping eyes, sobbing, and rhythmic, rocking behavior of the anguish of loss to the highly differentiated function of Sensation, and the Cultural Attitude of the Aesthetic. Yet if we focus on the function of that behavior, it can be seen that this autonomous reaction of the psyche assures a heart-rending experience of the significance of the loss that has occurred. It forces a total committement of consciousness to the devastating feelings and sensations which are evoked by loss, and the barren void into which one is driven. The myth of Demeter and Persephone brings these images vividly to mind; the rupture of the primal relationship of mother and child, expressed at the cosmic level of the Great Mother in Her two aspects as Mother and Daughter, chthonic Goddesses of Nature and the cycle of death and re-birth. Demeter's barren world of despair is the primal void that is constellated by loss. In the myth, her experience is raised to the highest level of cosmic drama in which the constancy of her longing for Persephone, and the limits to which she had to go to assure her return from the Underworld are emphasized. It is not our purpose here to go into the intricacies of this myth since we are only seeking to make evident the correlation of the basic images and theme of the myth with the "human" experience of loss. The expression of loss is a primal pattern which emphasizes the relationship of the earth to the underworld in its aspect as the source of the fruits and beauty of the world. This we may suggest is the channel of analogy at the primal level of the element earth through which ultimately evolved the Ego-Function of Sensation. As for the evolution of the Aesthetic Attitude we would call attention to the fact that the transformation of the ego that takes place in anguish is one in which consciousness is narrowed to include only the longing for the lost loved one. The human experience of loss and its transformation shows that the rituals of mourning, e.g. the traditional rhythmic lamentations and the iconic focus, serve to keep the positive image of the beloved enshrined in the heart. It seems but a small step from this thought to the role of the arts in depicting the images of nature and spirit for all humanity.

Terror

Let us look now at another archetypal affect for comparison. Our images of the expression of fear are distinctly different from those of anguish. The eyes are wide and staring, the mouth shaped into an audible or a silent shriek of horror, the hair stands on end, an uncanny feeling runs down the spine, and we quiver and quake. The primal behavior patterns are to run or fall in a shivering faint, i.e. play dead. This pattern in its noetic aspect is, we suggest, the prototypical form of the ego function of Intuition, in that consciousness is directed to a desparate entanglement with the dreaded possibilities of the situation. At bottom, the phenomenology of Fear can be understood only as a response to the "unknown," which in its spiritual aspect is Otto's "Wholly Other," and the "abyss" of Hellish terror. This is the channel of analogy which has led to the Religious Cultural Attitude. In *The Idea of the Holy* (1923), Rudolph Otto has shown in a compelling tour de force how the most exalted of religious feelings have evolved from the primal experience of terror, "demonic dread." We may present here only a single example of the myriad images with which that book abounds. Otto quotes here from the discourses of Chrystosom because of the vividness with which the "feeling tone," the numinous, is evoked:

> What does "fearfully" mean here? . . . terror and "fear" only seize upon us when we gaze down into its *depths*. So, too, here the Psalmist. When he gazes

down into the immeasurable, yawning . . . depth of the divine Wisdom, dizziness comes upon him and he recoils in terrified wonder and cries: . . . "Thy
knowledge is too wonderful for me; it is high above my power . . ." Dizzy before the unfathomable main and gazing down into its yawning depths, he
recoils precipitately and cries aloud: "O the depth of the riches both of the
wisdom and knowledge of God. . . ." (Otto 1923, p. 182)

Rage

Rage presents another face of emotion with eyes staring, brow con-
tracted in a scowl, face flushed. Every muscle is tensed, the body is thrust
forward ready to attack, and threatening growls or shouts may occur. But
perhaps the most distinguishing feature of Rage is the fiercely focused attention to freeing oneself from the perceived threat to autonomy. The
affect drives one to strike out, to remove the intrusion which is creating
chaos in one's world. There is perhaps no stronger engagement possible
with the object than in Rage. The primal behavior pattern is threat and attack. This pattern we suggest, is, in its noetic aspect, the prototypical form
of the ego function of Thinking, in that consciousness is single mindedly
directed to a confrontation with a chaotic situation of extreme frustration.
Is this not a first stage in thinking, that is the identification and engagement with a problem? What follows then in subsequent reflection may be
improved strategies for solving the problem. As we know from bitter experience, an angry outburst is often followed by a long period of "re-
hashing" the situation: I could have said that, or why didn't I do such and
such, and so on. This is thinking, pragmatic attempts to set things aright
in ones own mind at least; still under the sway of the emotion, to be sure,
but thinking nevertheless. There is still another way in which we may approach this difficult question. And here we may draw upon our understanding of the compensatory nature of the psyche—what cannot be
achieved in the everyday world appears in unconscious fantasy. This is
born out by studies of children, who at an early age of 3 or 4 years will respond to parental restrictions on their behavior by compensatory fantasies, often involving an imaginary figure who is able to do what they
would like to, and more. As the child develops, these fantasies evolve into
useful strategies for getting what it wants.

It seems more difficult, at first, to see the potential development of
the Philosophic Cultural Attitude from the expressive aspects of the behavior pattern of Rage. As we know philosophy develops in relation to
the value of the "True." The word itself derives from the two Greek
words, philo and sophia, which together mean love of wisdom. The philosopher William James saw philosophy as an unusually stubborn at-

tempt to think clearly, which captures a commonly held slant on the nature of a philosopher as one who thinks more deeply and obstinately than other people. The greatest frustration for a philosopher is not to understand something. Rodin's famous statue of the thinker shows a seated man with elbow on his knee, resting his head on his fist. His brow is furrowed as in anger, and he is obviously in a state of deep concentration. Is this not a link with the expressive qualities of the affect Rage? That is to say, the concentration of consciousness on gaining freedom from the restriction to autonomy, the fist and furrowed brow, expressive features related to such a response, whether it be the primitive one of a forceful physical attack, or the concentrated thought of the philosopher. A paradigm of the way in which reason must confront Chaos and discover the Cosmos within it, is to be found in the mythical imagery of the "Babylonian Genesis." In this ancient Babylonian creation myth the hero Mar-

The Archetypal Affects of the Self

Symbol and Primal Affect*				Evolved, Differentiated Functions**	
Stimulus→Image→		Affect	+	Expressive/dynamism→Cultural Attitude Noetic/apperception→Ego Function	
The Unknown→the Abyss→		TERROR	+	Ritual→ the Intangible→	Religious Attitude~ Intuitive Function
Loss→	the Void→	ANGUISH	+	Rhythm→ the Tangible→	Aesthetic Attitude~ Sensation Function
Restriction→	Chaos→	RAGE	+	Reason→ Quant. Order→	Philosophic Att.~ Thinking Function
Rejection→	Alienation→	DISGUST/ HUMILIATION	+	Relationship→ Qual. Order→	Social Attitude~ Feeling Function
Unexpected→	Disorien→ tation	STARTLE	+	Reflection→ Orientation→	Psychological Att. Ego Consciousness
The Familiar→	Illumina→ tion	ECSTASY	+	Play→ Being→	Imagination Eros
The Novel→	Insight→	EXCITE-→ MENT	+	Curiosity→ Becoming→	Memory Logos

*Janet's *parties inférieures;* Jung's Collective Unconscious.

**Janet's *parties supérieurs;* Henderson's Cultural Unconscious & Cultural Attitudes; Jung's Personal Unconscious and Ego Consciousness.

~Categories of the Imagination.

duk must do battle with the Goddess Tiamat, whose domain was the Chaos of the abysmal waters. The state of Chaos that Tiamat creates, and represents, is vividly portrayed at the moment when she is confronted by Marduk, who challenges her to single combat: "she became like one in a frenzy (and) lost her *reason*" [my emphasis]. But unswerving in the face of her fury, Marduk slays Tiamat whose body he divides in two to form heaven and earth, a new cosmos (Heidel 1941, pp. 40–43). The reciprocal relationship between anger and reaon has been perceived by thinkers throughout the ages, as for example these comments from Seneca's treatise "On Anger":

> Hesitation is the best cure for anger . . . The first blows of anger are heavy, but if it waits, it will think again. . . . Anger . . . is the foe of reason . . . nevertheless (it is) born only where reason dwells (Seneca, II 29)

The foregoing summary of the archetypal affects and their relationships to the differentiated functions of the psyche provides a background which will be of help in understanding the summary presentation of the following case of a schizophrenic child. This case provides an exceptional illustration of the devastating effects of the archetypal affects of the primal Self, Terror, Anguish, Rage, and Contempt/Humiliation, and their subsequent transmutations in symbolic play therapy, through the dialectical relationship of the archetypal affects of the libido, Joy and Interest, and their twin dynamisms Play and Curiosity.

The Case of Luci: Reconstruction of the Self in its Fourfold Manifestation as the Cultural Attitudes

This is the case of a 5 and one half year old girl referred to a child guidance clinic for treatment because of her "bizarre and destructive behavior." She was treated by Dr John A. B. Allan and an art therapist (Allan 1986). The diagnosis was childhood schizophrenia. Through the use of a "holding technique," with the mother's cooperation, Allan was able to bring the child out of her fantasy world sufficiently to allow for play therapy in which the two therapists engaged in active symbolic play with Luci. This play showed a progression of basic themes representing the expression and transformation of the four primal archetypal affects: Rage, Contempt/Humiliation, Anguish, and Terror. The play therapy was accompanied by art therapy. The treatment, which lasted for a year, was highly successful in bringing Luci to a state of normality which had persisted into adolescence when she was last contacted. The first theme of the play with the two therapists seemed to reflect the anger which was engendered by the "holding technique" and which reflected Luci's giving up her fantasy world. In her play Luci pretended to tie the therapists up and then pretended to attack them. She pushed them to the floor and shot arrows into them time after time during which they were commanded to die many times and to scream and plead for mercy. The rage persisted and became more violent. The therapists were dismembered, had pins shot into their eyes and genitals and were left lying in blood. Then the bodies were rotting, and wormy and floating in a sea of pooh and blood. (*Ibid.*, p. 159).

The "sea of pooh and blood" was the transition to the next play theme in which Luci would sit on the bench eating deluxe hamburgers while the therapists had to eat "pooh" burgers. This was clearly the phase of Contempt/Humiliation where Luci played out the role of the contemptuous one in compensation for the humiliation she must have felt during the period that her illness developed. At the end of this period of play sessions, Luci's drawings done in the art therapy sessions depicted her as grounded although very small in relation to the art therapist. (Allan 1986, p. 159)

Following the foregoing Rage and Contempt/Humiliation phases, Luci arrived one day in a state of Anguish (called depression). She was very lethargic and spoke only in whispers but related a dream:

I'm visiting the "dead land." There are no people, no fires in the fireplaces, no food in the refrigerator, no beds in the bedrooms and no furniture in the living room. Outside there are no flowers, no grass, only rocks. (Allan 1986, p. 159)

There could be no more vivid a depiction of the *void* of Anguish, Demeter's barren land. This state lasted about three weeks during which the child lay in her bed at home, getting up only for therapy. In the playroom she turned out all the lights, closed the blinds and totally darkened the room to create the "dead land." Slowly her mood changed and she divided the room into the "good" and the "dead" place and her mood would change as she travelled between the two. Here we see the transformation as expressed in the reuniting of mother and daughter, as in the Demeter-Persephone myth:

My mother is with us now and we're flying by jet to the good land. There's flowers, trees, grass and dirt and lots of food in the kitchen . . . Oh dear, it's time to go back to the dead land. Let's pack up and go . . . It's so dark and cold here in the dead land. I'm shaking with cold.(Allan 1986, p. 159)

At last a small windowless washroom off the playroom came to be used as the dead land. Her Anguish lifted and Terror appeared. This was heralded by another dream:

I am sleeping in my bed in my room. Above my bed are two posters, a happy face and a monster person with hands, who wants to touch me. Suddenly I wake up and there are monster "pumps" on top of me, above me, below me, all around me, squeezing my stomach and suffocating me. My Mom and Dad hear me yell and come running in. (Allan 1986, p. 160)

The nightmare reflects a mixture of shaming and frightening experiences: the "monster" who wants to touch her, and the attack of the pumps squeezing and suffocating her. This experience is obviously one of *alienation* as well as the *abyss* of Terror, a demonic world. The fear which was genuinely still felt in Luci's body lasted for about two months. She drew several "muscular 'Super girls' who were never afraid and could always fly away" (Allan 1986, p. 160). The washroom became the "pumproom" and Luci sat on the therapists' laps. She would then attack the therapists with flying pumps, saying, "the pump goes in your pee hole and pees on you" (*ibid.*, p. 161). They were to tremble, and cry out with fear. Luci acted out the dream over and over on the therapists' laps. Later she pretended to be the pump and suffocate them, clutch their necks, and land on their stomachs. The therapists felt that over time "her feelings of fear had changed to feelings of power and the wish to hurt us." They decided that she was not relaxing and that this play was a defense against enjoying human contact and intimacy. She seemed afraid of the experience of affection. This led the therapists to wonder about sexual abuse but ruled it out because of their feelings about the family. Eventually the therapists found themselves getting annoyed at the pump attacks and finally felt they had to set limits. They threatened termination of the session if this went on. The next week Luci came in with a friendly baby pump which she wanted to cuddle.

This initiated a stage of regression, but also led to the final theme in which Luci sat on the therapists' laps and pretended she was in a pump family "which had breakfast, lunch and dinner in bed. This theme was played out time and again. During this time her drawings changed completely. There were scenes of incubation and hatching, pregnancy, birth, a new baby, and nursing mothers." (Allan 1986, pp. 161, 166). In this sequence we see the reconstruction of a family and a social attitude through the birth of the divine child, a new generation with renewed hope and trust. The therapists "felt there was no longer any need for the fantasy enactment as Luci was now playing with objects and toys in age appropriate fashion."

The woman art therapist saw Luci for the last two months during which Luci worked on farm yard themes, separating wild animals from the domestic ones, and cowboys and Indians. She came to see herself as an Indian Princess. "She was returned to the public school system and after an adjustment period, therapy was terminated. Follow-up some years later indicated a happy, well-adjusted teenager" (Allan 1986, p. 162).

This remarkably successful treatment of the child Luci is very impressive. The sensitive response of the therapists in first of all inducing the child to come out of her fantasy world and enter into a therapeutic relationship is particularly notable. What is most interesting from the point of view of the issues being discussed here, is the way in which the sequence of play therapy reveals the transmutation of the effects of the four archetypal affects of Rage, Contempt/Humiliation, Anguish and Terror. The playing out of the Contempt/Humiliation theme comes at the beginning and the end of the sequence which reflects the probability that it is this archetypal affect which is the primary etiological factor, as is borne out by the symptomatology of schizophrenia, that is withdrawal from the everyday world and immersion in a fantasy world. As the therapists were aware, it is difficult to completely rule out the possibility of some incestual trauma, which even in Freud's cases turns out now to have been more reality than fantasy (Masson 1983). This, moreover, is the etiological experience in a large number, if not all cases of schizophrenia of this type, as witness Jung's case of the teenager who lived on the moon (see below), and others of his cases. The conclusion seems unavoidable that the archetypal affect Contempt/Humiliation has a significant etiological role in this case and in a many cases of schizophrenia.

Now we turn to etiology, the second important aspect of this case of Luci, as well as Allan's other cases of autism. (Allan 1986, pp. 152–56) Here we are raising the question of the significance of the archetypal affect of shame in the etiology of such cases.

The Etiology of Autism and Childhood Schizophrenia

First let us review some of the expressive features of autism and childhood schizophrenia. I shall mention just a few of the most universal and outstanding symptoms: the withdrawal from social contact; turning the head to avoid eye-contact; placing the hands before the eyes; and the generalized behavior of turning inward and away from others into a private "world," which for the autistic child invovles some sterotyped behavior of a universal nature, e.g., spinning, "pill rolling" of fingers, and the like; and which for the schizophrenic child may involve some stereotyped and universal thematic content. It is precisely the disruption of relationships, of social contact, and withdrawal into a private world which defines autism and schizophrenia, and which makes these disorders so difficult to treat. The inference to be drawn here is that, through excessive experiences of rejection in the family, or often the secret shame of incest, the autistic or schizophrenic child has withdrawn from the humiliating alienation they experience in the human community, into a private compensatory world. (We may suggest here that the differences in the two syndromes may turn out to be largely a function of the developmental timing of the experiences of rejection, although the role of incest would be different for the two syndromes, and, of course, other innate etiological factors cannot be ruled out in some, perhaps all cases of autism and some cases of schizophrenia.)

The foregoing is a very brief statement of the theory, but it should be sufficient for this brief review of the most salient themes of the case of Luci, which provides us with such a remarkable series of dreams and symbolic play sequences. First is the symbolic play in which the two therapists are dominated by Luci. This play takes the form of the compensatory inflation of Contempt which is the other side of her Humiliation, and leads to the humiliation of the two therapists who are tortured and in the end forced to submit to the "black" communion, or totem feast of "pooh", a prime symbol of Humiliation, i.e., having to eat shit. It is worth noting that this form of play follows the model of normal childhood play in which a potentially terrifying and humiliating experience such as the first visit to the dentist is subsequently played out by the child with the roles reversed.

The second theme is illustrated in the dreams of the "land of the dead" and the "invasion of the pumps" in which we recognize, first, the "void," Demeter's barren wasteland, and, second, the "abyss," abode of the demon monsters. These dreams are preludes to periods of Anguish and Terror, respectively. But it is also apparent that Humiliation is constellated in the experience of the alien pump family. In this sequence we see that the resolution of this "alienation" is the birth of a new pump family with benevolent human characteristics. The "void" of Anguish, on the other hand, is transformed, as we would expect, through the recovery of the "lost" mother as is shown in the symbolic play sequence where the mother's presence restores the wasteland to its natural beauty. This is obviously the Demeter-Persephone myth from the daughter's perspective. The transformation of the "abyss" of Terror is perhaps shown more clearly in Luci's drawings in which "super-girl", the Artemisian Goddess, appears (Allan 1986, p. 166). The trend of the symbolic play and the dream images seems highly representative of what might be expected.

At this point a reference to the work of John Perry (1974) with young adult schizophrenic patients may enlarge our perspective. The relevant imagery reported by Perry in his studies of young adult schizophrenic patients has to do with the destruction of society, usually in its form as "kingdom" or city state, which is followed, during the patient's recovery, by the reconstitution of a new society. In childhood schizophrenia it may be that such experiences as the invasion of the destructive demon pumps, and their subsequent transformation during the child's recovery into the benevolent, humanized family is the analogue to Perry's findings, in that society is but the family at large. This interpretation would fit with the findings of Petchkovsky's study of aboriginal Australians who become schizophrenic. Petchkovsky was attempting to validate Perry's findings, but to his surprise he found that the major etiological factor in the onset of the psychotic episode was violation of the incest taboo, that is marrying someone who was of a moiety which was forbidden by the incest taboo. (Not as we would interpret incest, that is as sexual relations with a member of the nuclear family.) The conclusion that he finally drew was that his findings did, after all, validate Perry's results in that incest, as so defined, was for the Australian Aborigine a rupture of the fabric of society:

> Just as the violent overthrow of the kingdom is an archetype of psychosis in Western man, so the radical disturbance of kinship structure through incest would seem to be an archetype for Aboriginal psychosis. (Petchovsky 1982)

I would suggest that it is, perhaps, more appropriate to speak of different representations of an underlying archetype, that is, the image/symbol of "alienation." In childhood schizophrenia (as in Luci's case) it appears as destruction of the family; in the adult Caucasian as violent overthrow of the kingdom; and in the adult Australian Aborigine as disruption of the kinship structure.

Jung's report of the case of a young woman eighteen years of age who in a catatonic state "lived on the moon," provides another example. As we know, Jung had recognized the symbolic meaning of incest as a return to the mother, to the maternal origins in the unconscious, in regression or in order to achieve a renewal and transformation. He also pointed out that since incest is the prerogative of the gods, then the effect of human incest is conscious alienation and unconscious inflation, and at its worst a complete withdrawal from life into a fantasy world of the gods. The Moon Lady illustrates this situation:

> Regarding them from the outside, all we see of the mentally ill is their tragic destruction, rarely the life of that side of the psyche which is turned away from us. Outward appearances are frequently deceptive, as I discovered to

my astonishment in the case of a young catatonic patient. She was eighteen years old, and came from a cultivated family. At the age of fifteen she had been seduced by her brother and abused by a schoolmate. From her sixteenth year on, she retreated into isolation. She concealed herself from people, and ultimately the only emotional relationship left to her was one with a vicious watchdog which belonged to another family, and which she tried to win over. She grew steadily odder, and at seventeen was taken to the mental hospital, where she spent a year and a half. She heard voices, refused food, and was completely mutistic (i.e., no longer spoke). When I first saw her she was in a typical catatonic state. (Jung 1961, p. 128)

Gradually Jung persuaded her to talk and she revealed to him that she had lived on the moon. In subsequent weeks she described her experiences on the moon. At first she had seen only men but they took her to a sublunar dwelling place where the women and children stayed. This was necessary to protect them from a vampire who lived on the high mountains and who kidnapped women and children thereby threatening the existence of the moon people. She decided to do something for the moon people by destroying the vampire. She exposed herself on a tower while holding beneath her cloak a sacrificial knife. When the vampire appeared, however, she was so fascinated by his wings and his complete covering of feathers that she moved closer to see what he looked like. Suddenly the wings opened revealing a man of unearthly beauty. Spellbound and held in his iron grip she was carried off.

It is not my intent at this point to attempt a statistical proof of the frequency of incest in the etiology of schizophrenia and other disorders, although a cursory examination of the cases reported by Jung, in which sufficient etiological date is available, is highly suggestive of a correlation. The interesting study by Petchkovsky of Australian aborigines reported above is relevant to this issue However, it is not just incest that I wish to focus on. We know that incest has occurred in some of these cases, but, it may be that it is the containment of the "secret" of incest which is a factor of etiological significance. It woul seem that the "secret" of incest kept over a prolonged period of time is likely to constellate the most powerful experience of humiliation, and thereby lead to an extensive withdrawal into a private fantasy world of a highly elaborate nature, as in the case of the "moon lady." At this point in our analysis, however, it is clear that it is the constellation of the archetypal affect of contempt/shame which seems of significance to the question of etiology. The importance of this fact lies in what we have said before, the archetypal affect of shame/humiliation has presumably evolved in direct relationship to the social domain of life. Its function appears to be that of forcing consciousness of any threat to the fabric of human relationships.

The Archetypal Affect of Contempt/Shame

We turn now to an exploration in some detail of the nature of the archetypal affect Contempt/Humiliation. First some comments by Sylvan Tomkins which will call to mind the significance of this archetypal affect and its toxic effects:

> We have argued that shame is an affect of relatively high toxicity, that it strikes deepest into the heart of man, that it is felt as a sickness of the soul which leaves man naked, defeated, alienated and lacking in dignity. . . . there is no claim which man makes upon himself and upon others which matters more to him than his essential dignity. Man above all other animals insists on walking erect. In lowering his eyes and bowing his head, he is vulnerable in a quite unique way. . . . the nature of the experience of shame guarantees a perpetual sensitivity to any violation of the dignity of man. (Tomkins 1963, p. 185).

> Men have exposed themselves repeatedly to death and terror, and have even surrendered their lives in the defense of their dignity, lest they be forced to bow their heads and bend their knees. The heavy hand of terror itself has been flouted and rejected in the name of pride. Many have had to confront death and terror all their lives lest their essential dignity and manhood be called into question. Better to risk the uncertainties of death and terror than to suffer the deep and certain humiliation of cowardice. (ibid., p. 133)

One is reminded of Dolores Ibarruri, "La Pasionaria," who in the face of almost certain defeat spoke the words that became a rallying cry for the Spanish Republic: "It is better to die on your feet, than to live on your knees" (Carroll 1986, p. 30).

Tomkins then raises the essential question:

> Why are shame and pride such central motives? How can loss of face be more intolerable than loss of life? How can hanging the head in shame so mortify the spirit? In contrast to all other affects, shame is an experience of the self by the self. At that moment when the self feels ashamed, it is felt as a sickness within the self. Shame is the most reflexive of affects in that the phenomenological distinction between the subject and object of shame is lost. . . . (Tomkins, p. 133)

What may we say about the innate basis of such a punishing affect? What is its survival value? In the evolutionary scheme of things it seems likely that it goes back to the primal affective reflex whose function was the rejection of noxious, potentially poisonous, substances. In the extremity of Disgust one may still experience this primal reaction of vomiting, either in expectation or in fact. Just how the evolution of this affect has come about is beyond the scope of our knowledge at the present time. We may venture the speculation, however, that it was through the intimate association of the early feeding experiences, which for mammals is nursing, thereby establishing a relationship between food and mother, and thus a possible evaluation of both food and mother in terms of the disgust affect. That is to say, any rejection of noxious foods, is in some unconscious sense a rejection of the mother's nursing and nurturance. And this rejection may carry with it an affective twinge of disgust. Further, since a realization of one's self as a separate being depends upon the prior recognition of the mother, it is possible to assume that the transfer of these associations is always a function of the growing separation of the individual, accompanied at the same time by a growing sense of relationship with the other. Thus we could argue that the first development of shyness, which occurs around the time of the awareness of the separate existence of another person, between eight to twelve months of age, is evidence of a reaction of shame, as well as the so-called "stranger anxiety" which has been observed at that age. This stage of development might as well be referred to as "stranger rejection." The "stranger" in early archaic societies is commonly the feared and contemptible "stranger" toward whom hostile reactions were common. Since the child at nine months of age has at its command very little in the way of defending itself against the intrusions of strange adults the reaction may be a primitive one of Contempt/Humiliation. There may be as well an element of fear in such early experiences of strangeness since there is a potential reaction to the unknown. Now we may ask about the relationship of Shame-Humiliation to Contempt-Disgust? In the very early stages of infancy it may be difficult to distinguish between contempt and shame reactions. The behavior pattern is essentially a turning away with a facial expression that lies between what will later on be 'seen as contempt and shame. But as the child develops out of the primal state of unconsciousness and the center of ego-consciousness is established, we can follow more clearly the emerging awareness of oneself and a sense of separate identity. One of the consequences of this development is the increasing ability to turn ones attention to oneself with both a benevolent and a critical eye. And as the feelings of confidence and inferiority fluctuate with the awareness of the complexities of human relationships, and of the inevitable ambivalence of all love committments, the child finds itself experiencing that painful human emotion, Shame-Humiliation; the emotion which strikes closest to the self. And what is it that evokes Shame? At first it is the rejection by parents, and other important family members, but soon it becomes the rejecting contempt of the child's own conscience. Finally it should be apparent by now that the devasting effect of an affect like Shame is only understandable if there exists in our inherited psyche an already prepared potential which needs but the spark of rejection to set it off.

What then is the specific domain of life experience which is pertinent to the evolution of Contempt/Shame? As we have seen, in its most ancient form, i.e. disgust and rejection of noxious substances, it serves a clear survival function. In its more recent evolutionary development its survival basis may appear more obscure. Nevertheless, if one follows out the evolution of the mammalian species we find an increasing degree of social responsiveness and of social cooperation. This development obviously has its general roots in the emotional nature of the mammals. Its more specific origin, however, is to be found in the increasing dependence of the mammalian young upon the mother for protection and nurturance, and, in turn, the mother's increasing dependence upon support from the group. From these needs has evolved social life. Social life is dependent upon cooperation, which means the willingness to subordinate individual freedom to the needs of the group. In this evolutionary process we can observe how submission to the authority of others is demanded, and how pride must give way to humility. The so-called dominance/submission rituals in many mammalian species appear to be examples of evolutionary stages in this development. One can see in the patterns of emotional reactions of the "dominant" and the "submissive," and in their ritualized behavior patterns of fawning on the one side and threat on the other, the seeds of the Contempt/Shame behavior of humans. It is only through a mutually agreed upon resolution of the conflict between the desire for individual autonomy and the equally strong need for cooperation that the social group can survive. It is no accident that *hubris* was for the Greeks the sin most repugnant to the Gods, and that it should again appear in the Renaissance, set in Christian dogma and in Dante's immortal poetry as the deadliest of the seven deadly sins, "*Superbia*, love of self perverted to hatred and contempt for one's neighbour" (Sayers 1955, p. 67).

Our conclusion must be, then, that the Contempt/Shame affect has evolved as the archetypal affect of the Self which assures consciousness of our dependence upon each other for survival, particularly in order that the dependent young and the nurturing mother may be protected. We may ask now just how this is achieved in human society. Here we need recall that the reason for its power to strike dread into our hearts is that it is directed at our innermost sense of self. The contempt we can feel for ourselves when we are in the sudden grip of shame is fathomless; we would disappear into the earth if we could. These effects of Contempt/Shame all revolve around this function it serves in bringing us face to face with ourselves. From this perspective we can see that Contempt/ Shame is an acute evaluative function which finds others or ourselves wanting. When we are contemptuous of others we turn up our noses and then find ourselves alienated; when we experience someone elses, or our own, contempt we hang our heads in shame, and find ourselves alienated. Nothing in the world has such a potential for inducing us to take stock of ourselves and our relationships with others. In the twinkling of an eye, shame can shatter what but a moment before was a comfortable sense of pride in our accomplishments, in our relationships, in our very being. Children are shamed by adults who point out to them the errors of their ways, often in a manner which for the child conveys rejection. How could you *do* that? You know better than that? For shame! Then may follow banishment; go to your room until you can behave! The withdrawal of love, the most potent punishment available to parents, is the ultimate meaning of rejection, and the most powerful stimulus to shame. And in the final analysis it is our own ability to turn contempt, in all its devastating force, upon ourselves which accounts for the desperate efforts made to fend it off, even to the point of choosing death over life. Finally in this dynamic of Contempt/Shame, we discover, surprisingly enough, the basis for a further evolution which has occurred in humans, namely the development of the ego function of feeling. As defined by Jung the feeling function is an evaluative function. It evaluates feelings, that is to say, it evaluates the state of relationships. What do I really feel about this person, this relationship? Is this right for me, or for the family, and the like. As an evaluative function it may be compared with the thinking function. The thinking function evaluates thoughts. The criteria against which the thinking function evaluates is *Truth*, defined as logic, verification, and in life terms, ultimately wisdom. Is there a criteria against which feelings are evaluated? Here we must look to the ideal value which underlies the social domain, namely the *Good*. This is the realm of human ethics and morality. Looked at from the broadcast possible perspective it is evident that society and the social order depend upon a continuing, sustained effort to achieve the best possible synthesis of the desires of the individual and the needs of the group. This human ideal is sustained through the efforts of individuals of good will who struggle to create a social order in which the contending desires for power and love may find an equilibration which maximizes justice and cooperation.

In conclusion then, we are suggesting that not only has the ego function of feeling evolved out of the Contempt/Shame dynamic, but in addition, the highest values which make possible a viable social order are similarly to be found imbedded in that archetypal affect. The end result of the evolutionary process which brought the affects into being in the mammalian species has, in the case of the archetypal affect Contempt/Shame, culminated in the development of psychic functions and cultural forms which have created and continue to sustain human relationships and the societal forms.

Finally it should be noted that the essential difference between Contempt/Shame and the other archetypal affects of Anger, Fear and Sadness is the extent to which self evaluation is involved. Quite simply, as we have seen, Contempt/Shame has to do with relationship, with others and with oneself. To be sure, Anger, Fear and Anguish are mediated by relationships. They inevitably become enmeshed in the web of interpersonal relationships, transformed and intermingled to create such subtle and complex emotions as jealousy, envy, greed, anxiety, depression, as well as respect, admiration, compassion, mercy, reverence and the like. But in contrast to the innate, primal affects, these are affective complexes, the emotions and feelings that develop in the family. On the other hand it is evident that the affect Contempt/Shame has evolved directly as a function of the social needs of the mammalian species.

Summary and Conclusions

Winnicott, the British pediatrician turned psychoanalyst, has suggested that child therapy is essentially completed when the child can play, alone, in the "ordinary" way appropriate to its age (Winnicott 1971, pp. 38, 49–50, 54ff); Jung said that dependence on further analysis was probably unnecessary when a patient could engage in active imagination, alone (Jung 1916, p. 91). From Plato to Schiller to Jung, play and the imagination are praised as the functions of the psyche which lift a human being from the state of "nothing but" into a state of being truly human. If this view is correct, and there is every reason to believe it is, then the wholeness of an individual rests on the readiness and the capacity to play and to engage with the imagination. Conversely, then, what is recognized as pathology is the consequence of the inability or failure to so engage.

Take autism and schizophrenia for example. The primary symptomatology which defines these disorders is the total withdrawal of the libido from ordinary life and human relationships, and its investment in "unconscious" fantasy, which now becomes the "only" reality. Individuals suffering from these disorders live in a "waking" dream. Thus it was necessary for the child Luci to first of all be "held" until she could once again invest the "world" with the archetypal affect of Interest. (See also Jung's case of the "moon lady" above.) This suggests a more precise definition of psychopathology as the inability to move freely from play and the imagination, on the one hand, to curiosity and constructive memory on the other hand; that is from the world of mythical reality to the world of empirical reality, and back again. The individual "lives," so to speak, suspended between the two "worlds." This, as we have suggested earlier on is a consequence of the natural, autonomous dialectic of the Syzygy, as it finds expression in play and curiosity, Eros and Logos, and through which is created self-reflective consciousness.

In these cases of autism and schizophrenia, the withdrawal from the everyday world into the world of unconscious fantasies is initiated by intrusions into the psyche of archetypal affects of the Self, which are constellated presumably, as Jung suggests, by the atmosphere of the family i.e. the unconscious complexes of the parents, and the influence of the zeitgeist. But this is what happens to every child in greater or lesser degree, and if the effects of these intrusions of the unconscious are not transmuted in play and imagination during childhood, they will inevitably find expression in life in one way or another as symptomatology of varying degrees, and, as potentially creative contributions to the collective.

This brings us, then, to consideration of other syndromes and to the experiences of analysis. Everyone who comes for analysis has a unique story to tell, woven of a thousand and one experiences, conscious and unconscious. Somewhere Jung spoke of the patient's story as the "hard rock on which the individual had been broken." That is a graphic image of the state that every analyst knows personally, and which makes it possible to listen empathically and intently to another's story. One of the prime features of every story is a sense of failure, a lack of ability or understanding, a feeling of inferiority, even in the face of obvious success and achievement in the world. Whether the individual shows the symptoms of depression, or anxiety, phobias or obsessions, illusions or delusions, inevitably, at the surface or not far below, there is an accompanying theme of inferiority, or compensating superiority, within which, or against which, all the other symptoms are to be understood, or so it seems to me.

This is the dynamic of inflation/deflation which Jung identified with "godlikeness," and the compensatory "inferiority," that accompanies the assimilation of new knowledge; eating of the tree of the knowledge of good and evil. It is apparent in what he has to say about the knowledge of good and evil that his discussion is relevant to the dynamic of Contempt/Shame as here understood:

> . . . godlikeness evidently refers to knowledge, the knowledge of good and evil. . . . But this same juxtaposition of good and evil can have a very different effect on a different kind of temperament. Not everyone will feel himself a superman, holding in his hands the scales of good and evil. It may also seem as though he were a helpless object caught between hammer and anvil. . . . For without knowing it, he is caught up in perhaps the greatest and most ancient of human conflicts, experiencing the throes of eternal principles in collision. . . . This would be "godlikeness" in suffering. (Jung 1966, pp. 140–41)

Jung proceeds to discuss "godlikeness" in more prosaic psychological terms and suggests that it be called psychic inflation: "The term seems . . . appropriate in so far as the state we are discussing involves an extension of the personality beyond individual limits, in other words, a state of being puffed up" (Jung 1986, p. 143). Reflecting further on this inflation which results from the extension of consciousness Jung notes that:

> This process is such a general reaction that, in Genesis 2:17, eating of the tree of knowledge is represented as a deadly sin. . . . I think that Genesis is right in so far as every step towards greater consciousness is a kind of Promethean guilt: through knowledge, the gods are as it were robbed of their fire, that is, something that was the property of the unconscious powers is torn out of its natural context and subordinated to the whims of the conscious mind. The man who has usurped the new knowledge suffers, however, a transformation or enlargement of consciousness, which no longer resembles that of his fellow men. He has raised himself above the human level of his age ("ye shall become like unto God"), but in so doing has alienated himself from humanity. The pain of this loneliness is the vengeance of the gods, for never again can he return to mankind. He is, as the myth says, chained to the lonely cliffs of the Caucasus, forsaken of God and man (*Ibid.*, p. 156*n*).

One cannot escape recognizing that Jung is no doubt speaking of his own experience as well. But this formulation is applicable to everyone, and to everyones experience, in greater or lesser degree. Let us turn then to the broader spectrum of psychopathology and to the experiences of analysis, keeping in mind the importance of the isolating alienation of Contempt/Shame with its self-reflexive dynamic of conscious humiliation compensated by unconscious arrogance, or vice versa. It is this latter dynamic which appears to be so significant in psychopathology. Why is this? First we must realize that the archetypal affects, in themselves, are not pathological; painful and scourging to be sure, but "normal" occurrences, nevertheless. Moreover, they carry the potentials of our highest human values. It is when these potentials are disallowed that psychopathology appears. And how are these potentials disallowed? Whenever the "atmosphere of the family", and the zeitgeist, invoke archetypal affective instrusions which arise from the unanswered questions of the ancestors.

Take for example Jung's early childhood experiences of the dreaded "Jesuit," and the underground "phallus," the "man-eater." Instinct and spirit are driven apart. And how is this? Because the unanswered questions of the ancestors, carried in the parental complexes, are "shameful" contents for the parents. The dreaded Jesuit was the father's bête noir, and the underground "phallus" was an expression of the mother's contemptuous attitude toward "heathen" images (Jung 1961, pp. 11, 17).

Jung was besieged by these terrifying experiences which dominated his life. They were shameful and threatening experiences which had to be kept secret. And why kept secret? Because he could not have counted on an understanding response from either parent, much as he sought ways to broach the subject with them. During his childhood and early adulthood he found ways in imaginative ritual to transmute to a degree the potency of the "secrets," primarily aspects of the Jesuit experience, through his little "manikin" bedded down with his "soul" stone and "wisdom" scrolls; and subsequent carvings following his recognition of the connection of the soul stone with the Arlesheim cache and the churingas of the Australians when he was writing *Symbols of Transformation* (Jung 1961, pp. 21–23). But the underground "phallus" remained, hidden, and actually lost to memory for years, only to be recovered as the first discovery of his "confrontation with the unconscious," when he began to play again like a child beside the lake. We may surmise that the final transformation of this experience waited on his writing of *Aion, Answer to Job*, and *Mysterium Coniunctionis*, but that is a topic for another time.

In Jung's theory of Analytical Psychology we have the contribution to the collective that sprang from those mysterious intrusions of "religious questions" in childhood, of which Jung said:

> The symbolism of my childhood experiences and the violence of the imagery upset me terribly. I asked myself:
>
>> *Who* talks like that? Who has the impudence to exhibit a phallus so nakedly, and in a shrine? Who makes me think that God destroys His Church in this abominable manner?' At last I asked myself whether it was not the devil's doing. For that it must have been God or the devil who spoke and acted in this way was something I never doubted. I felt absolutely sure that it was not myself who had invented these thoughts and images. (*Ibid.*, p. 47)
>
> These were the crucial experiences of my life. . . . I had been confronted with a problem to which I had to find the answer. And who posed the problem? Nobody ever answered me that. I knew that I had to find the answer out of my deepest self, that I was alone before God, and that God alone asked me these terrible things. (*Ibid.*, p. 47)

The gain for himself in his long, we could say lifelong, devotion to understanding those ideas and giving them a form which spoke to the individual and to the collective, was the experience of wholeness of which he despaired as a child, and again, as an adult following the break with Freud. His discovery of the function of play and active imagination in the individuation process was the touchstone of his work; this continual attention to the relationship of archetypal affect and image, of instinct and spirit. Critical in all this for Jung was the reconstruction of his Religious Attitude which had been shattered in childhood by those unwelcome visitors. How he suffered from this can be seen in many poignant comments about his experiences as a child, as for example in the following:

> My sense of union with the Church and with the human world, so far as I knew it, was shattered. I had, so it seemed to me, suffered the greatest defeat of my life. The religious outlook which I imagined constituted my sole meaningful relation with the universe had disintegrated; I could no longer participate in the general faith, but found myself involved in something inexpressible, in my secret, which I could share with no one. It was terrible and—this was the worst of it—vulgar and ridiculous also, a diabolical mockery. (*Ibid.*, p. 56)

In this context of the prima materia of Jung's life I should like to discuss further the topic of Active Imagination. For Jung it was a technique that was applicable to any of the art forms, drawing, painting, music, poetry, dance, and so on, and, of course, sandplay, which Jung was the first to demonstrate. But it was also a technique of dialogue with autonomous personifications of the unconscious, and perhaps particularly the Anima/Animus personifications. The basic aim, according to Jung, was to give free reign to fantasy while yet retaining a conscious viewpoint. This broad spectrum of experiences, which can include phenomena of the transference as well, is what I recognize as Active Imagination. The grounding place for me now-a-days in this realm of bewildering manifestations is the Syzygy; understood as the archetypal affects of the libido, Joy and Interest, and their dynamisms, Play and Curiosity. This means that there are differences in forms of the imagination at different developmental levels, and on the different planes of the unconscious, such that the symbolic play of childhood "pretend," as in the play therapy with Luci above, is a form of Active Imagination, just as is the experience in analysis when analysand and analyst may be seeking congruence for an image constellated in the transference/countertransference medium, as in the examples Nathan Schwartz-Salant describes (Schwartz-Salant 1986). Analysts may have their individual styles and terminology, and preferences for particular media, but, nevertheless, it is helpful, or so I believe, to be cognizant of the process as an archetypal manifestation of the libido, which fits many media, but which is forever preoccupied with the transformation of the archetypal affects of the Self. These transformations appear in normal development, and in re-creation in analysis, no matter the particular technique, in one or another of the four Cultural Attitudes of the ultimate Self, the Religious, the Aesthetic, the Philosophic, and the Social, and in the fourfold structure of the mandala symbols, or the two fold intertwining of the Tao, Yin and Yang, Luna and Sol, Eros and Logos.

Notes

1. I should like to acknowledge that during the early years of my interest in these subjects I was fortunate to have as collaborator my brother, Charles T. Stewart, the child psychiatrist. It is now sometimes difficult to sort out his contributions from my own, but I take full responsibility for the form in which the ideas are presented here.

2. I also wish to express my appreciation to James Hall for his very thoughtful critique of this paper when I first presented it at the Ghost Ranch Conference of 1986. Hall summarizes his position with respect to the affects as: "structure precedes affect." (In this context he means brain structures [Hall 1986]. Although my emphasis in this paper is less on brain correlates than on other aspects of the archetypal affects and their function in the psyche, I believe that Hall and I are more in agreement than not on this issue. His strong emphasis on structure fits well with my view that the affects are ". . . the bridge between body and psyche, instinct and spirit. They reach back into the physiology of the body, to the chemical processes of the hormones, and neurologically to the areas of the 'mammalian' brain. As for the structural position in general, it seems reasonable to think of Jung, in view of his theory of the complexes, as a "structuralist." The complexes are structures of the psyche which develop on the basis of innate archetypal affective responses to life experiences. But there are structures and structures and it is important, from my point of view, to recognize the developmental nature of such structures as the complexes per se. Prior to these complexes are the innate structures of the psyche, Jung's collective unconscious, which includes the archetypal affects, or so I believe. This I take it is what Hall would like to see explicated in more detail for the sake of clarity, and I welcome this reminder.

I may add that, as I see it, a good deal of apparent disagreement amongst Jungians could be cleared up if Henderson's concept of the Cultural Unconscious were more fully integrated into Jungian thought. For example, Hall speaks of "identity-structures or object-relation patterns" as "triggering" the brain mechanisms that lead to the expression of particular emotions (Hall 1986). If I understand these "identity-structures or object-relation patterns" correctly it would appear that some of them are emotional complexes that are originally structured in childhood within the crucible of the family. Moreover, the complexes, which arise from the structural features of the family, e.g. family constellation and family "atmosphere," make up what could be called the "family unconscious," and, as such, are a fundamental structure of the Cultural Unconscious which "behaves as if it were an aspect of the collective unconscious" (Henderson 1962, p. 9). Of course, all such structures are integrated with the primal, innate archetypal affective structures in the organization of the psyche as a whole (Stewart 1985, 1986 a, 1986 b, 1987).

References

Allan, J. (1986). The body in child psychotherapy. *The body in analysis*. Eds. N. Schwartz-Salant and M. Stein, pp. 145–165. Wilmette, Illinois: Chiron Publications.

Axline, V. (1964). *Dibs in search of self.* New York: Ballantine Books, 1976.

Bachelard, G. (1938). *The psychoanalysis of fire.* Boston: Beacon Press, 1968.

Campbell, J. (1959). *The masks of God: Primitive mythology.* pp. 22–23. New York: The Viking Press, Penguin Books, 1977.

Carroll, P. (1986). War Stories. *Image—San Francisco Sunday Examiner's Magazine of Northern California,* April 13, 1986:28–37.

Darwin, C. (1892). *The expression of the emotions in man and animals.* Chicago and London: The University of Chicago Press, 1965, fifth impression, 1974.

Ekman, P. (1972). Universals and cultural differences in facial expression in emotion. In *Nebraska symposium on motivation, 1971,* ed. J. K. Cole. Lincoln: University of Nebraska Press.

Hall, J. A. (1977). *Clinical uses of dreams: Jungian interpretations and enactments.* New York: Grune & Stratton.

———. (1986). Personal communication.

Heidel, A. (1942). *The Babylonian genesis.* Chicago and London: The University of Chicago Press, 1956.

Henderson, J. L. (1962). The archetype of culture. *The archetype, Proceedings of the second international congress of analytical psychology.* Zurich. New York: S. Karger, 1964, pp. 3–15.

———. (1984). *Cultural attitudes in psychological perspective.* Toronto: Inner City Books.

Hillman, J. (1961). *Emotion, A comprehensive phenomenology of theories and their meanings for therapy.* Evanston: Northwestern University Press.

Izard, C. E. (1977). *Human emotions.* New York: Plenum Press.

Jung, C. G. (1907). The psychology of dementia praecox. *Collected works,* vol. 3, pp. 1–151. Princeton: Princeton University Press, 1972.

———. (1916). The transcendent function. *Collected works,* vol. 8, pp. 67–91. Princeton: Princeton University Press, 1978.

———. (1919). Instinct and the unconscious. *Collected works,* vol. 8, pp. 129–138. Princeton: Princeton University Press, 1978.

———. (1921). *Psychological types. Collected works,* vol. 6. Princeton: Princeton University Press, 1977.

———. (1933). Brother Klaus. *Collected works,* 11. pp. 316–323. Princeton: Princeton University Press, 1975.

———. (1947). On the nature of the psyche. *Collected works,* vol. 8, pp. 159–234. Princeton: Princeton University Press, 1969.

———. (1952). Synchronicity: An acausal connecting principle. *Collected works,* vol. 8, pp. 419–519. Princeton: Princeton University Press, 1978.

———. (1956). *Symbols of transformation. Collected works,* vol. 5. Princeton: Princeton University Press, 1967.

———. (1959a). *The archetypes and the collective unconscious. Collected works,* vol. 9, part 1. Princeton: Princeton University Press, 1977.

———. (1959b). *Aion: Researches into the phenomenology of the Self. Collected works,* vol. 9, part 2. Princeton: Princeton University Press, 1968.

———. (1961). *Memories, dreams, reflections.* New York: Random House—Vintage Books, 1965.

———. (1963). *Mysterium coniunctionis. Collected works,* vol. 14. Princeton: Princeton University Press, 1976.

———. (1968). *Psychology and Alchemy. Collected works,* vol. 12. Princeton: Princeton University Press, 1974.

Kalff, D. M. (1962). Archetypus als heilender faktor. In *The archetype, Proceedings of the second international congress of analytical psychology, Zurich.* pp 182–200. Basel/New York: S. Karger, 1964.

Lynd, H. (1958). *On shame and the search for identity*. New York: Harcourt, Brace.

Masson, J. (1983). *The assault on truth: Freud's suppression of the seduction theory*. New York: Penguin.

Neumann, E. (1973). *The child*. New York: G. P. Putnam's Sons.

Osterman, E. (1965). The tendency toward patterning and order in matter and in the psyche. In *The reality of the psyche*. Ed. J. B. Wheelwright, pp. 14–27. New York: G. P. Putnam's Sons, 1968.

Otto, R. (1923). *The idea of the holy*. Oxford/New York: Oxford University Press, 1981.

Perry, J. (1974). *The far side of madness*. Englewood Cliff, New Jersey: Prentice-Hall.

Petchkovsky, L. (1982). Images of madness in Australian aborigines. *Journal of Analytical Psychology*, 27:21–39.

Piaget, J. (1962). *Play, dreams and imitation in childhood*. New York: W. W. Norton & Co., Inc.

Roberts, J. and Sutton-Smith, B. (1962). Child training and game involvement. In *Ethnology* 1:166–185.

Sayers, D., translation and introduction. (1955). Dante: The divine comedy, II: Purgatory. Harmondsworth, Middlesex: Penguin Books, 1959.

Schwartz-Salant, N. (1966). On the subtle body concept in clinical practice. *The body in analysis*. Eds. N. Schwartz-Salant and M. Stein, pp. 19–58. Wilmette, Illinois: Chiron Publications.

Seneca, L. A. (n.d.) On anger. In J. W. Basore, trans., *Moral essays*. Cambridge, Mass.: Harvard University Press, 1963.

Stewart, L. H. and Stewart, C. T. (1979). Play, games and affects: A contribution toward a comprehensive theory of play. In *Play as context*. ed. A.T. Cheska, pp.42–52. Proceedings of The Association for the Anthropological Study of Play. Westpoint, N.Y.: Leisure Press, 1981.

Stewart, L. H. (1976). Kinship libido: Toward an archetype of the family. In *Proceedings of the annual conference of Jungian analysts of the United States*. pp. 168–182, San Francisco: C. G. Jung Institute of San Francisco.

——. (1977). Sand play therapy: Jungian technique. In *International encyclopedia of psychiatry, psychology, psychoanalysis and neurology*, ed. B. Wolman, pp 9–11. New York: Aesculapius Publishers.

——. (1978). Gaston Bachelard and the poetics of reverie. In *The shaman from Elko*, ed. G. Hill, et al. San Francisco: C. G. Jung Institute of San Francisco.

——. (1981a). Play and sandplay. *Sandplay studies: Origins, theory and practice*. Ed. G. Hill, pp 21–37. San Francisco: C. G. Jung Institute of San Francisco.

——. (1981b). The play-dream continuum and the categories of the imagination. Presented at the 7th annual conference of The Association for the Anthropological Study of Play. Fort Worth, Texas, April 1981.

——. (1982). Sandplay and analysis. *Jungian analysis*. Ed. M. Stein, pp. 204–218. La Salle: Open Court Publishing Co.

——. (1985). Affect and archetype: A Contribution to a comprehensive theory of the structure of the psyche. In *Proceedings of the 1985 California Spring Conference*, pp. 89–120. San Francisco: C. G. Jung Institute.

——. (1986a). Work in progress, Affect and archetype: A contribution to a comprehensive theory of the structure of the psyche. *The body in analysis*. Eds. N. Schwartz-Salant and M. Stein, pp. 183–203. Wilmette, Illinois: Chiron Publications.

——. (1986b). Kinship libido: Shadow in marriage and family. Presented at the 10th International Congress for Analytical Psychology, Berlin (West), September 2–9, 1986.

——. (1987). A brief report: Affect and archetype. *Journal of Analytical Psychology* 32:35–46.

Tavris, C. (198). *Anger: The misunderstood emotion*. New York: Simon & Schuster, Inc., 1984.

Tomkins, S. S. (1962). *Affect imagery consciousness, Volume I: The positive affects*. New York: Springer Publishing Company, Inc.

———. (1963). *Affect imagery consciousness, Volume II: The negative affects*. New York: Springer Publishing Company, Inc.

Winnicott, D. (1971) *Playing and reality*. New York: Basic Books, Inc.

———. (1977). *The Piggle: An account of the psychoanalytic treatment of a little girl*. Ed. I. Ramzy. New York: International Universities Press, Inc., 1979.

An Extended Model of the Infant Self

Joel Ryce-Menuhin

*. . . the evolution of science reflects a basic polarity
in nature itself: a differentiation and integration.*
A. Koestler

Introduction

A. *The Childhood Ego*

Jung saw the psychic development of children as centering mainly
around ego formation within natural growth. He believed the origin of
the conscious ego was the unconscious. "The greatest and most extensive
development takes place during the period between birth and the end of
psychic puberty. . . . This development establishes a firm connection between the ego and the previously unconscious psychic processes, thus

---

Joel Ryce-Menuhin, B. Mus., B. Sc. (Lond.), M. Phil. (Lond.), is a Jungian analyst practicing privately in London. He is a Member of the Independent Group of Analytical Psychologists and a founding Board Member of the Dora Kalff International Society for Sandplay
Therapy. This paper is an excerpt from a book to be published early in 1988 entitled *The
Self in Early Childhood,* 320 pp. illustrated, London: Free Association Press. Mr. Ryce is married to Yaltah Menuhin, the pianist.

separating them from their source in the unconscious. In this way the conscious rises out of the unconscious like an island newly risen from the sea" (Jung 1954).

The archetypes, as organs of the unconscious and possibly bound up with the functioning of the central nervous system, are assumed to be formed before birth when the brain is formed. Jung originally thought that archetypal images in children's dreams and fantasies, because of their adult nature, related to the parents' psychology. But later Jung came to believe that children were expressing their own archetypal images which had an apparently adult character. In *The Development of Personality* (1954) Jung says: "The child's psyche, prior to the stage of ego consciousness, is very far from being empty and devoid of content. . . . The most important evidence . . . is the dreams of three- and four-year-old children, among which there are some so strikingly mythological and so fraught with meaning that one would take them at once for the dreams of grown-ups, did one not know who the dreamer was." And further: "These archetypes of the collective psyche . . . are the dominants that rule the preconscious soul of the child and, when projected upon the human parents, lend them a fascination which often assumes monstrous proportions."

Archetypal images in childhood dreams, play, and fantasy and in their pictures and sandplay are relevent to children themselves. Children unceasingly demand repetition of fairy stories and folk tales. This natural phenomenon represents the activity of archetypes within the child, and has little that is pathological or especially adult about it. It is very hard to eradicate in much parental experience. Jung describes children under the influence of archetypes as preconscious, here designating a state of consciousness in which the ego is very weak. Jung also believed that the images that represent unconscious vitality are high in libido. The general Jungian concept of libido is that this term includes all available psychic energy and does not refer only to sexual energies as in Freudian terminology. These highly energized archetypal images are described by Jung as "numinous." With a more developed or organized ego formation a more strongly coherent and unconscious mind emerges. A progression is postulated from unconscious to preconscious to an organized conscious mind.

In the child, Jung thought that the unconscious and preconscious stages included a primitive identity which he referred to as *participation mystique*. Jung thought that since identity derives at the start from the unconsciousness of the small child, this suggested a non-differentiated state. Without a clearly developed ego, the child cannot distinguish whether events belong to him or to another. All that is felt by the child, in Jung's view, is that someone should be affected by emotional reactions which become infectious to anyone in the vicinity, often involuntarily. The weak ego consciousness does not allow the child to yet say: "I am not reacting as you are because I am not you." The child doesn't know clearly his own ego separateness so this primitive identity enables the unconscious of parents to enter the child's psyche where children act out or interiorly live through the problems of their parents. Thus the concept of ego boundaries is hazy in the early stage of primitive identity and no boundaries of the self are apparent. This is clearly different from later more conscious identification with parents, as a part of cognitive development and of emotional feeling.

In infants, Jung traces libido as manifesting itself initially in the nutritional zone. By sucking, food is drunk with rhythmic movement. Contiguous with the first period of breast feeding there is rhythmic movement of arms and legs. This model of rhythmic movement moves to other functional zones and produces pleasure with sexuality its ultimate goal. Other body openings become an object of interest, then the skin. Rhythmic movements extend to picking, boring, and rubbing. Rhythm may influence the sexual zone and the first attempts at masturbation begin. Jung saw the period from birth to the first clear manifestations of sexuality as the "presexual stage." When the rhythmic activity no longer relates to breast feeding in the nutritional phase, it transfers itself to sexuality.

It is assumed that in the act of suckling and excreting that infants experience various fantasies which they cannot separate out from the physical experience. Jung sees these fantasy systems as preconscious and expressing archetypes. Libidinal zones, on this basis, are seen as preconscious centers of awareness having primitive images that form themselves into the first ego fragments. A linkage between libidinal zones is necessary for differentiated ego functions. These zones or preconscious centers will be described below as aspects of the original self which Fordham has named "deintegrates" which have a tendency to unite as they are derivatives of the archetypes of wholeness.

It is justifiable to set out these arguments as if there were no real parents or real environment because we are discussing the states of awareness of infants. The concept of having parents develops very gradually, as an image, to the baby. They have not appeared within the infant's scene as persons distinctly apart from himself.

Fordham (1957) argues that the development of consciousness in the child violates an original condition of wholeness and postulates a primary integrated state at birth. Although psychologists are ready to recognize that infants' important reactions are total ones of "self reactions" in the undifferentiated but complete sense, the current dichotomous nature of biological and psychological concepts makes it difficult to conceive of a state previous to descriptive units like psyche, soma; self, environment; mind, body; ego, non-ego; conscious, unconscious.

D. W. Winnicott (1953): "Let us assume that health in the early development of the individual entails continuity of being. . . . The early psyche-soma proceeds along a certain line of development provided its continuity of being is not disturbed." Winnicott then insists that a nearly perfect environment for the baby is essential at first. By this, Winnicott merely means that if parents face the conflicts of the baby in a normal way nothing else can go wrong psychically. "Continuity of being" implies a condition of wholeness but Winnicott is speaking of psyche-soma and environment which divides up the self even if the inner-outer fit be perfect. Winnicott's "continuity of being" implies time. Compared to Winnicott's concepts, Fordham's (1957) description, the original self, is theoretically a purer start getting rid of both the psyche-soma-environment duality and of time. The original self has retroactive evidence in that mature persons, when facing difficulties felt to be insurmountable, return to an original condition which can be named the original self or a primal condition of wholeness. Adults may approach this through memory or a regression.

B. Deintegration, Disintegration, Integration

In the development of consciousness, the child violates the original wholeness with a spontaneous division of self into parts. Fordham has proposed the term "deintegration" as a property of the self behind ego formation which is present first. This is distinct from the concept of disintegration, which presupposes an already formed ego which is split into a number of fragments. It explains the difference in Winnicott's and Fordham's view. Fordham sees the self as dividing itself up to form the ego and as being unintegrated or deintegrated from the level of the self until reintegration of the new formation. Winnicott sees a primary unintegrated state based on a viewpoint which is limited to Freudian ego psychology without a self-concept. Kohut (1977) has however put forward a theory of the self contained within a Freudian framework.

The Fordhamian position is that the self cannot disintegrate. Only the ego can be split or even destroyed. The ego integrate then regresses. If the process is at catastrophic level, the ego does not integrate to an earlier level of its history, either because there is not another earlier level available, as may be the case in schizophrenia, or because the disintegration has a high anxiety level which blocks a regression to an earlier ego level. If the disintegration is at complete level, a simpler ego integrate appears naturally and an earlier ego stability is re-established.

In the deintegration hypothesis of Fordham a spontaneous division of the self is proposed. Indirect evidence can be had from various sources. Jung believed that a new concept has certainly been reflected in ancient myths and this can amplify the concept of deintegration. The cosmic creation myths may be a source of parallel ideas to the deintegration theory. In the Orphic cult in Greece we find the cosmic egg as ". . . the symbol of what gives birth to all things and in itself contains all things" (Plutarch, cited in Harrison 1908). And again, "Orpheus likened chaos to an egg in which was the commingling of the primevel elements." Eros sprang spontaneously from the cosmic egg, he ". . . revealed and brought to light everything that had previously lain hidden in the golden egg" (Kerenyi 1951). The process is spontaneous like the deintegration concept.

Jung discusses the scintillae of the alchemists, which he describes as "seeds of light broadcast in the chaos, which Khunrath calls 'the seed bed of the future world'" (1960). Jung sees the scintillae as like the archetypes as he implies the origins of consciousness are in both and scintillae could correspond to "tiny conscious phenomena" and be closely related to the concept of the deintegrates.

How could the first element of consciousness as a formal image arise? We can easily but very incorrectly infer this by taking the image found in small children's circles as the representation of the original self at birth. This is incorrect because the original wholeness is imageless before the first deintegration achieves consciousness in Fordham's theory. Fordham postulates that a deintegrate may be described as a readiness to perceive and act which only enables a correct perception to occur if the object exactly fits the deintegrate because only then is the state of affairs possible where the baby cannot distinguish between subject and object. If the correspondence between object and deintegrate is not exact, it may at first not be perceived, but a tolerance later develops of the object not fitting the deintegrate until the distinction between subject and object dawns upon the infant.

1. The theory of con-integrates.

In the intense object-seeking of the infant I propose that there are seven "con-integrates," a term which I have originated, which are like storage bins for growingly recognizable areas of psychological experience which the ego develops as it separates out partially from the self. The seven con-integrates introduced here are speech, the shadow, the ego-ideal, the aesthetic, play, the persona, and defense-of-the-self. I suggest that the con-integrates can be thought of as huge, unifying, Gestalt-like complexes of de-integrates, conjoined to insure survival through effective performance and perception. It is argued that the con-integrates help clarify a group of very large de-integrated aggregates which re-integrate in special systems of great biological significance.

I wish to underpin Fordham's theory of the de-integrates, which has stated that as the self de-integrates outward to the object the re-integration gives a tendency of unity as re-integrates are a derivative of a wholeness or an original self. This postulates a global theory without any hierarchical postulates or more testable lower levels to consider. In proposing seven con-integrates which develop very early during the first two or three years of the child's development, I am proposing to clarify further what happens when de-integration is re-integrated back after the first ego differentiation from self begins. It is my contention that the seven con-integrates support not only overall psychic wholeness but specifically serve the most urgent developmental needs of the ego.

Why seven con-integrates? I believe the seven discussed below give the best illustration of what a con-integrate is, of what purpose or aim it serves and it restricts the number to be considered to the most essential for an introduction to the theory. There may be more and other theorists who may wish to bring arguments forward for others, or extend the hierarchical levels of the theory further than I shall attempt.

The con-integrates are closely allied in dynamics and structure to ego development; there are seven a priori psychological areas seen very early in childhood which are designated as con-integrates. They are universally present in western children and take precedence over lesser complexes as a linking and supporting part of ego-orientation. The boundaries of con-integrates are permeable to the ego as it re-integrates its de-integrates back for placement within psychological structure. The boundaries of the con-integrates are not permeable to one another. There is no reason to assume that over time brain cellular patterns cannot develop upon these a priori conglomerates, provided they develop normally, but it is postulated that the con-integrates are basically a priori in type and within the structure and process I shall postulate for the self/ego. The shadow, the ego-ideal and aspects of speech involve structurally unconscious components. The other con-integrates are conscious. Where a con-integrate has unconscious structure, it has permeable boundaries both to ego consciousness and to the personal unconscious;

the shadow, technically, also reaches to the collective unconscious (see Figure 1).

Multi-integrates are cognitive developments exclusively dependent on adaptation and reaction including physiological motility and are thought to be consciously built up. In the self-hierarchy multi-integrates stand underneath the con-integrate and are less ego-dependent and ego-related although all the integrates rely to some relative extent on the ego for their function.

Non-integrates are fragmented bits of cognitive material that the self stores in case a match to later input may require their use. If this seems unlikely, non-integrates are pushed out of the self entirely. Thus in this theory I believe there is some material processed through the self that is not retained in memory. Two kinds of memory stores are proposed; the first directly related to the acceptance of material by the ego as it de-integrates out to find a match either in archetypal images from the collective unconscious or in a highly differentiated memory store available to recall and to recognition. The second memory store is a non-differentiated storage of non-integrate material which may be available upon recognition of related bits or aspects of its material. This is not available to immediate recall, at least initially in the first months of life, but is more easily available to recognition.

The psychological areas put forward as con-integrates represent differing structural types in existing theory. They may be archetypes themselves, complexes or functions in existing Jungian theory. But in view of the self/ego re-integrating back distinctive and definite de-integrates, it is maintained theoretically that it is unclear to allow no further differentiation than does Fordham's theory as to possible systems developing around the gradually differentiating ego and essential to its growth. Before proceeding further the ego-self relationship should be redefined.

The term ego is being used here as the seat of consciousness. This concept is based on the theory of the ego's original state as being unconscious at birth or contained within the self as the original totality. Neumann (1954) symbolically describes the original psychic state before the birth of ego consciousness as the Uroborus or the circular image of the tail-eating serpent as a representation of the self or totality out of which the individual ego is born. During the first stage of life the separation of ego from self and their constant re-union shows an emerging ego which retains its primary identity with the self or self-system. The ego processes all incoming input as the free center of the psyche, which can differentiate, store, or reject incoming perception either out of the self entirely or into the personal unconscious as repressed material.

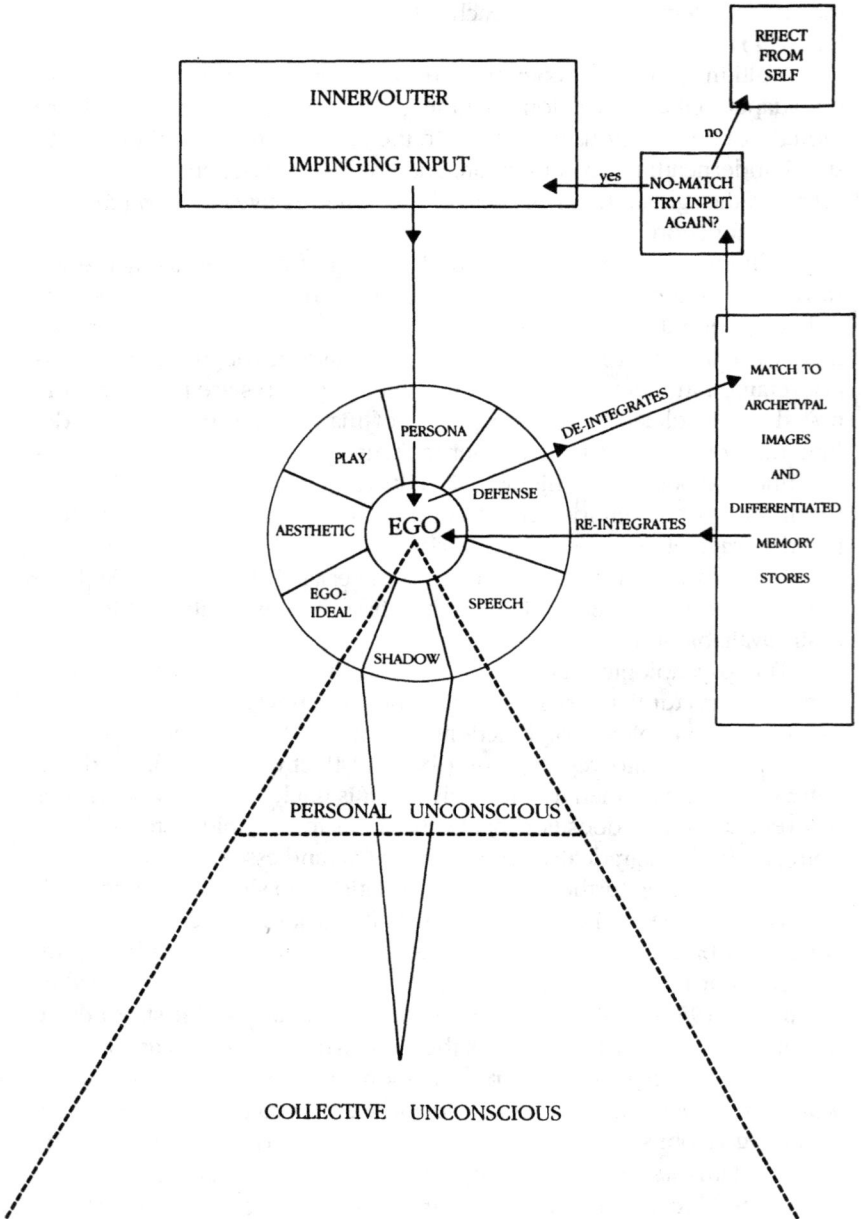

Figure 1. DIAGRAM OF SELF/EGO CON-INTEGRATES

The ego orders and focuses capacities of awareness as the presiding seat of consciousness. This process illustrated in a flow-diagram below is a process which enlarges its own structure as it develops. In elaborating the ego's surrounding structures into a new model, an attempt is made to clarify theoretically the process and its structure of the ego itself, as it separates out from the self. Because the ego can split or be destroyed, it must have a protective system around it, metaphorically like a "cluster" of con-integrates, which separate out and unite incoming stimuli received by the ego into at least seven categories. Where stimuli do not fit these con-integrates, a lower hierarchical level of multi-integrates is proposed and discussed further below. Beyond these postulations one could propose that incoming stimuli not interpreted as con-integrates or multi-integrates would simply re-integrate to the less differentiated portion of the self named as a less differentiated store of non-integrates.

Operationally, the con-integrate has permeable boundaries to the ego but not to other con-integrates except via the ego. Where ego development is noticeably weak or undifferentiated in the child, it is postulated that part of the problem is a too-slow development of con-integrates which defend, delineate, and strengthen the ego and clarify areas of awareness necessary to performance and perception. Con-integrates are both adaptive and interpretative. They coagulate, or bring together, via their permeable boundaries to the ego, the re-integrates of their specific "area" which are fundamental to the early ego growth and its participation in infancy and childhood. It is proposed that, with the exception of the play con-integrate which merges into a play-work content over time, the other con-integrates remain throughout life in their original focus and have in this regard the closest access to ego material and ego process.

2. The flow-diagram of the self/ego system

In the following flow diagram a basic conceptual sketch of the con-integrate system within the self, including the multi-integrate and non-integrate levels, is attempted. The flow-diagram gives a binary and conjectural formulation of how input material may be processed through the archives of the self and its integrates' system of allocation (see Figure 2).

The self/ego system has an Input Control Center (A) in which initial registration of ectophysic and endophysic input occurs. As the ego's task is to focus the capacities of consciousness, the facts and data of the outer ectophysic environment are processed through the same system as the inner endophysic input from the matrix of inner psychic life, e.g. memo-

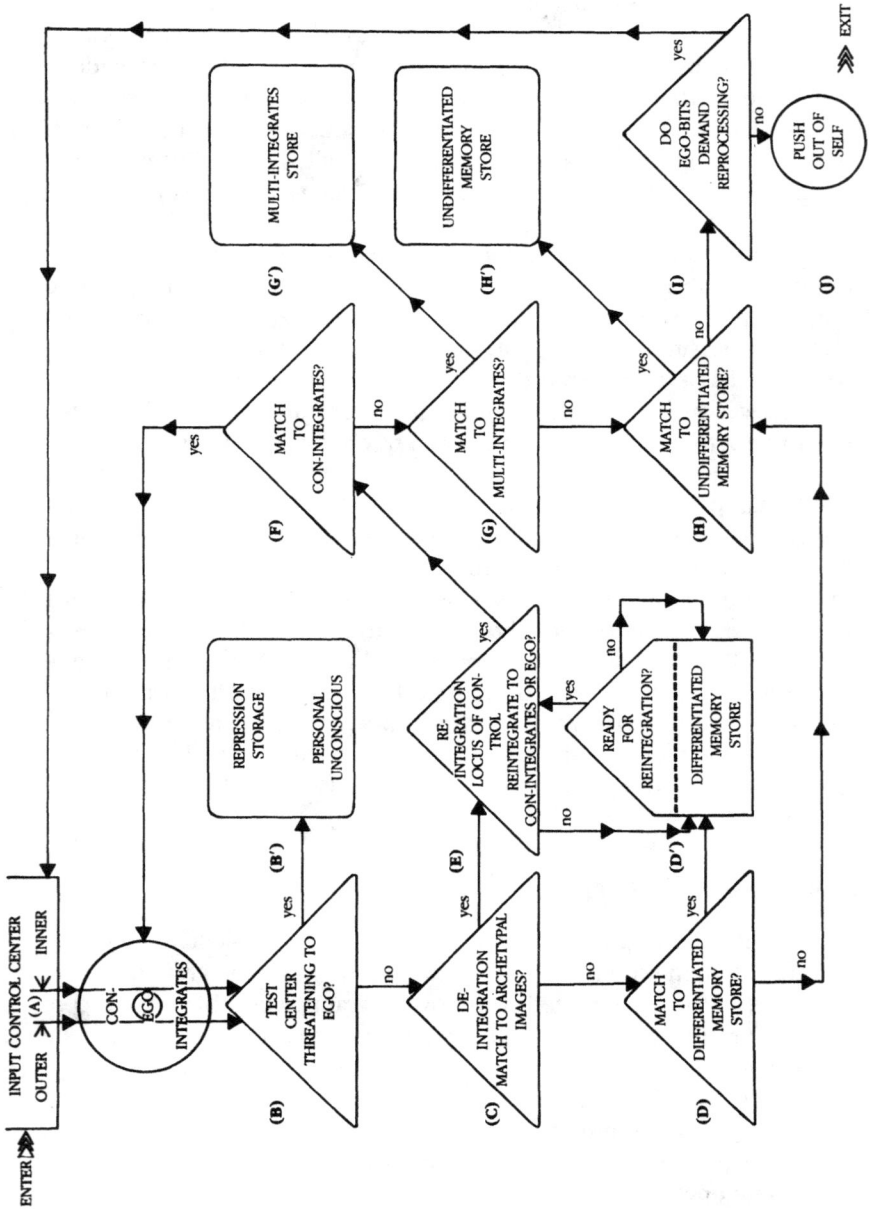

Figure 2. Flow Diagram of the Ego Processes

ries and recollections, affective emotions and the subjective components of conscious functions (thinking, feeling, sensation, and intuition) and invasions from the unconscious. All incoming material passes the Threatening-to-Ego Test Center (B), where contents which are threatening to the function of the self/ego system may be taken from processing into the personal unconscious for enforced storage in the Personal Unconscious Repression Storage (B').

a. Repression

Repression occurs to make inoperative contents which threaten the ego. The ego gives more strength in avoiding pain via repression than to accepting it. This rejection implies that ego development must be sufficiently conscious to resist that which is dangerous to itself and to keep it out of consciousness by relegating it to the personal unconscious. ". . . (Ego) is the mental agency which supervises all its own constituent process . . ." (Freud 1914). As the ego begins to de-integrate and re-integrate, the conscious begins to emerge. "Repression is not a defence mechanism present from the very beginning. . . . It cannot occur until a sharp distinction has been established between what is conscious and what is unconscious" (Freud 1925). The ego, which is in direct contact with the external world during de-integration/re-integration, is adapted to the reception and exclusion of stimuli and is governed by considerations of self-preservation and safety. The ego must also defend itself against overwhelming demands of the internal input, such as threatening instinctual contents of great power from the collective unconscious. The weak and immature ego of the child is particularly vulnerable to external dangers; parents ideally create a security for the child's ego but the child pays for this security by a fear of the loss of love from caretakers which would render him helpless to some of the dangers of the external world. Repression of these security fears often occurs and if ego development lags behind libidinal development generally, the precondition for neurosis occurs. The phylogenetic influences also act on the ego and if very intensified can become intolerably painful and repression is attempted. It is assumed that associative material to the repressed will also be repressed, but the present state of knowledge is less than clear about this. Unpleasant mental content probably covers a wide field, but repression itself is initiated by anxiety that arises from interference with conscience or other means of preserving the parents' love, or interference with the maintenance of self-esteem. Internalization of the primitive threat from parents influences the repression sequence. Culture influences parents' opinions as to what behavior in the child should be punished. Ideas or memories relating to motives that are punished would be what Freud considered unpleasant content that might be repressed.

Early experiments have been full of methodological defects (Sears 1942) but Kline (1972) argues there are some significant exceptions. Wilkinson and Carghill (1955) studied the recall of two stories from dream sequences, one neutral and one containing symbolic Oedipal material. Recall for the Oedipal story was significantly worse. Levinger and Clark (1961) took reaction times and galvanic skin responses to emotive words and to neutral words. Further rotated factor analysis of all variables gives this experiment the quality of irrefutable evidence for repression theory. The multivariate statistical check ruled out response competition as the determining factor of the results although its influence must be estimated, and failure to recall was shown to be related to the emotionality of words. Jung's Word-Association studies (1918) give impressive clinical evidence for the return of the repressed. Subjects when asked to repeat a list of word associations sometimes responded with difficulty, were reduced to silence, changed responses, or were unable to associate again to certain words. Galvanic skin responses were higher for disturbed responses than for undisturbed responses. These indicators of emotionality can be regarded as evidence for the return of the repressed.

Problems with testing repression lie with what the criteria for normal can be; an apparently neutral stimulus might be related, for some persons, to repressed material. Anxiety, as studied in experiments, has not been related to Freud's concept of the specific areas discussed above, which constitute unpleasant content for the ego in relation to repression thresholds. Virtually no repression experiments have been devised for very young children nor does it appear likely that the laboratory can concoct Oedipal or castration wishes or other profound anxieties.

b. De-integrates and archetypes

If the Input (A) is not sent to Repression (B'), it moves to the De-integration Matches (C and D). De-integrates are like islands of consciousness in the sea of the self; they are archetypal predispositions for objects and experiences that activate bits of ego consciousness when they meet and link up. The de-integration process refers to cognitive and conative processes and applies to the entire development of infant, child, and adult. Through the self-ego process system, de-integration and re-integration continually take place and the re-integrated parts of the self-ego become more realized "in terms of flesh and blood, space and time and also have more consciousness attached to them" (Lambert 1981). The ego emerges, through the coming together of the initial pieces of ego consciousness, into a whole ego capacity. The ego can link the archetypal potentialities tested in the model by a match of the archetypal image (C) to a conscious reality, and this forms the internal archetypal self-objects spontaneously. "If we were to ask what the difference is between the original self-integrate and the re-integrated self, after an appropriate series of de-integrations, at the level of maturity suitable for the stage of life that has been reached, we could describe it in terms of content" (Lambert 1981). At birth, the infant's primary self-integrate is a conglomerate restricted to archetypal potentiality and nothing else. But at later development stages the ego-center makes coherent not only archetypal potential but archetypal images not yet fully experienced as well as archetypal internal objects fully identified by the ego.

Re-integration begins to occur if an archetypal match is made at (C) and the content moves to (E), the Re-integration Locus of Control, for further processing. Where a direct archetypal match is not made, the Differentiated Memory Store (D) is searched in case associated differentiated material be stored there and indicate that integration to the ego-integrates is possible. If the content is less-than-ready for the integrates, it remains stored (D'); otherwise the differentiated material is sent for re-integration (E). If the content does not find any match in (D) at all, it is sent to a secondary memory store, the undifferentiated memory store (H') where it is matched to any fragmented ego-bits it may contain or include. It is stored there or sent back through the whole system for rechecking if at (I) the identified ego-bits demand reprocessing. If no ego-bits are identified, the content is pushed out of the self-ego system (J). Before discussing the integrate-system (E,F,F',G,G',H,H') further, I wish to elucidate the difference between the two memory stores of the system, the differentiated (D') and undifferentiated (H') stores.

c. Memory stores

The critical difference between the differentiated memory store and the undifferentiated store is that the latter only stores non-integral ego-bits of information, not yet in a form suitable for recall but readily available to recognition where the original stimulus is present. In the absence of the original stimulus, recall involves an ego-oriented process in order to generate reconstruction within memory search and its verbal correlates. Recall develops much later in infants than recognition, which Friedman (1972) tested at only a few days of age in babies. As quite substantial development is required for the ego's role in recall and the differentiated memory storage (available also to recognition, but recall from the non-integrate undifferentiated storage would be expected to be poor or even non-existent), it comes as a support for the self-ego model that recall is present only after one year of age (Piaget and Inhelder 1973). It is only then that the ego-oriented differentiated memory store could develop as a function and as a growing structure. Here I lean on Gottlieb's (1970) model for recall which assumes that there are "reciprocal effects in the relationship between structure and function whereby function can significantly modify the development of the structures that are involved in the events." Gottlieb admits structural development is probabilistic against a norm but argues it is unique to each child's endogenous and exogenous stimulation. For fostering and channeling prenatal physio-anatomical growth, the stimulative events that determine the sequence and outcome of prenatal behavior are: 1) presensory mechanical agitation, 2) interoceptive stimulation, 3) proprioceptive stimulation, 4) exteroceptive stimulation, 5) neurochemical stimulation, and 6) musculoskeletal effects of use or exercise.

Gottlieb (1970) reports supporting experimental evidence from chick and duck embryo studies and from experiments on unborn kittens and guinea pigs. In chicks, movements are required from the embryo's own skeletal muscles to create articulated cavity formation and the sculpturing of cartilaginous surfaces. In duck embryos prenatal responses to strong flickering light enhances electrical responses at the retina, telencephalon, and the optic lobe. Hormones injected prenatally can alter the sex direction of male chicks and guinea pigs. If structure were unidirectional, the structure would continue to determine function blindly and simply throw off these manipulative exogenous stimulations. Gottlieb's bidirectional structure-function hypothesis assumes reciprocal effects: that function can modify development of both peripheral and central structures.

Ego development is not an invariant course of development but is reactive to stimulational developmental factors at all of its stages. This tallies with the integrate-theory in that recall would be available as ego-growth permits a wider scope of differentiated storage to occur and be accessible. Both recognition and recall depend on acquisition and retention of information and both involve a match-decision process. Recall needs additional processing such as complex encoding skills, linking stimulus items, elaboration, generative representation, verbalizations, etc. These processes are facilitated in the self-ego model in that the check with the differentiated memory store comes first before integrate-matches and the secondary non-integrate store are reached. Of course, the process remains slower in recall than recognition because of its complexity and later partly because of the huge storage in the differentiated store.

Recognition failure of recallable words (Tulving and Thomson 1973) has been claimed: however superior recall was only found in testing recall in the presence of contextual clues, but recognition was not so tested. This experiment is really a test of recognition more than a test of recall as contextual clues contain the presence of partial stimulus. Tulving admits that his free- and forced-choice experimental designs bring problems underlying his procedure that are unknown. Light and Carter-Sobell (1970) argue that recognition tests should include a control of the semantic aspect; retrieval would need to be tagged the exact way a noun is used. "Squash," for example, would be tagged in several ways; squash, the noun, as a sport or as a drink, and as the verb, "to squash."

In the self/ego model recognition would take perceptual input directly to each memory store; with recall it is assumed that self-generated representations requiring an independent ego integration are matched with memory representation and that this is principally linked to the differentiated store under normal circumstances.

In psychopathology the undifferentiated store of non-ego material may flood verbalization as in the "word-salad" of full-blown schizophrenia. The differentiated store where recall may evoke a full impression—in the absence of a model—that an object or event has been experienced or perceived at a prior moment in time, requires symbolic representation. Such internalized images are dependent on a healthy ego for the correct mnemonic process of recall involving figurative knowledge under a mnemonic referent. Obviously ego-damage seriously impairs the control of mental imagery and language, so here too a "word-salad" may develop in psychopathology from the differentiated store.

The original healthy ego re-integrates a sufficiently whole image or clear mnemonic referent to differentiate integrate-memory back into language in the process of recall I would argue that it is the role of the ego and its memory storage as an integrate (differentiated store) or a non-integrate (undifferentiated store) that is the initial criterion for the structure and function of storage.

Perlmutter and Lange (1978) report that two-year-olds are sometimes better than adults in recognizing old items presented again. Recognition involves, on the self/ego model, the quick scan of both memory stores. In the two-year-olds' life the differentiated store is still rather empty, which could explain their speed in recognition scan. Later the differentiated store is very full but improvement in encoding strategy via rehearsal would enable test results almost to equal out up to middle age. Recognition rarely improves much with age; that points significantly to the early availability in the first year of non-integrate memory—bits which the self/ego system scans as strategy and practice during the gradual tuning-in of the ego-integrate differentiated storage which becomes active at about one year. This postulation of memory stores within the self/ego model can assimilate the theoretical dual-process information models (see Kintsch 1970, Klatzky 1975) and Piaget's intelligence-dependent developmental memory model.

d. Re-integration and the Integrates

If contact reaches the re-integration (E) center it is first matched to the con-integrate prototypes (discussed at length in the next section). The seven con-integrates are closest to ego-identity and process and they have first choice of assimilating the material which the self/ego de-integrate accepts into re-integration. The con-integrate builds up residues and implications from ego-direction as it balances, directs, and processes the inner and outer impingement which re-integrates into the con-integrates' nature of function. All con-integrates are intrinsic to the infant's need to interpret experience and they incorporate the infant's most ego-related needs.

Ego re-integrates that do not belong to the con-integrates move to the multi-integrate match (G). These are conscious bits of self which fall outside the con-integrates but which the self-ego can use progressively and developmentally. They cohere in the principal sensory, perceptual, and motility systems. Multi-integrates might be the cognitively and conatively developed areas when very complex, like the learning of a second language and other skills requiring combinations of integrates secondary to the con-integrates and beneath them hierarchically among the integrates. It is outside the task of theory at the level of the con-integrates to comment further on multi-integrates. They deserve separate empirical study.

Where no multi-integrate match is made, content is matched to the undifferentiated memory store (H). It remains there should it contain sufficient ego-bits for retention. If not it is checked at (I) for a repeat processing through the self/ego system if any ego-bits are identified in the content at this last check point; if not sent back for reprocessing, the content is pushed out of the self/ego system altogether (J).

The binary-process scheme is an efficient descriptive method for imaging these processes and was introduced to clarify my model of the self-ego and its integrate system. The entire system is dependent on the ego as a growing locus of control within and relative to a self that integrates its a priori archetypal configurations against the endophysic and ectophysic real ties of the infant's psychic life. This model has the advantage of being suitable for all developmental stages in the life of the self-ego and its emerging consciousness through its match-storage system. It has parsimony in its model-construction of great economy, and I could not discover a simpler conceptual framework that will integrate the extraordinarily complex data, i.e., everything a person can relate to and integrate into himself or herself at any stage of life.

3. Description of the Con-integrates

The seven con-integrates will be defined and described with reference to the self-ego relationship that begins in infancy.

a. Speech

With the influx of tape recording and videotaping, the analysis of linguistics and acoustics has assumed vast proportions. Details of the infant's approach to speech have never before been so fully documented. Much of this work is reported for its own sake; some of it is related to theory. The overall quality of experimental work in the last two decades emphasizes the sense of utterances as more important than their form to the infant child. Work has often centered on distinguishing speech sounds in terms of phones, phonemes, distinctive features, phonological rules, and intonation. These are the elements usually classified in the scores of recent publications on language development in children.

Some of the valuable discoveries in this literature relate to the development of speech perception in the very young baby. In work by Eimas *et al.* (1971) one-month-olds were discovered to have categorical perception of phonemes. This is well before the child begins to approximate speech sounds in babbling, usually placed at three to four months. By ten to fifteen months some words are intelligible and after age two there is more evidence reported by the de Villierses (1978) that the correct reproduction of distinctive features on their own as a learning device becomes important to children at this time. Studies on deletion and substitution which are based on later babbling suggest that in its last stages babbling is already partially governed by restrictions similar to those of the phonological development in early words. Between two and four the child learns a rather limited scope of grammatical rules using agent, possessive and locative. Simple two- or three-term propositions are first mastered and then shades of meaning, signaled by grammatical morphemes, are added in a realtively stable order.

The relationship between a child's world-knowledge, intentions to communicate, and early word-strings is a difficult study. The boundary line between the sense in which the child may have an idiosyncratic linguistic category in his head and its similarity/dis-similarity to the generally accepted system of the category is difficult to judge or delineate. Experts argue over early semantics in child language. Bloom (1973) believes the child's correct use of words like "this," "more," and "all gone" means children understand the semantic relations involved (nomination or existence, recurrence, and nonexistence). On the other hand, Braine (1976) believes the semantic status of such terms is narrower in child's grammar than in adults. He points to the groping patterns of early speech and suggests children express a meaning before they learn word position in linguistic strings. Both Nelson (1976) and Rosch (1973) point out that the exemplars of nouns such as "cat" or "chair" may share some physical features, but a search for common features among all proper exemplars fails and leads to null sets. This suggests that the child searches for semantic meanings, not physical elements of syntax, and that core meanings, feeling, function, and experience combine into prototypically organized experiences in which core meaning is lodged. Further experience then elaborates this. Language enables the child to demand, to question, to blame and to deny. The de Villierses (1978) believe children comprehend more information than they can express in language at first, and that they use conceptions of events that are based on stored information as to what is likely in a situation and what is expected of them.

Condon and Sander (1974) report the results of a decade of films of neonate and caretaker taken during the first hours of life. Their interest is the connection between linguistics and kinesic body movement. Condon hypothesizes that the neonate moves synchronously with adult speech as early as the second day of life. Body motility is seen as partly growing out of sound patterns around the child as well as its well-documented relation to touch. Film was analyzed in 1/6th of a second "units" and a self-synchronous rhythm-hierarchy in babies' motility characteristic of human speech behavior was discovered. The unit is a segment in which several body parts will sustain whatever direction or speed in which they are moving for brief duration. This reveals a behavioral "mode" that contrasts with previous and following "bundles" of speech-movement. This may be characteristic of all nervous systems. A listener moves synchronously with a speaker in an "entrainment." In videotaping infants from twelve hours to two weeks of age, the stimuli used were an adult speaker and audiotapes of English, Chinese, vowel sounds, and tapping sounds. Precise synchrony of infant movement with the articulatory structure of adult speech was discovered.

The infant, by moving into the organization of his cultural speech structure, gains a huge number of repetitions of linguistic forms before he uses them in speech. The neonate participates immediately in communication from the first day of life through entrainment of body movement to environmental speech patterns. This behavioral evidence suggests that entrainment to speech may be innate and that a con-integrate is developing within the self/ego from the first or second day of life. It could only become delineated with the ego's own development.

The use of continuity in early child language suggests the early participation of the ego. "She came it over there" was a sample from a child's use of "come" while watching a dog take a piece of food into the next room (Bowerman 1974). This child had always used "come" with a meaning "move." She thought it could also mean "cause to move" by hypothesizing that it might operate as "walk" in "the dog walked" and "the man walked the dog." Children tend to build on what they already know. Early objects are usually named only after they are noticed, picked up and studied. This choice of objects suggests the ego is involved in naming objects and that language has the formation of a con-integrate in close relation to ego-object delineation from the first weeks of life.

E. Clark (1978) has traced the use of continuity and hypotheses in the development of deictic terms which in person-deixis involves "I," "we," "you," or "they." Deixis relates to objects with locatives or demonstratives like "here" or "that." The study of deixis also includes place, movement and cause. Gestures start off and are built into directives in language by children in a series of developmental stages. The learning of "here" or "there" is dependent on the ego's separation from the outer object or speaker in order to comprehend where the point of view originates. This is essential within deictic language.

Personal interaction and the shyness of a child dynamically affect the way linguistic ability develops. Language is closely related in its idiosyncratic development to the complexity of ego-needs and the way these are met in the child linguistically. The speech con-integrate develops in the early weeks of life and continues as a principal mode of expression throughout life. The speech con-integrate is postulated as indispensable, important to ego-object separation and as taking to itself all the linguistic signals for cognitive development that it can. The large area of the left hemisphere usually used for much of speech development shows its great biological significance. For the self to utilize its complete sphere of ego-consciousness, speech becomes enormously important to the self-expression of ideas as information and as theory.

b. Ego-Shadow

C. G. Jung designated the shadow generally as a principal archetype in the collective unconscious and also as the repressed material in the personal unconscious. To avoid confusion, my term Ego-Shadow relates not to all repressed material but to repression intimately connected to the ego itself and particularly to the birth of the ego. On the flow-diagram model above (Figure 2), this material would be automatically repressed by the Threatening-to-Ego repression center and then that material most closely related to the stage which ego-development had reached would be filtered into the Ego-Shadow con-integrate for unconscious storage of ego material. This process which is unconscious is not shown in the model diagram itself. I insinuate it here. The ego would control release of Ego-Shadow material in projection as it becomes tolerable to the ego from its conscious standpoint.

I put the Ego-Shadow into self theory as a con-integrate because repression is present in the baby as he de-integrates out from the ego to incoming phenomena, tries a match to the archetypal level to achieve re-integration into the self, and may quite early on begin to project the repressed material of the personal unconscious which is specifically relegated to the Ego-Shadow con-integrate onto his growing conscious ability to tolerate a mismatch between ego/self and de-integrates. This toleration prevents distintegration and I believe all babies would experience disintegration without a repression system for ego protection. For example, we can consider that at the moment the mother stops a breast feed, the infant may cry in rage having no cognition that he will get another feed later. Eventually he may be able to repress the anxious feeling as the nipple is withdrawn, or as he spits it out, and this repression into the Ego-Shadow con-integrate may enable him to tolerate the wait between feeds *prior to a cognition* that he is in a secure feeding schedule. In this way the Ego-Shadow would be serving the need of ego-development and preventing disintegration from the first days of life. Repression can initially serve a positive role to increase the child's toleration of delay in meeting immediate ego-needs and to help delineate the curious or de-integrating "I" from a fearful and anxiously repressed nature. The shadow as an over-all term contains all the non-conscious aspects of personality over time from both collective and personal levels of the unconscious and can only be measured in its projections. When a child begins to play, he can project good and bad repressions onto toys or the play situation, enabling child therapists to catch glimpses of unconscious material.

Where there is a birth trauma through late or difficult delivery, oxygen problems or surgery directly after parturition, the shadow itself as a whole and the Ego-Shadow as a prefiguration in the con-integrate system can protect the birth of the ego out of the self by repressing and containing birth traumata so that something like normal ego development can begin. There may be a birth-archetype which would coordinate other elements of the fight-for-life outside the womb in the baby. Birth traumata bear a relationship to psychic life whether they remain unconscious or are later raised to consciousness.

The ego separates out gradually from the self until the child no longer refrains from saying "I," drawing "me," or acting out "myself" in play. However difficult a problem the general shadow may be in the personality of adult life, the Ego-Shadow as a con-integrate is indispensably helpful to the initial survival of the ego-complex in infancy as it begins to separate out from its initial fusion with the self. As the child's ego gains in stability and range the Ego-Shadow con-integrate functions when inhibitions and repressions, especially close to the ego, occur.

c. The Ego-Ideal

The Ego-Ideal con-integrate is conceptually based on Freud's super-ego but, it is argued, takes effect earlier in the child's life than Freud postulated. Freud believed the super-ego to be the residues of the earliest object choices of the unconscious and not formed until the resolution of the Oedipus complex in the child. It was derived from a transformation of the child's earliest object-cathexis by identification with the object and introjection with it. Freud did not realize that it could be formed before the resolution of the Oedipal complex because he conceived of the super-ego as partly a reaction formation against the Oedipal complex. But an earlier formation of ego-ideals in infancy is in no way dependent on a reaction formation to Oedipal or Elektra complexes. The existence of narcissism in infants before the ego is differentiated enough to risk non-narcissism suggests an early identification with the lengthy childhood helplessness and dependence of self/ego upon parents or caretaker and the beginning of a permanent expression to the influence of the parents. The Ego-Ideal even if it does begin with the mother and her nutritive role normally includes the father at a very early stage. There is no reason to assume that the feminine and masculine side of environmental influence on the infant do not begin almost at once in the infant from the atmosphere of the caring situation forward. This is particularly true now that fathers are tending to take a more active role with babies from their birth (Parke 1979).

The Ego-Ideal gives a "permanent expression of the influence of the parents . . ." (Freud 1927). In the young child this spreads to include the influence of siblings and older relatives and friends of the household. Whatever personal evocation of the parents that archetypal development enables a child to have, much happens psychologically as this influence moves into the development of external personality traits. "We know that the loss of the mother (without adequate substitute) during the first year of the child's life can lead to death, severe deteriorization and psychotic disturbances, whereas if the loss occurs after a normal primary relationship in the earliest developmental period the chances of the child's healthy development are much more promising even if he becomes ill" (Neumann 1959).

Jung maintained that the real mother evokes the mother archetype in the psychic structure of the child and that this can function independently of the mother's reality as a compensating psychic reality. The same would be true for the instigation of a father archetype. Both archetypes would make secure the ego-self relationship achieved in a successful primary relationship (usually to the mother, but possibly to a maternal father). If the primary relationship is the basis for security, nourishment and containment in the long dependency of the baby on its caretaker, then the Ego-Ideal has ample time to develop as a con-integrate. It would influence the regulation of development within the child's psyche, between him and other individuals and later between him and society. In childhood, the overall intrapsychic development can be described as an initial "interdependence of ego and self, conflict between ego and self, growth of ego and consciousness out of the unconscious and conflict between ego consciousness and the unconscious as a result of increasing independence" (Neumann 1959).

At every stage the Ego-Ideal must be developing in its hierarchical, conservative, and authoritative influence on the ego. Freud was very defensive in his arguments about the Oedipal situation and the super-ego and he overlooked the realization that ego-ideals were developing much earlier and that this influences the child's ego in the first year of life.

It is proposed that the con-integrate of the Ego-Ideal begins its long development early in the infant's development through the discipline and learned strictures of behavior from the parents or caretakers and continues to operate with modification, throughout life.

d. The Aesthetic

The aesthetic appreciation of the beautiful has been documented by C. W. Valentine in *The Experimental Psychology of Beauty* (1962). The bulk of the statistical summaries referred to children over the age of four and is just outside the age-range considered here, although the individual case material involving Valentine's children is very helpful. It is a part of common experience to hear children of two, three, and four years of age show a recurrent use of the word "pretty" when referring to flowers and pictures. This showed up in Valentine's child "Y," who took Binet's Faces Test (see Burt 1921) and always showed preference for "pretty" faces. Burt found when using the Binet test that 33% of three-year-olds chose the "pretty" face in each of three pair-choices presented, 67% of four-year-olds did so, and 91% of the five-year-olds. The criteria for "prettiness" would be widely debated today. Was Binet simply measuring "average" types of faces against "non-average" which the children responded to as "like" or "unlike" their normal daily environment? Was Binet measuring evenness of photogenic facial features as against unevenness?

Spontaneous verbal description showing feeling for aspects of the aesthetic may be a truer indication of the aesthetic in the very young. Wilhelm Stern in his *Psychology of Early Childhood* (1924) reported that his daughter "L. E." at four years and four months said: "Who has made the dish so beautiful—just like a picture? How nice it looks—apples and vine leaves, you see yellow below and green above."

It is important in arguing that the development of aesthetic discernment should be a con-integrate to establish that the aesthetic dynamic is closely related to the growth of ego-consciousness. To get to the stage where children can abstract themselves from their needs and experience pure will and self-control while making aesthetic choices involves previous developmental processes (Abenheimer 1968). In the early oral phase of development, related to needs for being fed, protected, touched, comforted, and brought into some sort of dialogue with caretakers (in vision, sound, holding and playing), the less good responses the baby experiences make it exhibit defenses. Self-awareness begins as the need for survival and help. In the anal phase that follows, the Freudian school believes that in the conscious expulsion of feces the infant becomes aware of his own power. The omnipotence that results is neurotic. It becomes non-neurotic when the infant can show aggressive power without needing to feel omnipotent and achieves another development of flexible self-awareness. A third level of self-awareness, essential to aesthetic experience, comes out of the oral and anal phases. It occurs when a child can abstract himself under pressure of needs or dangers with self-control, in an authentic self, as the agent of controlled will.

An ultimate essence of all aesthetic experience has been described by Worringer (1908) as the need for self-alienation. He means that in the sense that the contemplation of the aesthetic takes the self away for a time from the problems of existence and its dangers. At the same time, there is a bi-polar quality in aesthetic experience. It requires empathy, which can objectify self-enjoyment and is a self-affirmation as well as requiring the capacity of self-alienation. In empathizing our will into another object (art, music, nature, etc.) we absorb outself into the outer object with our urge to know it and accept, momentarily, its fixed boundaries. These boundaries limit the usual ongoing differentiation of individual needs and a self-alienation occurs. "In empathy . . . I am not the real I, but am inwardly liberated from the latter . . ." (Lipps 1903).

As the ego builds itself through the de-integration/re-integration process, it reaches a level of function where it can afford to fuse temporarily with an object of aesthetic pleasure and thereby gain distance through alienation not only from the ego but from the self-defenses. In what is felt as an empathetic ego fusion to the object, we are witnessing an ego-choice which is a self-affirmation in terms of need or taste, but a technical self-alienation in terms of the intensity with which the ego merges "into" the chosen aesthetic object. In the development of ego-consciousness the child seems to experience two directions simultaneously. "On the conscious level he goes on developing even finer differentiations among the appearances of the real things around him, while in his unconscious fantasy life he undoes even the most fundamental differentiation of commonsense reality and so creates images that cannot have any possible correlate in rational thought" (Ehrenzweig 1967). Both of these developmental aspects, conscious and unconscious, play into the aesthetic experience which involves a fine conscious choice and differentiation as well as the projection of unconscious image.

Aesthetic experience is paradoxical in its combination of objectified self-enjoyment and a temporary self-alienation in the urge to abstraction and fusion outside the self and its normally fixed ego boundaries. The aesthetic experience is a con-integrate because of the accumulation of these experiences which began in early childhood and because of the particular relationship the aesthetic has to ego development and temporary separation from total control of the self. The feedback of the aesthetic can reflect upon the significance of the self and facilitate its authentic realization. The aesthetic builds ego-consciousness, which contains "its enabling awareness and consciousness, its focus of perception and its factor of mediation between itself and the environment within and without" (Lambert 1981).

e. Play

Play is a universal element of childhood. Play is a concept on its own not reducible to any one socio-psychological view of the universe or to any one stage of civilization. The play element has existed in all cultures and in all known historical periods. It may be described as a supra-biological form through which society expresses its interpretation of life and the world (Luria 1966). Why is play civilizing? The play element introduces certain rules and the concept of fair play into civilization. This enables civilization to presuppose limitation and some mastery of the self which gives persons the ability to understand that personal conduct within any civilization must remain within certain freely accepted bounds. A general characteristic of play is tension and uncertainty. "Will we win? Will it come off?" are conditions of uncertainty fulfilled in card games or football, in crosswords or archery, in shaking a rattle or reaching for one's toes. In the play world if the rules are transgressed, the whole play world collapses. In the same way, nations go to war if the currently accepted lawful rights of national sovereignty are overstepped.

Play has been considered both as a physiological phenomenon and a psychological reflex. These approaches overlook an aspect of "at playness" in play that imparts meaning to action. The fun of playing is rarely measured when experimenters view play as quantitative. In some types of play, biological functions are to be seen. A biological approach assumes play must serve something which is not play. Theories about this mention the need for abreaction, for outlets of harmful impulses, for wish-fulfillment, and for a means to bolster the feeling of personal value. This may involve the release of extra energy through imitation, experimentation, assimilation, and competition.

The contrast between play and seriousness is a fluid one. For the very young child, serious play was thought by Vygotsky to mean that the child was not separating the imaginary situation from the real one. In this way aspects of play are irrational. Tension and its solution are often present in play. A game can represent a contest or it may become a contest for the best representation of something. Both Luria (1966) and Piaget (1951) agree that play is the leading source of development during pre-school years.

In viewing play as a con-integrate it is important to note how useful play is to early ego-strengthening. The child both pretends and tries to master adult situations through accommodation to the external situation and assimilation of experience into meaning. Play is an activity occurring before a behavior is fully organized, suggesting that aspects of ego-development are at an under-developed stage. Play can be a preparation for life via the realization of the environment that it can demonstrate, as a repetition of experience, and as the communication of symbolic fantasy. Symbolic play is assimilative in that it organizes thinking in terms of symbols and images already partly mastered. The child's ego-centric position during symbolic play enables him to make a transition over time to a more and more accurate representation of reality. As the child is more adapted, play becomes constructive and eventually the child very gradually plays less by himself or herself after entering the arena of school life (Millar 1968).

The idea that play may be an antidote to under-stimulation or boredom suggests that the building of more ego-experience is needed within an optimal amount of stimulation. But the concept of optimal stimulation has a wide application, given the great variation in individual babies' metabolic and environmental stimulation levels. Both in its inner and outer reality for the child, play constantly challenges the ego through its directedness, concentration, and release of another form of play or non-play activity. Play is very much the child's own private ego-directed world and as such a strong conglomerate integrated very early around the ego.

As the child grows, he learns through play's zone of proximal development: the imaginary is often near to the memory of the real, and voluntary intentions may combine with the formation of real-life plans and volitional motives. In creating imaginary situations abstract thought develops. These abstractions, when expressed as rules, lead to the understanding of rules and the later division between work and play at school age. Play is a preamble to work.

In the young child there are many unrealizable tendencies and desires. Under age three, the infant wants immediate gratification. Play can be said to be invented at the point when the unrealizable tendencies appear in development. What interested the infant no longer interests the toddler. The transitional nature of play is described by Piaget as an intermediary between the situational constraints of early childhood and play ideas free of an actual situation. In game rules, the child can set the rules by himself free of the one-sided influence of an adult or make rules he jointly establishes with his parents. Freely chosen game rules include both self-restraint and self-determination. The ego is being relativized and has a close developmental relationship to the play-con-integrate.

f. Persona

Jung defines the persona as "a function-complex which has come into existence for reasons of adaptation or necessary convenience, but by no means is it identical with the individuality. The function-complex of the persona is exclusively concerned with the relation to the object . . ." (Jung 1960). Throughout the stages of life one adapts one's persona constantly to pressures of the environment and of one's own evolving value system. Persona is "a psycho-physical attitude that mediates between the inner and outer worlds, a kind of mask we develop to maintain a relatively constant or consistent front to the outside world, through which those we meet may relate to us fittingly" (Jacobi 1976).

Where in early childhood do we see signs of adaptation that are reflected in external behavior? The infant's early persona is immediately involved with smiling. Ende and Harrison (1972) measured this to be at a rate of 11 times in every 100 minutes. They related this to internal arousal state or a change of state and to recognizable EEG patterns. The social smile appears in the third week when a mechanical noise no longer elicits a smile as well as a human voice does and as eye-to-eye contact begins to further alter smiling patterns (Macfarlane 1975), I would argue that the first almost embryonic appearance of a persona in the baby begins with his use of the social smile, at first unconsciously, and later very consciously and manipulatively Schaffer (1971) argues that reciprocal behavior, which would involve the baby's use of cognition and a conscious persona, begins at the very end of the first year of life. Reciprocal intentional signaling to the mother requires comprehension of the difference between self-behavior and the behavior of the other and some awareness of feedback from self-produced behavior. Feedback also requires the ability to anticipate the outcome of behavior from past memory and to regulate responses in relation to this feedback.

The close connection with ego development is obvious if the persona helps the signaling processes and enables the child to begin to test details of his behavior against the feedback received from caretakers. Although the persona is very gradually socially developed during early childhood, it becomes such an important aspect of adult behavior as to give it sufficient force to be a con-integrate from the beginning of infancy. Behavioral studies have tended to quantify measures of smiling, crying, eye movements, and the like without picking up the idiosyncratic differences within these modes in individual children as their persona develops and acts to alter their manner of appearing and doing. Families mold persona so individually that by the time the child enters school he or she will need a major change of persona adaptation towards the group. The persona's adaptive function deals with incoming stimulation in a principal way from very early life and is, I believe, a con-integrate in its great influence upon the ego's role in behavior and style of response throughout life.

g. Defense of self

Self-defense as a con-integrate refers to the ways the infant can defend the self constellation psychologically. This is particularly dependent on the early sources of security and competence and of ego-defense. A study of how personal relationships begin in childhood suggests that they are dependent on having elements of security and competence between child and caretaker. Whether the child is socially advantaged or disadvantaged does not give us a probability statement about what damage may occur to the self at psychiatric levels of disorder. Often children from stable homes do show disorders of the self, and children from disadvantaged homes may come through unfortunate experiences and still develop competence and psychological security.

In children's earliest social development in the first months of life, infants respond in much the same way both to familiar adults and to strangers. At about 7 months infants usually attach to a specific person, although it can happen from 3½ months to 15 months (Ainsworth 1967). Neither feeding nor caretaking is the essential feature. The intensity of interaction seems to have the greatest effect in bonding (Stayton and Ainsworth 1973). Increased anxiety and fear, expressing an ego needing defense, or illness when the self is attacked, increased the baby's attachment seeking (Bowlby 1969). There is a persisting hierarchy among attachments (Schaffer and Emerson 1964).

The reduction of anxiety if a familiar person is present in a strange situation proves how important bonding is (Cohen and Campos 1974). Bonding is differentiated from attachment by the selectivity in relationships in which the infant persists over time and place. It is associated with older children at one or two years when the ego is being used by the child in this lasting selection of relationships more apparently than in infant attachment where ego competence is still not ripe.

Newborn infants react in a specific and individual way to frustration since de-integrates do not yet re-integrate easily. A similar reaction is present in surprise when the ego must try cognitive appraisal. Fraiberg (1968) points out that every baby defends or protects itself in very specific ways. Anxiety can become attached to ideas where previous experience produced pain, frustration, instinctive denial (hunger, cold, pain, and general somatic distress), loneliness, or the need to be autonomous. Macfarlane *et al.* (1954) studied 100 infants of 21 months of age and found 30% had specific fears. At 3 years, 70% were affected by fears.

By the third week the normal baby is using smiles to insure that adults will interact with him. This is a primary defense of the self. The grasping reflex in the first two days enables a baby to hold onto a hand or finger and gain stability and contact at once. At six weeks amidst the gurgles and babbling and crying, some syllables can be heard. There is a rapid read-out of defenses for the self as the ego de-integrates out to objects to assimilate them and re-integrate those which match its self/ego development. Self-defense is, like the other con-integrates, a very early vital reservoir of experience and capacity to cope with attacks to security, competence, and survival. It would occupy a central position of control among the con-integrates, filtering incoming stimuli from the ego to see if defense of the self were needed. Then the incoming stimulus would filter into other con-integrates, or if more general in nature and further down the hierarchy of self, it might be designated to a multi-integrate level and find its way to the more general store of integrative aspects of the self.

4. Theory and empirical evidence

It is not the task of the theoretician to provide complete empirical evidence. Other workers in the field can continue to build that up. Postulation requires a strong conjecture to be put forward as scientific theory and defended within the present knowledge in psychology. When experimental psychology is more ready to acknowledge the unconscious through its projection into conscious behavior we will have the requisite foundation to explore what experiments can achieve for a self theory. In the past experimenters have rarely been sufficiently close to the work of depth psychologists to comprehend what is being claimed and to determine if it is testable by experiment. Basically depth psychologists cannot be blind to human experience or convert it very easily into a laboratory setting. Individual experience and its detail is important to them. "Individual" implies that a self involving a total personality is what needs to be tested by experimenters in broadly-based open-ended psychometric approaches. If experimenters could work more effectively with depth psychologists and analysts it might be possible to begin to quantify depth psychology with carefully designed research and strictly controlled experiments. The chief problem has been that the postulates of depth psychology are difficult to frame in an experimental design. To do so, experimenters have often so altered the meaning of the behavior to be tested as to be testing something other than the postulate under question.

Using Jung's totality definition of the self, it can be argued that the self theory should be the principal framework for human psychology as a whole. For all psychological work is the psyche talking about and working with the psyche. That includes everything that can occur to the psyche, all of which must occur within some self or selves. To bring back the self theory to its inherent position of importance would be an important goal for the future of a total psychology—one that includes the richesse of the unconscious and its manifestations in conscious experience. In a hierarchical self theory to which this paper contributes, we have suitable boundaries for a unity among workers' approaches to the psychology of the self in all of its ramifications.

The great challenge to empirical study of the con-integrates is that it is essential to include experimental criteria of what only the subject knows about his or her own behavior, not just what another can measure. In the young child it is notoriously difficult to interpret experimenters' description and interpretation of early language but archetypally projected images can be studied by photographing the child's art or sandplay creations while taping any spoken interaction and photographing the child's movements and manner of using toys. Where the function of the archetypes is not included in the psychological study of early childhood, empirical work may remain full of unrelated detail in hundreds of thousands of experiments unrelated to any complete theory of the self/ego and hence become both parenthetical and perseverative. Babies cannot be reduced to organism or process alone. They are persons and however obscure the form of the personal has remained in psychology as a whole, the self/ego system is inevitably involved in behavior. As the self is mediated by the ego's constructions and interpretations as agent, then experimentalists run a danger of incompleteness in that statements about personality should include deductions both from laboratory data itself and from the self-evaluation of those tested where age allows. The predictive capacity of experiments is questioned because the individual self cannot predict itself. The ego and the con-integrates have sufficient freedom of response within their archetypal framework to be simultaneous agents of the psyche. This precludes laboratory measurement of past behavior as totally predictive of future behavior. The influence of outside objects and their study neglects the fact that the self/ego system can adapt its interpretation and meaning concepts constantly, so that over time the person's interactions change. The standpoint of the agent is in flux.

A parallel study to this idea concerning the indeterminism of self-prediction is found in K. R. Popper's work (see Popper and Eccles 1977). While the probability of events may be predicted from precise information, provided that similar conditions are present for their occurrence, events between the subject and object and their closed system of interaction lead to the unpredictability of events. Popper points out that it is impossible for a calculator to have up-to-date information about itself. I assert here it may also be impossible for the self, in each ego-decision process, to be up-to-date with the present and complex incoming demands. Past states can be explained in detail. It is self-prediction while constantly interacting with an on-going self system that cannot be accurate. The interaction introduces a disturbance into the system whose magnitude is unpredictable.

If a standpoint within this total ongoing action of self is not the paradigm for psychology, i.e., the self/ego-integrates system proposed here, the alternative is a scattered, broken up set of aggregates of extreme psychological specializations lacking coherence or an organizing principle. Disconnected data demand a self theory inclusive of childhood leading on through to old age. Hypotheses need a developmental procedure that is open to what persons of any age can do and become. The self and the ego-integrates are the processing systems which can include a knowledge of what the person knows about his own behavior as well as what others observe that behavior to be. The amalgam of inner and outer experience of self/ego, including the repeated experiencing of the archetypes, is the totality within which psychology should be conducting its investigations. Personality is not only what it seems to be for others, it is also what one knows it to be oneself. It is both about what one can do and about what is experienced in the doing. Action is experiential. This gives two sorts of proposition that lead to higher order theoretical propositions; one of the behavioral action and one of the experience of the actor.

Conclusion

The con-integrates are proposed as the self's chief concept-carriers. They function under the direction of the ego and unify the self's objective input to its own subjective connectedness of experiencing. The influence of the archetypes is seen as the a priori categories of universal human experience as they read out in projection from the collective level of the unconscious. The archetypes contribute a degree of regularity within the self's innate propensity to interpret sequences of impressions as unity within complexity, but their influence over time will be altered by the ego's propensities.

References

Abenheimer, K. 1968. The ego as Subject. In J. B. Wheelwright (ed.), *The Reality of the Psyche*. London: Bairie and Rockliffe.

Ainsworth, M. D. S. 1967. *Infancy in Uganda: Infant Care and the Growth of Love*. Baltimore: Johns Hopkins Press.

Bloom, L. 1973. *One Word at a Time*. The Hague: Monton.

Bowlby, J. 1969. *Attachment and Loss*, Vol. 1. London: Hogarth Press.

Braine, M. D. S. 1976. Children's First Word Combinations. *Monograph for Social Research in Child Development*, 31(4):1–92.

Burt, C. 1921. *Mental and Scholastic Tests*. London: London County Council.

Clark, E. V. 1978. From Gesture to Word: On the Natural History of Deixis in Language Acquisition. In J. S. Bruner and A. Garton (eds.), *Human Growth and Development*. Oxford: Clarendon Press.

Cohen, L. J., and Campos, J. J. 1974. Father, Mother and Stranger as Elicitors of Attachment Behaviours in Infancy. *Developmental Psychology*, 10:146–54.

Condon, W. S., and Sander, L. W. 1974. Neonate Movement is Synchronized with Adult Speech. *Science*, 183:99–108.

Ehrenzweig, A. 1967. *The Hidden Order of Art: A Study in the Psychology of Artistic Imagination*. San Francisco: University of California Press.

Eimas, P. D. *et al.* 1971. Speech Perception in Infants. *Science*, 171, 303–06.

Ende, R. N., and Harrison, R. J. 1972. Endogenous and Exogenous Smiling Systems in Early Infancy. *Journal of Child Psychology and Psychiatry*, 2:177–200.

Fordham, M. 1957. *New Developments in Analytical Psychology*. London: Routledge and Kegan Paul.

Fraiberg, S. A. 1968. *The Magic Years*. London: Methuen.

Freud, S. 1914. On Narcissism: An Introduction. *Standard Edition*, vol. 14.

———— 1927. *The Ego and the Id*. London: Hogarth.

Friedman, S. 1972. Habituation and Recovery of Visual Response in the Alert Human Newborn. *Journal of Experimental Child Psychology*, 13:339–49.

Gottlieb, G. 1970. Conception of Prenatal Behaviour. In L. R. Aronson, E. Tobach, D. S. Lehrmann and J. S. Rosenblatt (eds.), *Development and Evolution of Behaviour*. San Francisco: W. H. Freeman.

Harrison, J. E. 1908. *Prolegomena to the Study of the Greek Religion*. Cambridge: Cambridge University Press.

Jacobi, J. 1976. *Masks of the Soul*. London: Darton, Longman and Todd.

Jung, C. G. 1918. *Studies in Word-Association*. New York: Moffat, Yard.

————. 1954. *The Development of Personality*. In *Collected Works*, vol. 17. Princeton: Princeton University Press.

————. 1960. *The Structure and Dynamics of the Psyche*. In *Collected Works*, vol. 18. Princeton: Princeton University Press.

————. 1960. *Psychological Types*. In *Collected Works*, vol. 6. Princeton: Princeton University Press, 1971.

Kerenyi, C. 1951. *Gods of the Greeks*. London: Thames.

Kintsch, W. 1970. *Learning, Memory and Conceptual Processes*. New York: Wiley.

Klatzky, R. L. 1975. *Human Memory: Structures and Processes*. San Francisco: W. H. Freeman.

Kline, P. 1972. *Fact and Fantasy in Freudian Theory*. London: Methuen.

Koestler, A. 1972. *The Roots of Coincidence*. London: Hutchinson.

Kohut, H. 1977. *The Restoration of the Self*. New York: International Universities Press.

Lambert, K. 1981. *Analysis, Repair and Individuation*. London: Academic Press.

Levinger, G., and Clark, J. 1961. Emotional factors in the forgetting of word associations. *Journal of Abnormal Social Psychology*, 62:99–105.

Light, L. L., and Carter-Sobell, L. 1970. Effects of Changed Semantic Context on Recognition Memory. *Journal of Verbal Learning and Verbal Behaviour*. 9:1–11.

Lipps, T. 1903. *Aesthetik: Psychologie der Schonen und der Kunst*. Leipzig: Voss.

Luria, A. R. 1966. L. S. Vygotsky and the Problem of Functional Localization. *Soviet Psychology* 5(3):53–60.

Macfarlane, A. 1975. The First Hours and the Smile. In R. Lewin (ed.), *Child Alive*. London: Temple Smith.

Macfarlane, J. W. *et al*. 1954. *Behaviour Problems of Normal Children*. Los Angeles: University of California Press.

Millar, S. 1968. *The Psychology of Play*. London: Penguin.

Nelson, K. 1976. *The Conceptual Basis for Naming*. New Haven: Yale University Press.

Neumann, E. 1954. *The Origins and History of Consciousness*. Princeton: Princeton University Press.

———— 1959. The Significance of the Genetic aspect for Analytical Psychology. *Journal of Analytical Psychology* 4(2):125–38.

Parke, R. D. 1979. Perspectives on Father-Infant Interaction. In J. D. Osofsky (ed.), *Handbook of Infant Development*. New York: Riley.

Perlmutter, M., and Lange, G. 1978. The Development Analysis of Recall-Recognition Distinction. In P. S. Ornstein (ed.), *Memory Development in Children*. New Jersey: Erlbaum.

Piaget, J. 1951. *Play, Dreams and Imitation in Childhood*. London: Routledge and Kegan Paul.

————. 1966. *The Origins of Intelligence in Childhood*. New York: International Universities Press.

———— and Inhelder, B. 1973. *Memory and Intelligence*. New York: Basic Books.

Rosch, E. 1973. On the Internal Structure of Perceptual and Semantic Categories. In T. E. Moore (ed.), *Cognitive Development and the Acquisition of Language*. New York: Academic Press.

Schaffer, H. R. 1971. *The Growth of Sociability*. London: Penguin.

————, and Emerson, P.E. 1964. The Development of Social Attachments in Infancy. *Monographs Society for Research in Child Development* 19(3):1–77.

Sears, R. R. 1942. Repression. In S. G. M. Lee and M. Herbert (eds.), *Freud and Psychology*. Harmondsworth: Penguin, 1970.

Stayton, J. J. and Ainsworth, M. D. S. 1973. Individual Differences in Infant Responses to Brief, Everyday Separations as Related to Other Infant and Maternal Behaviour. *Developmental Psychology*, 9:226–35.

Stern, W. 1924. *Psychology of Early Childhood*. A. Barwell (trans.). London.

Tulving, E., and Thomson, D.M. 1973. Encoding Specificity and Retrieval Processes in Episodic Memory. *Psychological Review*, 80:352–73.

Valentine, C. W. 1962. *The Experimental Psychology of Beauty*. London: Methuen.

de Villiers, J. G., and de Villiers, P. A. 1978. *Language Acquisition*. London: Harvard University Press.

Wilkinson, F. R. and Carghill, D. W. 1955. Repression Elicited by Story Material Based on the Oedipal Complex. *Journal of Social Psychology* 42:209–14.

Winnicott, D. W. 1953. Transitional Objects and Transitional Phenomena. *International Journal of Psychoanalysis* 34:89–97.

Worringer, W. 1908. *Abstraction and Empathy*. London: Routledge and Kegan Paul.

Chiron's Wound: Some Reflections on the Wounded-Healer

M. Whan

Let me begin with some lines from T. S. Elliot's "East Coker":

> *The wounded surgeon plies the steel*
> *That questions the distempered part;*
> *Beneath the bleeding hands we feel*
> *The sharp compassion of the healer's art . . .*

It is the nature of this "distempered part" and "sharp compassion" that I wish to explore in my discussion on the archetype of the wounded-healer and its constellation in the psychotherapeutic relationship.

Theoretical Wounds

Examining the connection between Jung's personality and his theoretical ideas, the Jungian analyst, Satinover, has put forward the suggestion that the theory served a self-healing purpose for Jung himself. Satinover relates this restorative function particulary to the period of inner disorder which followed Jung's break with Freud. For Satinover Jung's ideas may be regarded as "symptoms," as an attempt to heal what he calls "the narcissistic wound" (1985, p. 51).

Michael Whan, M.A., is a psychiatric social worker and preliminary candidate in Jungian analytic training in London.

It is not my intention to argue for or against this re-assessment of Jung and Jungian theory. Rather I would like to approach Satinover's proposition in a different sense: as exemplifying an underlying archetypal meaning of the *woundedness in Jung's theory.* I would like to relate this *to the mythos of the wounded-healer.* Besides Satinover, others have said things similar. Ellenberger, for example, has drawn attention to the role of "creative illness" in the life of both Freud and Jung. Such periods of psychological disturbance may act as a catalyst in which the personality undergoes transformation, and out of which insights of various kinds may be gained.

This notion of "creative illness" is reminiscent of the shaman's "sickness-vocation," serving as a initiatory experience, a "rite of passage" into the career of healing (Eliade 1974, p. 33). Similarly, through their own psychological sufferings, Freud and Jung were moved into a new relationship with their vocation. Their wounds helped to shape their work, and, in turn, the work re-shaped the wounds. They deepened their understanding of psyche. One could say that both Freudian and Jungian depth psychology carry a fundamental experience of infirmity which is itself part of their shaping spirit.

This connection between healing and wound was evident very early on in Jung's theoretical understanding of neurosis and psychosis. He regarded pathological material as containing a potential healing element. For instance, he observed that the content manifested in schizophrenia expressed archetypal motifs, the nature of which is to compensate the onesidedness of the conscious attitude. Because of this understanding, Jung believed, in contradistinction to Freud and the "conventional wisdom" of the day, that schizophrenia might be treatable by psychotherapy. Jung's theory of psychological compensation, then, exemplifies an instance of a "healing wound." Woundedness is not without hope.

Recognition of the wounded-healer archetype signifies how we cannot altogether separate the healer from the wounded one. And conversely, it reminds us of the splitting processes in some other forms of healing where there *is* a sharp psychological and social division between healer and patient, healer and wound.

Compare the ambiguity of the wounded-healer, for instance, with a god of healing such as Apollo. Unlike the wounded-healer, who is "infected" and affected in his very being by the healing work, Apollo is a "mortally clean" god (Kerenyi 1976, p. 39). He works his medical art by means of catharsis, purification and sublimation. In Apollonic forms of medicine there is a definitive split between healer and "contaminated" patient. Apollo is the god of rational enlightment, objectification and intellectual distancing. Archetypally, Apollo brings the benefits of rational order and clarity by way of objectifying thought. Illness and suffering are to be explained in terms of "objective factors" such as "cause and effect." This entails a separation of thought from being. In order to represent something, it must be rendered object-ifiable, requiring it to be completely unhidden, wholly accountable. Only what can be so represented is worthy of thought. When this rationalistic spirit holds sway in depth psychology, psyche is, in principle, totally objectifiable, representable; but its *ontological mystery* is denied.

Guggenbuhl-Craig has pointed out the clinical implications for therapist and patient when the archetype of wounded-healer is so split. He describes (1970, p.134) how this splitting can prevent the work of the healing factor in the patient. The therapist represses his own wounded nature, and projects it onto the patient, who therefore comes to incarnate it. But because it is repressed the therapist attempts to overcome his inner division by trying to dominate the patient. This splitting process becomes reinforced when the therapist overlays it with a further distinction between himself and the patient, that of consciousness and unconsciousness. The therapist identifies his own position with being conscious and that of the patient with being unconscious. Again, the therapist projects his own unconsciousness onto the patient.

When such splitting takes place, the connection between healing and wound becomes severed. In the split a shadow and will-to-power forms in which the therapist attempts to sustain invulnerability and isolation from the experience of pathos, thereby trying to defend a sham self-esteem of being "healthy." Guggenbuhl-Craig's remarks argue for constant relatedness on the therapist's part to his own woundedness, recognizing projection and splitting-off and how this depletes his capacity to experience pathos. In other words, identification with the healing pole of the archetype alone may lead to the adoption of a schizoid position by the therapist. The therapist introjects the "good" healing part and projects the "bad" wounded part onto the other. Because of projective identification the patient may be kept in the role of the ill one of the pair. Then the therapist distances himself from the patient, negating possibilites of intimacy since this would lead to a blurring between healer and wound. The patient is increasingly perceived in a depersonalized way, and the therapist compensates his denied woundedness by grandiosity and overestimation of himself. Thus he defends against the experience of guilt, anxiety and depression which may be engendered in the psychotherapeutic relationship.

One should remember, as against over-identification with the healing end of the wounded-healer archetype, that the patient too carries healing propensities within himself. Searles (1979) has drawn attention to the way the patient may suffer on behalf of the therapist in order to heal the therapist's illness, and how this may work itself out in the transference relationship. The other side of this hardly explored interaction between therapist and patient is that the therapist in his countertransference may offer his illness to the patient for treatment and resolution: Stein (1984, p.80) writes: "This reversal of the therapeutic direction is the great unanalyzed shadow of the shamanic type of countertransference." We shall explore this term 'shamanic countertransference' later on.

In the history of psychiatry and depth psychology there are a number of patients who have made profound contributions to the development of theory and practice: Charcot's Blanche Wittman; Breuer's Anna O (Bertha Pappenheim); Freud's Elizabeth von R.; and the Wolf-Man; and for Jung there were, among others, Helene Preiswerk and the schizophrenic, Babette S. The point to be emphasized is not only that some of these played a most active part in their own treatment, but also in the development of therapy and depth psychology. Freud's method of free association was partly suggested to him by Elizabeth von R.; likewise Anna O "directed her cure, explained it to her physician, and prophesied" the termination of her treatment (Ellenberger, 1970, pp. 892-893). Freud was so grateful to the Wolf-Man, from whon he learned much, that he later analyzed him gratis, collecting money to support him (ibid.). All of this shows how much is to be learned concerning *healing from* the patient, how the archetype of wounded-healer may be constellated as much in person of the patient as in the therapist.

Chiron

Reflection on the wounded-healer is aided by recourse to a mythic image, one that is found in the figure of Chiron. Through contemplation of the Chironion mythologem we may make the meaning of the wounded-healer more ample. In Greek mythology Chiron was considered the wisest of the centaurs. He was also noted for his kindness, but particularly for his role as primordial physician. It is said Apollo gave Chiron his son, Asklepios, to educate and nurture. This suggests that Chiron was also at the heart of the Asklepian healing mystery. Perhaps here is the "sharp compassion," the spirit of care that infuses the healing vocation. Through Chiron Asklepios was initiated into the medical arts. Chiron was involved as well with the upbringing of various heroic figures, such as Herakles, Jason and Achilles. These he instructed in the art of healing, so tempering the wounding, aggressive propensity of the heroic ego with a quality of reparation and care. It is thus both tragic and ironic that Chiron received his fateful wound accidentally from Herakles. The "Chironion wound" (Meier 1967, p. 9) was caused by an arrow Herakles intended for Elatos, one of the other centaurs. The arrow wounded Chiron in the knee, bringing about the lameness of the wounded-healer. On the arrow was venom from the Hydra, and though Herakles attempted to cure the wound his attempt failed. Chiron too was unable to heal himself, and so suffered the pain of an incurable wound. The centaur withdrew to his cave, but being immortal there remained in agony, unable to die and find release from suffering. Eventually, however, Chiron could offer himself in the place of Prometheus, and so bearing Prometheus' suffering and death, Chiron descended into Hades.

Before attempting an account of the myth of Chiron in terms of depth psychology, an apology is necessary. For when we ask our questions concerning meaning, we must have regard for our own hermeneutic situation. We cannot know the meaning of the mythic image directly, we approach it from a 'hermeneutic distance', from a position of estrangement. The image has to be interpreted, and in this instance that interpretation is determined from within the sphere of depth psychology. An interpretation, however, is not an answer, but a response. What meanings may we, therefore, draw from this mythologem? How might we understand some of its elements from the perspective of depth psychology?

We could begin perhaps with Chiron's wound and journey to the Underworld. Chironion suffering leads into the morbidities of body and soul. The wound signifies to the physician that he, himself, is in need of healing. The wound to Chiron's knee, to the equine part of his nature, bears upon the movement, the characteristic motion of the centaur. His possibilities of being are severely curtailed, and he is drawn into the slow, lame world of chronicity and pain. Chiron loses the flexibility of movement that is natural to him. Consciousness of the wound's incurability establishes for the great physician his limits. Yet contained in this is "the knowledge of a wound in which the healer forever partakes" (Kerenyi 1959, p. 99).

In the figure of Herakles Chiron meets the bearer of his fate. Herakles' act points towards the shadow side of the heroic ego. The arrow that he shoots wounds Chiron *at a distance*. It is the 'distance', the remoteness of the heroic ego from the other; the violent, unreflected action which erupts from the dark unconscious. Here alienation wounds.

As half-man, half-theriomorphic god, Chiron is a liminal being, a mythical figure of the threshold or borderline. His world encompasses that of gods, mortals and animals. Chiron's liminality is suggested by his habitat, his mountain cave which epitomizes "outsiderhood". His figure also combines "wisdom and animal force" (Turner 1978, p. 253). Divinity, humanness and creaturely being are all part of Chiron. This last aspect is important to remember when dealing with illness, for even the most sophisticatedly 'human' of ills, those associated with the 'higher' problems of civilization and culture, entail a suffering animal, a wounded *nature*. Chiron's endless suffering, until released into Hades, suggests the pain of existence. The House of Hades may come to seem a gentler abode for the wounded psyche, the agonized body, than endlessly living out one's pain. Chiron's choice to enter Hades signifies the *need for a limit to suffering*. It is here that we find the relevance of the management of pain, both in its mental and physical manifestations.

Empathic woundedness, transference and countertransference

Chiron's fate as a wounded-healer gives, then, an archetypal meaning and depth to various patterns of woundedness and healing in the psychotherapeutic situation. Constellation of this archetype can indicate the way the therapist has become profoundly involved with and vulnerable to the patient's psyche. It is these patterns of involvement, in both a positive and negative sense, that I now wish to look at more closely.

Central to the nature of the wounded-healer is the problem of empathy. Chironion woundedness represents an 'open wound', and in this sense is connected with empathic understanding and experience. An "open wound" indicates interiority: the punctured, torn flesh, open to the world; the body's raw, red depths; lacerated feelings, exposed, tender, bruised and swelling; the pierced access to what is within. It signifies *an archetypal image of an empathic consciousness which is in its own way a wound*; a wound which brings consciousness. The therapist's very capacity for empathy, his ability to 'feel into' and share the patient's inner life also lays him open to become wounded. To be open empathically is to be open to the other's shadow and disturbance.

Whenever we are touched by Chironion woundedness, we undergo a slowing down which may lead to a greater therapeutic patience, a capacity to tend and hold onto the wounds of body and soul. Chiron symbolizes a threefold perspective on illness in terms of divine, human and animal nature. Sickness for the gods is not what it is for men and beasts. Chiron tends to the injuries and ills of the gods: that he can remedy these distinguishes them from mortal afflictions. For humans, however, such afflictions are of the morbidity of flesh, and hence they become a mortal condition. According to Homer, the boundary between gods and men is absolute and inviolable. It is the boundary between eternity and time.

As a divine physician Chiron figures a compassion by which he is "involved in the un-Olympian world of life and death" (Kerenyi 1959, p. 80). It is this involvement in the temporal world which provides the fundamental experience for the wounded-healer's empathy. Illness and suffering always entail an awareness of time: the wound shows us our mortal nature. This mortal sense of things, our common lot, is found in Freud's notion that the function of insight deepens our consciousness and experience of the human condition. Freud wrote: "much will be gained if we succeed in transforming your hysterical misery into common happiness" (1953–73, p. 305). Jung too spoke of the aim of psychotherapy in much the same vein: *"The patient has not to learn how to get rid of his neurosis, but how to bear it"* (1964, para. 360). The purpose of insight is to let us down into our human condition, to enable us to carry our wounds of being human. Consciousness means here perceiving the latency of death-in-life. Being wounded we begin to live our dying and death. The Chironion wound introduces something medial between life and death, especially when we have set them apart as warring principles, as life against death. Woundedness may initiate us into an intermediate zone where these polarities find their connection, where being less estranged from death, we may find, by way of the experience of mortalness, a more humanly compassionate sense of life.

A number of studies concerning the effects of their own illness upon doctors have shown how many of them subsequently felt their practice and sensibilities enhanced. One commented: "New zeal as a therapist seemed to emerge from the straitjacket of my former training alongside my experience of illness. I was able to treat my patients in a more active and participating manner" (Todes 1983, pp. 977–78). An American psychiatrist declared: "My wounds become my spectacles, helping me to see what I encounter with empathy and a grateful sense of privilege" (Lipp 1980, p. 107).

The question of empathy further directs one into the nature of the relationship between therapist and patient: namely, to the issue of transference and countertransference. From a clinical perspective the Hydra's venom on the arrow of Herakles is representative of archaic destructive energies, venomous feelings of hatred and envy projected onto the other. Chiron's wounding can signify that the therapist has come to stand for a hated inner image, the object of a displaced aggression expressed in the transference. This hated image need not only be a familial one, but as epitomized by the figure of Chiron himself one of divinity, humanness or animal nature. There can be a hatred of God or the gods; a misanthropy extending not only to hostility towards others, but to oneself as well; and there may be, as in our own Western conciousness, a deep antithesis toward body and nature.

Such feelings and attitudes manifest themselves in the to-ing and fro-ing of the transference and countertransference with their concomitant processes of projection, projective identification and introjection. Jung's dialectical model of psychotherapy implies this light and dark aspect of the mutuality and co-transformation that goes on between patient and therapist. He writes of "psychic disturbances or even injuries peculiar to the profession," and goes on to say:

> One of the best known symptoms of this kind is the counter-transference evoked by transference. But the effects are often much more subtle, and their nature can best be conveyed by the old idea of the demon sickness. According to this, a sufferer can transmit his disease to a healthy person whose powers then subdue the demon—but not without impairing the wellbeing of the subduer. (1954, para. 163)

Elaborating this theme of the wounded-healer, Stein has described a countertransference response based on what he refers to as "the shamanic process":

> As this process of psychological identifiction takes hold, the empathy flowing between the partners tends to intensify; what happens in the one also occurs in the other; they resonate psychologically to one another. And this is when the analyst becomes "infected". Psychic ailments like depression, anxiety, schizoid withdrawal, invasions of unconscious figures and impulses are experienced, often simultaneously, by the analyst as well as by the analysand because the two psychic systems run on parallel lines, the analyst's psyche bending to the features of the analysand's inner landscape. Through this kind of mirroring, the analyst's psyche absorbs and comes to reflect the analysand's "illness." (1984, p. 77)

Having introjected the patient's illness or wound, the possibility of healing lies in the resonance of the therapist's own psyche; in what the introjection constellates within. There are questions here as to what extent the therapist's psyche responds in terms of its own wounds. Does the therapist deal directly within himself with the patient's problem, or does he respond to it more indirectly in terms of his own woundedness? The "shamanic countertransference" suggests that healing may occur partly by way of the constellated woundedness which belongs to the therapist's psyche. A further pattern, however, occurs when healing is by way of the therapist taking into himself the inner disturbance of the patient. The therapist then tries to understand and integrate the problem, and eventually works towards handing the difficulties back in "a repaired form," so that the patient too can understand, assimilate and contain them (Lambert 1981, p. 162). The work of the therapist in these exchanges is to differentiate inwardly his own from the patient's wounds. For the patient's wounds contain part of his individuality. The empathic wounding and openness of the therapist to the patient takes place in the context of the unconscious bonding between them. Hence each may lose parts of their individuality to the other in a process of con-fusion and projection.

The wounding of the therapist, however, is only one side of the interaction. Corresponding to it is the patient's capacity to wound either by the expression of aggressive feelings or by projecting the wounded part onto the therapist. Such a possibility depends upon a capability for ambivalence; that is to say, *the ambivalent nature of the wounded-healer in which healing and illness are present in the one person.* For some patients though it is this very ambivalence which is problematic. In order to protect the idealized healer, wound and healing must be split off. The association of woundedness with fantasies of destruction or punishment, for instance, represents too great a threat to the "wholesomeness" of healing and healer. Such patients repress emotions of rage or hatred toward the therapist because of their fear of damaging, of making the therapist ill. Often they cannot express depression for fear of burdening the therapist with it. Some patients, who are closely identified with their shadow, with feelings of worthlessness, with a self-image of being damaged, may come to envy the apparent "healthiness" of the therapist. Least these feelings realize themselves in attacks on him, the patient must deny them. By various defences they seek to preserve the therapist's "health." This can lead them to identify wholly, in an almost scapegoat fashion, with woundedness, perhaps even taking on the therapist's suffering for that reason. In such ways the healing process may become blocked, and the therapist be unable to develop an empathic woundedness.

What may be necessary, therefore, in order to develop a capacity for ambivalence, and hence for the constellation of the wounded-healer archetype, is for the patient to be able to wound, to feel anxiety and guilt, and to be able to experience the possibility of himself as an agent of healing: namely, through *reparation.* Such reparation requires the patient face his depression, and not escape into manic or omnipotent forms of repair. If this occurs, especially with borderline personalities, there is an underlying sense of increasing damage to the other and thus of despair (Steiner 1979, p. 389).

The patient needs to experience the therapist as able to contain both wound and healing in his person. For this to be, the therapist's own attitudes and relationship with mental and bodily illness and pain are crucial. These will be communicated unconsciously to the patient. Inherent in this is how the therapist relates to death and dying. Chironion wound-edness leads into Hades. When he is in flight from woundedness and morbidity, the therapist's ego defenses may close off from empathy, because that way lies the Underworld.

The wounded-healer's empathy though is also his vulnerability: Chiron's wound did not heal. The recent interest is "burn out" in the helping professions bears witness to the "wear and tear" of the therapeutic relationship. Perhaps many who enter psychotherapeutic work come already wounded; they may have chosen a vocation of healing because of this experience of suffering. Some will succeed, yet some will fail; their depressed feelings more disturbingly constellated. In America suicide among psychiatrists is the highest for any occupational group.

This negative aspect of the wound realizes itself in many ways. A therapist, for instance, who, because of guilt or self-hatred, accepts the whole of a paranoid or other derogatory attribution, may collude in self-denigration, deepening the injury to his Selfhood. The attempt to empathically follow a borderline or psychotic patient down into the depths of his illness brings the therapist up against his own areas of madness. So he may "mirror" the patient's pathology leading to disturbances within himself (Sanders and Beebe 1984, pp. 327–28; Kernberg 1972, p. 271). The hermetic nature of psychotherapy may intensify such effects, the therapist coming to have his own self-image reflected solely in the patient's communications to the point when he begins to lose himself in the other.

In a study of therapists who worked with schizophrenic patients, the psychoanalyst, Farber, has noted the particular forms of despair and wilfulness that developed among them. These therapists became "increasingly impatient of relation" and assumed "public self-assertive gestures" that were "unfaithful" to the person each might have become. Farber concludes that the despair and distortions of personality among these therapists were a response to working with schizophrenia (1972, p. 98).

These instances show the propensity for destructiveness in the psychotherapeutic relationship, a destructiveness which belongs, in part, to the archetype of the wounded-healer. The factors and dynamics of this configuration are obviously complex, and for this reason there is always the risk of the woundedness being uncontained in a manageable way.

Conclusions

Thus to end this excursus on the wounded-healer: in Chiron we find an archetype which encompasses both healing and wound. The wounded-healer is present whenever there are equivocal possibilities for both healing and sickness, hope and despair, nature and nurture. Chiron's "open wound" signifies the painful openings into ourselves which require nursing attention: a palpable experience of archetypal value. Acknowledging one's wound represents the beginning of a felt responsiveness towards it. In life Chiron is unable to forsake the world of chronic suffering because that world is part of his own. The pathos of his injury is the existential price of his kinship with human beings and animals. Yet out of this sense of finitude, of self-limitation, the wounded-healer finds the condition of his self-understanding, his compassion and empathy, whether for gods, mankind, or animals. His is the experience of life, suffering and death, and for this reason he is close to the human condition. Do we not hear of him in the lines:

> *Our only health is the disease*
> *If we obey the dying nurse . . .*

References

Eliade, M. 1974. *Shamanism: Archaic Techniques of Ecstasy.* Princeton: Princeton University Press.

Ellenberger, H. 1970. *The Discovery of the Unconscious.* New York: Basic Books, Inc.

Farber, L. 1968. Schizophrenia and the Mad Psychotherapist. In *The Ways of the Will.* New York: Harper & Row. Also in *Laing and Anti-Psychiatry,* R. Boyers and R. Orrill, eds., 1972. Middlesex: Penguin Books.

Freud, S. 1953–73. *Studies on Hysteria, Standard Edition,* 2. London: Hogarth Press and The Institute of Psycho-Analysis.

Guggenbuhl-Craig, A. 1970. Must Analysis Fail Through Its Destructive Aspect? *Spring: An Annual of Archetypal Psychology and Jungian Thought.* 1970: 133–145.

Jung, C. G. 1931. Problems of Modern Psychotherapy. In *Collected Works* 16: 53–75. London: Routledge & Kegan Paul, 1954.

———— 1934. The State of Psychotherapy Today. In *Collected Works* 10: 157–173. London: Routledge & Kegan Paul, 1964.

Kerenyi, C. 1959. *Asklepios: Archetypal Image of the Physician's Existence.* New York: Pantheon Books.

———— 1976. *Hermes: Guide of Souls.* Zurich Spring Publications.

Kernberg, O. F. 1972. Treatment of Borderline Patients. In *Tactics and Techniques in Psychoanalytic Therapy,* P. L. Giovacchini, ed., London: Hogarth Press and The Institute of Psycho-Analysis.

Lambert, K. 1981. *Analysis, Repair and Individuation.* London: Academic Press and The Society of Analytical Psychology.

Lipp, M. R. 1980. *The Bitter Pill: Doctors, Patients and Failed Expectations.* New York: Harper & Row. Quoted in *Wounded-Healers: Mental Health Workers's Experiences of Depression.* V. Rippere and R. Williams, eds., Chichester: John Wiley and Sons. 1985.

Meier, C. A. 1967. *Ancient Incubation and Modern Psychotherapy.* Evanston: Northwestern University Press.

Sander, D. F., and Beebe, J. 1984. Psychopathology and Analysis. In *Jungian Analysis.* M. Stein, ed., London: Shambhala Publication; 294–334.

Satinover, J. 1985. At the Mercy of Another: Abandonment and Restitution in Psychosis and Psychotic Character. *Chiron: A Review of Jungian Analysis.* 1985: 47–86.

Searles, K. 1979. The patient as therapist to his analyst. In *Countertransference and related subjects*. New York: International Universities Press: 380–459.

Stein, M. 1984. Power, Shamanism, and Maieutics in the Countertransference. *Chiron: A Review of Jungian Analysis*: 67–87.

Steiner, J. 1979. The border between the paranoid-schizoid and the depressive positions in the borderline patient. *British Journal of Medical Psychology*. 1952: 385–390.

Todes, C. 1983. Inside Parkinsonism—a psychiatrist's experience. *Lancet*. i, 977-978. Quoted in Rippere and Williams.

Turner, V. 1978. *Dramas, Fields, and Metaphors*. London: Cornell University Press.

Book Reviews

Anatomy of the Psyche: Alchemical Symbolism in Psychotherapy
Edward F. Edinger. La Salle, Illinois: Open Court Publishing Company,
1985. 260 pp. $14.95.

Reviewed by John Beebe

    This remarkable book is modest neither in its intent nor its scope, yet it manages to compress a veritable mine of information about alchemical symbolism into less than three hundred unhurried pages. These comprise the literal body of Edward Edinger's psychological masterpiece; the spirit within it, as those who have attended his magisterial lectures on psychological topics will expect, speaks for itself; and, as a subtle, unexpected gift, a generous soul makes the entire experience of confronting archetypal alchemical symbolism a refreshing and nourishing one, like a bath after a long journey, in which the trip's meaning and purpose are restored to the traveller.
    The long journey that Edinger refreshes with his understanding is the individuation journey; he shares Jung's faith that the peculiar, often unpleasant, vicissitudes of human emotional experience are not without point, that indeed they

---

John Beebe, M.D., is a member of the C. G. Jung Institute of San Francisco, where he is editor of *The San Francisco Jung Institute Library Journal.* A graduate of Harvard College and the University of Chicago Medical School, he did his psychiatric residency at Stanford University Medical Center and his analytic training at the C. G. Jung Institute of San Francisco. He is the editor of *Psychiatric Treatment: Crisis, Clinic, and Consultation* (1975) and *Money, Food, Drink, Fashion, and Analytic Training: Depth Dimensions of Physical Existence* (1983). He has a private practice in San Francisco.

do point to a major work in progress that can be compared with great profit to the alchemical opus, that grand and bizarre effort to make mineralogically corrupt *prima materia* into an incorruptible Philosopher's Stone with transcendental properties. In this volume, he compares the emotions of individuation to the "operations" to which the alchemists subjected their base materials in the effort at refinement. He makes it clear that he thinks the seven central alchemical operations—*calcinatio, solutio, coagulatio, sublimatio, mortificatio, separatio, and coniunctio*—were projections onto material processes by the alchemists of aspects of the archetype of transformation, the innate property of psyche to transform itself which the alchemists projected onto the as yet mysterious capacities for chemical transformation of physical substances. He retains the Latin alchemical terms "to distinguish the psychological processes from the chemical procedure" (p. 15). He leaves little doubt that the purposive, transformative aspect of the psyche is to his mind entirely expressed within the imagery connected with these operations:

> Each of these operations is found to be the center of an elaborate symbol system. These central symbols of transformation make up the major content of all culture-products. They provide basic categories by which to understand the life of the psyche, and they illustrate almost the full range of experiences that constitute individuation. (p. 15)

Although I think it is possible to verify these claims, they seem to me, for all the majesty, clarity, and integrity of Edinger's subsequent presentation of the rich symbolism which abounds in the alchemical writings about these operations, somewhat seductive. The book is based in the advantages and pretensions of modernism, which even with the concept of the Self and the lip-service to Heisenberg's uncertainty principle, really does retain the 19th-century notion of the hero with its belief that a structural map of existence can be found. Its red cover seems less to suggest the alchemical *rubedo* than to bid for its place beside Gray's *Anatomy*. Many post-modern readers will want to deconstruct this work and place it into the ongoing text of Jungian thought, as one of the fascinating perspectives on the possibilities of the psyche, to which we can be drawn for nourishment. But *Anatomy of the Psyche* insists, heroically, on being more that that: it wants to define the grand design of self-realization, to be a basic medical school text of the psyche; and its author seems to believe that he can be a sort of Virchow of the soul.

This is a great pity, because this is a great book on quite another scale; a beautiful effort at clarity within an almost inchoate field; and a labor of love by one of the most unusual psychotherapists of our day. This book will go on the shelf beside Henderson's *Thresholds of Initiation,* von Franz's seminars on fairy tales, and Hillman's Eranos lectures as one of those quintessentially Jungian efforts to mine a cultural tradition for psychological understanding, in the process enriching, not just psychology, but the culture itself, which springs to renewed life when freshened with the dew of loving depth psychological attention.

For example, where but in this book, in the midst of the brilliant and subtle analysis of *separatio,* would one be able to find the following passage?

> The early geometers attached special significance to an ideal proportion achieved by the so-called *golden section.* This is done by bisecting a line of

given magnitude in such a way that the lesser part is to the greater part as the greater part is to the whole. Thus, if a line of length c is bisected into a shorter part a and a longer part b, the proportion will be $a/b = b/c$; b will be the so-called golden mean. This proportion was considered to be the most beautiful one.

The golden section is a very interesting *separatio* symbol. It expresses the idea that there is a particular way to separate the opposites that will create a third thing (the proportion or mean between them) of great value. The value is indicated by the term golden and by the presumes beauty of the proportion. The same image of the mean was used by Aristotle in an ethical context to define the nature of virtue. . . .

The image of the golden mean can be understood psychologically as a symbolic expression of the ego's relation to the Self. This accounts for the numinosity of the idea of the golden section to the ancients. This slender geometric parable contains the same mystery as the dogma of the Christian Trinity. (pp. 197–98)

The entire book is studded with such jewels, moments of patiently created illumination in which Edinger carefully and generously explains a piece of the Western tradition that usually is delivered to us (if at all) hurriedly, in passing. (A painter friend had long ago explained the principle of the golden section in helping me to decide where to hang a painting on a wall, but not until I began to peruse Edinger's book did I really feel this bit of information lock into its cultural context, as part of the history of the idea of wholeness). In this same chapter Edinger lists the "pairs of opposites" as established by the Pythagoreans as well as, Jung's own rather idiosyncratic list of the opposites in the *Seven Sermons to the Dead.*

One senses that Edinger is passionately connected to the educative effort that permeates this book. Its informative spirit is beyond and beside its effort to make alchemy and personality transformation clearer. I once chanced to hear from him that he felt that he had had a very poor education, as a chemistry major in college preparing for medical school. It looks as if he has in the course of writing this book, returned, so to speak, to that college, now as an alchemy major, and found the humanities from which he was excluded the first time around. The book is redolent with the freshness of discovery of poetry, philosophy, literature, art, music, and drama, as if its author had listened to that recurrent theme in the dreams of so many of us, of being back at school and behind in one or more of our courses, and really gone to college in the midst of his psychological maturity, when he could finally learn something rather than feel overwhelmed and depressed, as so many young college students do, faced with the demand to integrate material they are not truly ready for.

Edinger's is the scholarship of the passionate *afficionado* rather than the professional scholar, so that the amplifications of specific alchemical motifs are based on the feeling-investments of the author rather than an intellectual logic. I was in the audience the first time he presented one of the papers that became this book, what is now the chapter on *calcinatio,* the operation by which the body is intensely heated by fire to drive away moisture, often to the point of becoming purified white ash. As Edinger moved from a patient's dream of being in a fiery place from which he could not escape to a careful amplification of the patient's own association (Nebuchadnezzar's fiery furnace), to Eliade's discussion of shamanic "mastery of fire," to the Christian doctrine of purgatory, to a remarkable passage from the great church father Origen, who interpreted hell psychologically in the third century A.D., to Robert Frost's "Fire and Ice," to (later on) the fifty-ninth sonnet of Michelangelo, and to T.S. Eliot's intense conclusion to "Little Gidding" ("Love is the unfamiliar name/Behind the hands that wove/The intolerable shirt of flame/Which human power cannot remove"; the image, a shirt of Nessus in the Heracles myth, was carefully amplified), I was myself calcined by the heat of Dr. Edinger's passionate commitment to the affective track of his subject. I could see that this was not scholarly fidelity to an idea so much as love of learning as much as possible about a psychologically gripping experience, the love of learning taking on a life of its own. This example of psychological writing—writing from a genuinely psychological place—was profoundly inspiring to me and forever changed the course of my own writing. I was able to see beyond the usual advice to "write from experience" to a model that seemed to let genuinely felt experience be the guide for the effort at intellectual amplification, with its multitude of cultural and conceptual footnotes to primary imaginal data.

Now, with the book as a whole in my hand, with its clear introductory chapter followed by seven chapters on the individual alchemical operations, I can see that this book about individuation (from the standpoint of its symbolism) is in many ways the individuation of its author. That's why it inspired me so when it first started being born. Without being intrusively autobiographical, the author's own relation to his material gradually makes itself evident as the opus proceeds. At first, in the introductory chapter, the choice of a particular passage from Thomas Norton's *Ordinal of Alchemy* suggests only Edinger's sly, dry humor. He compares Norton's description, without further comment, with "the experience of psychotherapy":

Anyone who gives himself up to this search must therefore expect to meet with much vexation of spirit. He will frequently have to change his course in consequence of new discoveries which he makes. . . . The devil will do his utmost to frustrate your search by one or the other of the three stumbling blocks, namely haste, despair, or deception. . . . He who is in a hurry will complete his work neither in a month, nor yet in a year; and in this Art it will always be true that the man who is in a hurry will never be without matter of complaint. . . . If the enemy does not prevail against you by hurry, he will assault you with despondency, and will be constantly putting into your mind discouraging thoughts, how those who seek this Art are many, while they are few that find it, and how those who fail are often wiser men than yourself. He will then ask you what hope there can be of your attaining the grand arcanum; moreover he will vex you with doubts whether your master is himself possessed of the secret which he professes to impart to you; or whether he is not concealing from you the best part of that which he knows. . . . The third enemy against whom you must guard yourself is deceit, and this is perhaps more dangerous than the other two. The servants whom you must employ to feed your furnaces are frequently most untrustworthy. Some are careless and go to sleep when they should be attending the fire; others are depraved, and do you all the harm they can; others again are either stupid or conceited and over-confident, and disobey instructions . . . or they are drunken, negligent, and absent-minded. Be on your guard against all these, if you wish to be spared some great loss. (A. E. Waite, trans., *The Hermetic Museum.* London: John M. Watkins, 1953, 2: 22–25, quoted in Edinger, p. 5)

With little personal reference to himself, Edinger goes on to plunge us deeply into the alchemical/personal transformative work. He describes the way the four elements go about transforming us—fire (whose method is *calcinatio,* which purges us); water (whose method is *solutio,* which dissolves us); earth (whose method is *coagulatio,* which grounds us); and air (whose method is *sublimatio,* which gets us outside and above ourselves). Only then does he let us see more deeply into the nature of the person who has been taking us through such complex material with such thoroughness and patience. (He goes deeply into seven major aspects of *solutio* alone.) His last three chapters will be about the deeply transformative stages which occur when the process has really taken hold, following the initial operations at the hands of the four elements. (These operations may of course be required again and again during the later stages of producing the Philosopher's Stone, an incorruptible integrity, but they are now subordinate to other big changes taking place in the character of the *prima materia.*) The *prima materia* is starting to go through its famous color changes, known to alchemists as the *nigredo, albedo,* and *rubedo* stages. It has suddenly turned black (as a consequence of the operation of *mortificatio*) and will turn white (as a consequence of *separatio*) and will turn red (as a consequence of *coniunctio*). It is in discussing *mortificatio,* which inaugurates this really deep sequence of the work, that Edinger "kills" his own characteristic professional reticence with a most revealing personal example. Within his description of *mortifactio* (and its related *putrefactio*) is an account of the head symbolism associated with this *nigredo* phase that leads him to relate an experience of his own at this level:

One reason seems to be the connection between the term "head" and top or beginning. Blackness was considered to be the starting point of the work. A text says, "When you see your matter going black, rejoice: for that is the beginning of the work". . . .
The dead, worthless residue is the stuff of the *nigredo* phase. The fact that is it called a *caput* or head indicates a paradoxical reversal of opposites. The worthless becomes the most precious, and the last becomes first. This is a lesson that we each must learn again and again. It is the *psyche* that we find in the worthless, despised place. By the conventional standards of our environment the psyche is nothing, nothing at all. A personal example: I feel empty and out of sorts; I sit for hours in my chair seeking my lost libido. What a painful humiliation to be subjected to such catatonic impotence. Even active imagination refuses to function. Finally I get one meager image —a small, black, earthenware pot. Does it contain something, or is it empty like me? I turn it over. One drop of golden fluid comes, which solidifies on contact with the air. That was all I needed! That single drop of solid gold released a stream of associations, and with them, libido. It has come from the black pot, the black head of Osiris, which personified my dark and empty state, a state I despised while I was in it. (pp. 165, 167)

Edinger's is clearly a personality with an archetypal bias, as well as a passionate commitment to the individuation process.

We all have the faults of our virtues, and my only serious criticism of this commanding author's effort is that he sometimes seems to confuse an openness to the archetypal with commitment to individuation. This is nowhere more evident than in his chapter on *coagulatio,* in which he seems to insist against the psyche's own doubts on the necessity of integrating archetypal qualities of the Self into the ego. He gives a case example; it sounds as if it may be one of his own patients.

> A young man who had come to the end of his analysis and was in process of taking on more substantial life responsibilities had this dream: I go out for dinner at a very special place. It is not really a restaurant, but the basement of a monastery. The food is served by monks. For dessert they serve "cow-dung cokies"—supposedly a delicacy like filet mignon. However they warn me to be careful, for some may not have crystallized out of their prior form. The idea of eating them causes me great distress. (p. 111)

Edinger's comment is, "Whenever food is offered one in a dream, the general rule is that is should be eaten no matter how unpleasant it seems" (p. 112). This is an attitude which seems to stem less from the psyche than from the Jungian idea that the archetypes ought to be integrated whenever they offer themselves. Yet if we look at this dream (and I have seen many like it), I am not at all sure that this dreamer ought to be advised to eat those "cow dung cookies." Such advice would violate his own sense within the dream that there is something wrong about doing so, and our common sense. I suspect that this basement of a monastery has something to do with the shadow side of the Jungian reverence for the archetypal, which can include half-baked suppositions about the value for individuation of all archetypal material, a countertransference problem of the archetypally biased therapist.

And elsewhere, Edinger's tips about psychotherapeutic technique based on the possibilities and dangers of the operations seem inadequate as the basis for a general theory of technique. But this is a minor cavil in a book that is really opening the door to the archetypal dimension of clinical material and warns frequently enough of what comes from premature, simplistic, or incautious exposure to archetypal elements. It reflects a consciousness trained by much experience with archetypal material, one that can discriminate between "lesser" and "greater" *coniunctios, solutios, separatios,* and so on, and point out that each of the operations can have negative as well as positive aspects. The charts of the symbolic ideals that cluster around each of the operations (I reproduce as figure 1 the one for *calcinatio*) show a real understanding of the way one successfully completed emotional experience leads quickly into another, so that a continuous process of emotional work is to be expected once psychological life starts to develop. It is not surprising that a "lesser" *coniunctio* should occur when the conscious mind makes premature identification with archetypal ideas and affects just making their appearance, and that further *separatio* will be needed, often after the "mortifying" recognition of inflation and contamination of the conscious attitude by insufficiently worked-over unconscious material.

By reference to great individuals, Edinger makes convincing his belief that the "greater" aspects of the operations need not lead simply to archetypal infla-

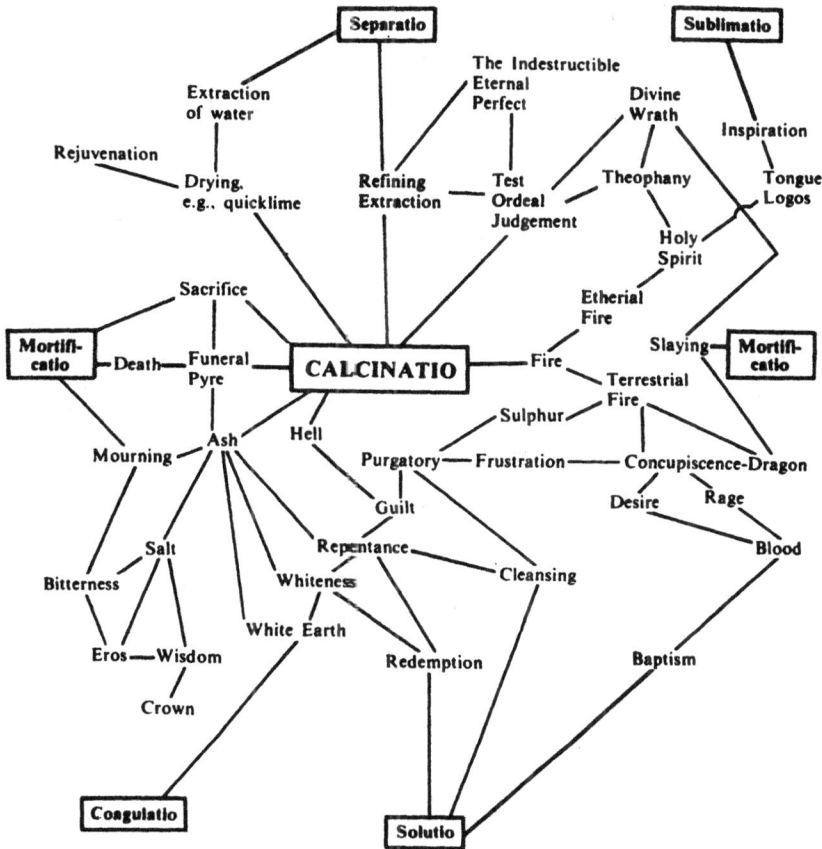

Figure 1.

tions of a more subtle sort but to quite recognizably valuable living in the world. He cites a dream of Ralph Waldo Emerson, dreamed in 1840 when, at the age of 37, the great American author was just preparing his *Essays: First Series* for publication:

> I floated at will in the great Ether, and I saw this world floating also not far off, but diminished to the size of an apple. Then an angel took it in his hand and brought it to me and said "This must thou eat." And I ate the world. (Ralph Waldo Emerson, *The Journals and Miscellaneous Notebooks of Ralph Waldo Emerson.* Edited by W. H. Gilman et. al. Cambridge, Mass: Harvard University Press, Belknap Press, 1960, 7:525 quoted in Edinger, p. 126)

Edinger's comment seems quite "cn" to me:

A dream of floating in the "great Ether" seems symbolically appropriate for the author of Emersonian transcendentalism. This dream is grand rather than grandiose. In contrast to the previous dreams, this one contains its own corrective factor. The extreme *sublimatio* is compensated by the *coagulatio* image of eating the apple of the world. (pp. 126–27)

To really understand the various operations and the symbol systems that cluster around them, one must of course turn to this book. Yet the interested reader may want to know how this reviewer related them to his own glimpses of individuation. I can give three examples. My first is a clinical case I worked once with a woman having the diagnosis of borderline personality, who had set herself on fire in a fit of rage at the frustrations of her life. She had immediately rolled herself on the ground to put out the fire and sought treatment. After many years of working with me analytically, which involved for her a remarkable initiation into her own unconscious life and into the mysterious worth of the Self that lay therein, she dreamed that she set herself afire again but, this time, let herself burn until she became ash. I think this dream, which had a peculiar sense of rightness to its dreamer, meant that therapy had promoted a profound acceptance of her frustrated desirousness, so profound that it had become a vehicle of alchemical transformation for her entire personality, a greater *calcinatio*. She did in fact become a more effective presence in the world than she had ever imagined being.

A second example comes from my own process several years into my analysis in my own psyciatric residency when I had a dream in which my leather briefcase turned from its natural tan to an unaccountable black. About six years later, with the end of my analytic training in sight, I dreamed that I had received a new pair of shoes of the sort I would wear to work (leather again); though they were exactly suited to me, they were as yet not cordovan but a creamy white color; I would have to apply the red stain myself. I take the first dream to represent the onset of the *nigredo,* whereas the second indicated that the stage of the *albedo* had been reached, with the *rubedo* still to come. The "tincture" that would produce the *rubedo* had not yet arrived; that might refer to the special characteristics of a seasoned professional personality, which waited more years of practice as an analyst. In these dreams, the *prima materia* for my individuation seems to be my own development as a doctor, symbolized by briefcase and shoes.

A final example is from the movies. I recently looked again at the great John Huston film, *The African Queen,* the quintessential romantic adventure so satisfyingly full of the energy of individuation, and during this viewing I was able to verify Edinger's hypothesis that the alchemical categories cover almost the full range of individuation-experience. I could identify all of the alchemical operations as prime movers along the journey along the supposedly unnavigable African river that makes up the action of the film and is its metaphor for individuation. Humphrey Bogart plays a Cockney steamboat captain spurred on by Katherine Hepburn, playing a spinster British missionary, to turn his craft, the *African Queen,* into a torpedo that can blow up the German steamer, the *Louisa.* The film begins with the outbreak of World War I in Africa; the Germans set fire to Katherine Hepburn's missionary compound, a *calcinatio* which helps her to get past her cold identification with collective attitudes toward the feminine. Her resulting anger sets her free to pursue her individuation journey, symbolized by her task of blowing up the *Louisa,* which is an image of the controlling patriarchal anima. At first Bogart is simply a means to her end, but a bath in the river is followed by a rainstorm (*solutio*), which softens her enough to let him at least sleep in the dry region of the boat near her. This is still a lesser *solutio*; a lesser *separatio* based on unreflecting discriminations between male and female opposites on the basis of social and cultural prejudices is only gradually being broken down. Then, an exciting triumph over the rapids provides an exhilarating experience of *sublimatio*; they forget their differences, and, thoroughly drenched by the river (further *solutio*), they embrace. Her eros for him and his for her have been released. But then he gets drunk and their first, lesser *coniunctio,* is followed by *mortifactio*: he humiliates her, and, in retaliation, she humiliates him. (They are mortifying each other's pride.) They reconcile around the repairing of the propeller, a metallurgy involving principles of *solve et coagula.* Their increased level of *coniunctio* is followed by further *mortificatio*; leeches attack Bogart, terrifying and sickening him. Yet the leeches are also performing an *extractio* (variant of *separatio*) of the tincture, in the form of his blood; the essence is his courage, which is experienced by her at last as equal and opposite to her own. The couple now experience *coagulatio*: the boat is run aground, and they finally go to sleep imagining they must die. But then a rain storm produces a truly great *solutio,* a real solution which allows the ship to float free again. They are captured by the *Louisa,* and the incisive German officers effect a greater *separatio* on the partners by questioning them separately and condemning them individually to death. But they are brought together for hanging and in fulfillment of their last request, they are married, a greater *coniunctio* before they are to be executed. Instead of death, this greater *coniunctio* leads to a release of energy (the Philosopher's stone, which can work miracles). The *African Queen,* which they have abandoned, strikes the *Louisa,* and its nitroglycerin detonates as they had hoped. In this explosion, which lands them in the water safe from the ship they have destroyed, elements of *sublimatio, calcinatio, mortificatio, coniunctio, separatio, solutio,* and *coagulatio* all are involved in a final recapitulation of these themes as the partners realize that they have actually accomplished the opus. This is the triumph of the authentic female principle—the goddess, represented by *The African Queen*—over the controlling patriarchal anima, represented by *Louisa.* Their vital unexpected relationship (a true union of opposites: Hepburn and Bogart!) is a symbol of the liberated Self.

The last example, particularly, will remain controversial to anyone who does not like the argument by analogy, because it depends so much on analogy. How can the images of a popular film have so much to do with medieval alchemy? Such analogizing, as Edinger makes clear, is the essence of the modern psychological effort; in effect, such reasoning—disreputable in certain circles, essential to others—continues the old alchemical tradition.

It is important, now that Edinger has so clearly defined the various alchemical operations, that each who employs his system continues to breathe life into them with analogies to image nets and symbol systems—mine, here, in film—that are fresh. We need to relate to the alchemical "operations" with imagery that matters to us. Otherwise, all we will gain from the creative psychological opus that has produced this volume is a fresh set of concepts, which will not really help us see the psyche. In commenting on an alchemical text, Edinger makes some statements inspired by Plato's *Timaeus,* which praises analogy as a basis for bonding the body of the universe. Edinger says, in a passage of his book that might serve as his recommendation for the psychological style of this effort, and for the style we might employ in taking it seriously:

> Analogy is a process of relationship, a making of connections by "as if." [The] texts tell us that analogy corporifies or coagulates spirit. This is what makes alchemy so valuable for depth psychology. It is a treasury of analogies that corporify or embody the objective psyche and the processes it undergoes in development. The same applies for religion or mythology. The importance of analogy for realization of the psyche can hardly be overestimated. It gives form and visibility to that which was previously invisible, intangible, not yet coagulated.
>
> Concepts and abstractions don't coagulate. . . . The images of dreams and active imagination do coagulate. They connect the outer world with the inner world by means of proportional or analogous images and thus coagulate soul-stuff. (p. 100)

Forms of Feeling: The Heart of Psychotherapy
Robert Hobson. New York: Tavistock Publications, 1985.

Reviewed by Lee Zahner-Roloff

"Growing up," Robert Hobson writes, "is a matter of engaging in a never-ending personal conversation." (vii) Because it is the first sentence of his book, and it haunts by the last, it deserves a meditation about that elusive element in life. It is the heart of psychotherapy, it is the enduring monologic paradox of intrapsychic conversations, and it is the outer manifestation of abdicating autism. It is a phenomenon of many moods, closest in the male psychology to the presence of the enduring feminine, or, lamentably, her absence. If one imagines masculine conversation, or phallic discourse, the presentiment suggests that conversation has turned to probes, lines of defense, and, even, petite battles or grand wars of words. Masculine conversation is conversation, but with different aims. It is closer to argumentation, tortes of the mind that have litigious purposes—to convince, to win, to obtain *the* decision.

Entymologically, conversation as an archetype of talk, is aligned with psyche's basic modality of movement: to meander, to wander, to be in the presence of the ultimate hermaneut, "the sudden find." Conversation is discovery, and it discovers because it is without the commitment to convince, to persuade in Aristotle's sense of "examining the available means of persuasion." Conversation is a consenting to the unknown, a reminder of what Alexander Pope might be sug-

Lee Zahner-Roloff, Ph.D., Professor, Department of Performance Studies, Northwestern University, is the author of *Perception and Evocation in Literature* (1973) and is a practicing Jungian analyst in Evanston, Illinois.

gesting when he advises that "consenting sets one free." We discover, for example, that conversation originates from the Latin *conversere*, to turn often, or surprisingly, *convertere*, to turn around. The psycholinguistic hint of conversation's ground of being is its early meaning of *to live or move about*. Here, to converse would be that peregrination, that journeying, that menadering that witnesses effortlessly, to be in conversation with nature, with a city, with a moment of intense awareness of where one is. Conversation carries, even, the intimacy of love-making in its obsolesence of meaning suggesting sexual intercourse. (See Webster, 498). So, "growing up," one might observe, is being free to discover, to turn in many directions, to become intimate, to be privy to soul's desire for an intercourse with meaning, image, a sudden find. Conversation is revelation, healing, witnessing, consenting, of knowing the flexible moment when mind is supple, toned, attuned, and free to wander into trouble and out of it. It is an activity we witness in dreams when they converse in the discovery of the *bon mot*, in that sudden slip of speech that has meandered into consciousness. Conversation, Hobson would say, is the heart of psychotherapy. Without conversation, psychotherapy is many other things, but it is not a form of feeling in a professional activity of valuing conversing above all else.

What Hobson is addressing, to my mind at least, is the western Cartesian split that would place concepts before experience, or psychological theorizing and metapraxsis before psychological conversation and experiential discovery. Conversation is the praxis of psyche. In an ego-dominated world of Cartesian dualism, the reality of concepts precede experience, and *that* is the *angst* of not only contemporary life, but contemporary psychological praxsis. What would psychological praxsis look like, Hobson wonders, if experience preceded conceptualizing? What *then* would experience be conceptualized as? The answer is phenomenological: psychological praxsis would become a conversation, and that conversation would become purposeful, painful, revelatory, indirect, metaphorical, healing, disastrous. *Disastrous?* Disaster is the failure of conversation, and it is on a disastrous failure that Hobson ends his essay. We will be left, as we shall see, with the realization that *experience can more powerful, more telling, more insistent than any concept.* But I am ahead of myself. Disaster is Hobson's final warning, his final caveat in a stunning *tour de force* of psychological writing.

The conceptual underpinnings of Hobson's work are his own self-disclosing conversants, including Freud, Jung and their encounters with the unconscious, but also, and the list is but a partial one, Bowlby, Buber, Bruner, Chomsky, Klein, Kohut, Langer, Levi-Strauss, Piaget, Polyani, I.A. Richards, Tillich, Winnicott, and Wittgenstein. These, the conceptualizers of experience, are for the reader in nearness to the forerunners of the English romantic tradition, particularly Wordsworth, Coleridge, Keats, and Shelley. He persists, as it were, in maintaining a conversation with two distinct modes of discourse, the rhetoric of psychological discourse and the poetic of metaphoric experience. For him the struggle is an eternal one not to split into a Cartesian dualism of antagonistic discourse, but, rather, to enjoin the mental faculty of psyche to be present during those healing hours of meeting those who have chosen in inquire *into the nature of experience*. It is conversation which humanizes, it is the breadth of human inquiry which inspires. The book's remarkable conceit, or embedded metaphor, is that Hobson himself meanders from the intellectual conversations of his mentors, scientific and poetic, from man as thinking to man as playful, supple. Conversation is that interface between *homo mentalis* and *homo ludens* (and *homo fantasia*). The heart of the psychotherapist is that which knows both dynamics, both languages, both hermaneuts.

Hobson admonishes that learning how to engage in a personal conversation is that heart of psychotherapy.

> I conceive of psychotherapy as a process of learning, and learning how to learn, within a personal conversation. The central feature of this relationship is the mutual creation or discovery of a feeling-language—a language of the heart. (15)
>
> In psychotherapy we need to learn, and to share, the language of our patient in developing a conversation. An important activity is that of giving life to significant metaphor. (60)
>
> A very important feature of the developed Conversational Model is 'staying with' immediate 'bodily experiencing' and waiting for 'living symbols' to emerge, Such symbols intimate possibilities which are as yet unknown, inexpressible. (170)
>
> The Conversational Model is designed for the therapy of patients or clients (the words are used interchangeably) whose symptoms and problems arise from defects or disturbances of significant relationships. Closely associated with a general theory of psychoneurotic disturbance, it aims at the promotion of *unlearning and of new learning in a dialogue between persons.* A situation is created in which problems are disclosed, explored, understood, and modified within a therapeutic conversation. (182) (Italics mine)
>
> The Conversational Model is concerned with the promotion of a state of aloneness—togetherness within which inevitable anxiety associated with loss can be revealed and tolerated. It involves a discovery and resolution of maladapted and unnecessary means of avoiding those conflicts which arise from the fear of damaging separation. (217)

To be in conversation is, in greater part, to abandon being in role, and paradoxically, not altogether abandoning being in role. This inexpressible dilemma is, naturally, enormously threatening. There are expectations of role, of being "in the hands of a healer" not a personal friend. Role, after all, exclaims "who I am" and "who you are." The issue is identification. When role is predominate, one cannot get around it. The conversational model is one which leans towards the potential expression of a spark, of a generative moment of excitement wherein two persons forget roles for the overwhelming presence of a third thing. This "third thing" is that ineffable transcendent realization that something else is being uttered, something else is being witnessed, that a remarkable poesis is present. This poesis is the speech of psyche that makes, shapes, and creates the truthfulness of what is present for both conversants to seize upon as the linguistic reality of psyche. It is what I have tried to summarize in the statement, "As surely as I speak, I am spoken." Hobson puts it, "The combination of concentrated attention to detail, together with a nebulous receptiveness, is the unattainable ideal of a psychotherapist." (142).

What the poetic frame induces is the phenomenological witnessing of the present moment. Poetic concentration is that concentration that goes to the heart of the matter, or, reflexively, to that which matters to the heart. The heart of psychotherapy for Hobson is the heart of what matters, of the effortless motility, or movement, towards that which which *is*, transcending it-ness for interpretation. of what phenomenologists suggest *in holding beings open to their fields of being*. Of what David Michael Levin suggests when he observes ". . . that we relate to the various beings of our world in a way that *maintains* their contact, and our own, with the primordial clearing of space that let them, and us, first meet in the enchantment of presence." (Levin, 139). Spontaneously moving towards being is the ground that Hobson maintains in the psychopoesis of Buber's I-Thou. This motility of Being, Hobson qualifies in the following way:

> A therapeutic dialogue involves the use of varied languages. Buber stresses that every human Thou must become an It; but to speak of, and act towards, another as if their reality consisted only in his or her being simply a He or a She (an It) is disloyalty to the truth of the meeting with the Thou. Then, there is alienation with a loss of mutuality, trust, and personal exploration. For Buber, knowing a person is what it means to be a human being: 'All real living is meeting', 'Where there is no sharing, there is no reality.' (22)

The qualities that Hobson lists as those of a personal relationship which are at the heart of conversational therapy are these: what occurs happens between experiencing subjects, what is happening can only be known from 'within', what is happening is mutual, what is experienced is always aloneness-togetherness, that conversational therapy is a language of disclosure that is 'private' information, and the therapy is always here and now. (25).

For two hundred and fifty seven pages, Robert Hobson explores the poetic inventiveness of psyche's motility toward the healing possibility in conversation, and the worldly possibility of living more fully, deeply, and meaningfully in a problemmatic world at best. It is the work of an artisan, a culminating work of his discovered and tutored practice. Having lived fully and richly with the intellectual investigators of his own time, he has shared his unique synthesis of his own protean reading and reflection, integrating them into a professional's statement and testament of praxsis in the service of psyche. Readers will be rewarded with the achievements of his results. Why then, one might ask, does the book conclude in its final section, "The Heart of a Psychotherapist," with a meditation upon the heart of darkness, the black hole of psyche's potential errant entry, and the confrontation with failure, and worse, suicide, of a psychotherapist? Why, indeed, a confrontation with disaster? It is a shattering, ennobling, memorable, grounding, and inspired conclusion to another inexorable movement of psyche towards loneliness, alienation, and death. The epithet of the final section points the way. It is from Thomas Hardy and his *Poems of Past and Present*: "if way to the Better there be, it exacts a full look at the Worst."

Sue's voice is dull and monotonous.

"It is all a waste of time . . . we just go around in circles . . . nothing changes . . . just the same. Now Jim has dropped me. . . . Oh, I know, I know, I made him reject me, but knowing is no damn use. We were talking like this twelve years ago . . . You are fed up with it too. . . . And then I give you hell ringing you up ten times over the weekend . . . and taking those pills . . . sleeping in your garden and throwing stones through your windows . . . I can't cope . . . I really can't cope . . . I'm no good . . . You are fed up too. I know you are."

Sue is right. I am fed up: but that is to put it too mildly. Psychotherapy is no good. *I* can't cope. Sue's vicious attacks have gouged out my inside and all the weekend with my family life has been in chaos. Today my wife has a big wash, and I have to get through a day of difficult interviews and interminable committees. She has failed and feels that she herself is a failure. I have failed. I am a failure.

There are no fresh words. No words to carry on the "mutual, asymmetrical conversation" of psychotherapy. Just the same sounds growing colder in a repetitive round of empty phrases.

It is often like that: nothing more to say. (262)

The contemplation of failure is the contemplation of another turn for the worse, the inversion which silences conversation, the turning inward away from another, the journey away from being with to that of non-being, no-being, cutoffness. This is the journey towards loneliness, and it is the dark side of psychotherapy, the black heart of loneliness, the heart of darkness. The suicide is a failure in life, but for the analyst the temptations are such that the analyst is poised between two statements. Either "I have now known failure," or, "I am a failure." It is this existential *angst*, this that-which-must-be-endured, this agony that shatters the compacency of professionalism.

I suppose Hobson would observe that we never become an analyst, that we, rather, are always in a condition of arriving, of becoming, hopefully, a person who by happenstance of life is a professional. We are, he reminds us, always in a neverending task of our own lives and their most poignant awareness, that we are called for the growth in all of our relationships. However, more shadowily, we are also called to other recognitions: how we can use patients for our own purposes and ends, how we satisfy our own limited needs through our patients, and how, more determinedly, we avoid our own fears, guilts, fears of meaningless by avoiding our felt loneliness, and, ultimately, deaths. Finally to admit that we know very little, that we do not even know ourselves, maintaining our defenses, our addictions, our own avoidances of darkness. This is what failure confronts us with.

In one of the more startling acts of self-disclosure, Jung remains in his own admissions pre-eminently the model for those who would confront their inner core of being. It was re-articulation of the archetypal realities that, in a sense, provided the "imaginative grammar" of the soul to overcome its loneliness through the "rainbow bridge" of the symbolic function. For Jungians this remains a form of the Ultimate Conversation, but even here isolation can be a despairing experience. It is the presence of the human Other, the thou-ness of witnessing, that provides an alternative to the aloneness of what Anne Sexton acknowledged as "the awful rowing towards God." By all accounts Jung himself was something of a paradigm in his "being with-ness," of his setting aside of concept for the interaction of conversation. Yet, we might well ask how the chill factor has been allowed to contaminate the potential of genuine conversation in therapeutic encounters? Hobson suggests an answer.

Perhaps it is the therapeutic defense to avoid a confrontation with no-being.

Perhaps, as professionals, we substitute genuine presencing of conversation with glibness, and worse, pseudo-intimacy. What is it that has created the "taboo on tenderness?" It might well be that until the psychological professional admits that it is darkness itself that lies at the heart of psychotherapy, psychotherapy itself will resist the moments of motility towards the Other. As Hobson puts it, it is that Moment that is "the experience of a meeting in and out of time." (278). The Moment: the heart of psychotherapy. In the Moment of awareness, I can truthfully acknowledge that "I have known failure," that "I have known disaster," that "I have known the heart of darkness." This does not mean that "I am a failure." Failure is pseudo-intimacy, pseudo-mutuality, pseudo-being. "To go on growing up to be a person means to explore new ways of resting in and speakin out of our loneliness. Then, there is the hope of a meeting in the space *between* lonely persons." (281).

Sources Cited

1. Robert Hobson (1985). *Forms of Feeling: The Heart of Psychotherapy*. (New York: Tavistock Publications).

2. *Webster's Third New International Dictionary of the English Language* (1966). (Springfield, Massachusetts: G. and C. Merriam Company, Publishers).

3. David Michael Levin (1985). *The Body's Recollection of Being, Phenomenological Psychology and the Destruction of Nihilism*. (London: Routledge and Kegan Paul).

Down to the Bones

Karin Lofthus Carrington

Five-thirty in the afternoon is a luminous time on a summer's day in the New Mexico desert. The work of light on all the expanse is breathtaking. Clarifying. Awesome.

All the preceding articles in this volume (with the exception of the book reviews) were delivered at the Annual Ghost Ranch Conference for Jungian Analysts. Since Ghost Ranch is Georgia O'Keeffe's painting studio/home, this reflection and the photos by the author are included here in honor of the artist.

Karin Lofthus Carrington, M.A., is a candidate-in-training in the Jung Institute of San Francisco and has a private practice in Berkeley.

And so we came, my four New York friends and I, at just this time of day, less than a year ago, to see Georgia O'Keeffe's Ghost Ranch home. The woman had always been more than a remarkable artist to me. Her life was an original. She was also a lover of the ordinary daily round, and was neither widely traveled nor an adventurer in the world. The richness of her vision, her art, and her daily existence came from turning inward—wholeheartedly, courageously, perhaps at times with wonder and at other times with dread, to travel the far reaches of her soul. The richness came too from her contact with the natural world—with the desert, where life and death cannot be separated, where the sky and the earth so distinctly meet and yet are never parted. Here one can see and know the meaning of the ancient alchemical proclamation: "In truth certainly and without doubt, whatever is below is like that which is above, and whatever is above is like that which is below, to accomplish the miracles of one thing."

And so we came. My breathing was rapid as we approached the house. I felt expectant, devout, wide open, like the Pilgrims I had seen coming to the sacred Hindu village of Muktanath in the Kalhi Ghandaki Valley of the Himalaya. They came to pay tribute to Shiva. I came to be in the presence of another greatness, knowing intuitively that this woman who carried so much for me would soon be dead.

There was nothing unusual about this rambling U-shaped adobe house, just off a rarely used road on a treeless piece of desert. The house had many windows, some facing out toward the distant hills and flatness of this place, others turning in toward the patio at the center. Sagebrush was growing out of control everywhere. The view in all four directions was as dramatic, blue, and endless as O'Keeffe's art.

Heart pounding with a sound like a herd of wild horses galloping at full speed, I walked on tiptoe all around the house. We peered into all the windows like scuba divers loose in the ocean for the first time. I felt self-consciously voyeuristic, critical of our intrusiveness and yet determined to see all that I could see. Though there was no one at home, this was clearly a home, one that had been carefully lived in. The rooms we could view were sparsely furnished, open, aesthetically mirroring the spirit of the surroundings. The interior was like a Shaker home or the quarters of a Zen monk. On the second go-round of the house, we stopped at the patio. There was a fence of tiny meshed wire enclosing the open end of this area, undoubtedly to keep snakes out. And other predators. Like us.

At that moment I felt a strong instinct to take something from this place and make it mine. A rock from the driveway, a stick from the yard, something to remember me, to hold in my hands, to make this moment of discovery lasting. This impulse felt embarrassing and shameful, but I could also feel compassionate and good-natured about my very human response to finding a treasure. Buddhist practice teaches us to watch the feelings. And then let them go and come back to our breathing. There was so much to pay attention to—both within and without.

My focus came back to the patio, and I was taken by several crudely made wooden tables and benches covered with rocks of every shape and color. Hundreds of rocks. Evidence that this was the home of a true introvert. Rising out of the desert camouflage was the very sturdy handmade ladder which O'Keeffe said she ". . . climbed several times a day to look at the world all around . . ." when she first bought this house in 1945. 1945. Two years after I was born. The year my mother died. The year the war ended. The year of Hiroshima and Nagasake. These juxtaposed images of life and death kept flooding my consciousness.

The ladder led to the roof, like in the Himalayan villages of Nepal, where people retreated to sit and absorb the full three hundred-and-sixty degrees of vastness and wonder surrounding them. My friends and I were taking it all in from the ground, from behind the fence and whispering to one another occasionally. There was obviously no one else there, but still we whispered, like children in church on a Sunday morning.

My eyes scanned the patio several times to see if there was anything we might be missing. I caught my breath. Gesturing with reserved excitement, my voice still a whisper, I was able to attract the attention of my friends. There before us, at the far end of the patio, almost concealed by a combination of sagebrush and dusk, were the pelvic bones, skulls, and antlers which O'Keeffe painted. I pointed out the ledge of bones to them, incredulous and mute. My heart was racing again, and I knew I had to see the full array more clearly—up close. I found a small, easily opened gate so we made a silent procession to the altar ledge covered with bones, rocks, and natural wood sculptures. With the reverence of an initiate, I held my breath. The bones reminded me—breathe in, breathe out. Stripped of all flesh, disengaged, dried white by the sun and beautiful in their starkness, these bones reminded me to breathe. In that moment I knew with absolute certainty that even bones and rocks breathe, and there is no death. Only continual transformation, then the final formlessness of our great return to the earth. I was comforted in the presence of these holy bones and rocks and adobe.

The impulse to take something returned. But to move anything would be to defile the temple. And so I went on—touching, looking inside and out, taking in the gift of the present. Everything fascinated me and nothing was too small not to notice. It seemed all her rocks and bones and pieces of wood had been touched —some many times—and carefully placed. The rooms were tended with the same care, and I remembered the passage from the biography, *Portrait of an Artist*, in which O'Keeffe is quoted: "My center does not come from my mind. . . . It feels in me like a plot of warm moist well-tilled earth with the sun shining hot on it. It seems I would rather feel starkly empty than let anything be planted that cannot be tended to the fullest possibility of its growth. I do know that the demands of my plot of earth are relentless if anything is to grow in it worthy of its quality . . . If the past year or two or three has taught me anything, it is that my plot of earth must be tended with absurd care. . . ."

Turning away from the ledge of bones and the house, I was able to see the Pedernal pushing up from inside the hills with all of the grace and drama that she captured again and again in her paintings of this desert mountain. Everywhere I look I see what she was inspired by. All that O'Keeffe revealed in her work, content, and spirit felt available to me. Utter simplicity, what is fundamental and of the earth. This was the lead for O'Keeffe's alchemical opus.

After forty-five minutes of exploration and reverent greed, we left feeling exhilarated and somewhat overwhelmed. And during the week, in between presentations at the Jungian Ghost Ranch Conference, I returned several times. I came at various times of day, in different states of mind. Alone. With a friend or two. I came to pay homage to a woman who so clearly lived in harmony with the nature within and without. As an artist she seemed committed to that threshold region in our collective consciousness where life and death are one. O'Keeffe, like the medieval alchemists, was intent on finding the spirit in matter and had the generosity to share her passion with the rest of us.

Almost a year later I still return often to this sacred place in the desert and the private interior richness it holds for me. And I am reminded of the importance of journeying to this source of creativity and wonder within myself. I learned there how all that surrounds me, and the care with which I hold it, determines how deeply I can travel toward my own source. And I discovered something about my own integrity as I struggled with the desire to take something away with me. I left knowing that to have taken anything from this place would have been to betray my Self. And knowing that to leave without taking in all that the experience gave me would have been a far greater betrayal.

In the spirit of Georgia O'Keeffe, my teacher, I pass on to you the gift of my visit.

CHIRON. *The most celebrated of the Centaurs, son of Cronos and the nymph Philyra. Dreading the jealousy of his wife, Rhea, the god is said to have transformed Philyra into a mare, and himself into a steed. The offspring of this union was Chiron, half man and half horse. To Chiron were entrusted the rearing and educating of Iason and his son Medeus, Heracles, Aesculapius, and Achilles. Besides his knowledge of musical art, which he imparted to his heroic pupils, he was also skilled in surgery, which he taught to the last two of this number. In the contest between Heracles and the Centaurs, Chiron was accidentally wounded in the knee by one of the arrows of the hero. Grieved at this unhappy event, Heracles ran up, drew out the arrow, and applied to the wound a remedy given by Chiron himself. But in vain; the venom of the hydra was not to be overcome. Chiron retired to his cave longing to die, but unable on account of his immortality, until, on his expressing his willingness to die for Prometheus, he was released by death from his misery. According to another account, he was, on his prayer to Zeus for relief, raised to the sky and made the constellation of Sagittarius. In art, Chiron is represented as of noble and intellectual cast of countenance, while the other Centaurs exhibit brutal and sensual traits. (Adapted from* Harper's Dictionary of Classical Literature and Antiquities.)

www.ingramcontent.com/pod-product-compliance
Lightning Source LLC
Chambersburg PA
CBHW061014280326

41935CB00009B/963